ECONOMIC

MAN *The Anthropology of Economics*

HAROLD K. SCHNEIDER

SHEFFIELD PUBLISHING COMPANY
Salem, Wisconsin

For information about this book, write or call:

Sheffield Publishing Company
P.O. Box 359
Salem, Wisconsin 53168
(414) 843-2281

ISBN 0-88133-400-6

Printed in the United States of America

7 6 5 4 3 2 1

DEDICATED TO MELVILLE J. HERSKOVITS
AND EDWARD E. LECLAIR, JR.,
WHOSE WORK AND INSPIRATION
LAID THE GROUNDWORK
FOR THIS VOLUME

CONTENTS

LIST OF
ILLUSTRATIONS

1989 PREFACE

With characteristic clear and forceful style, Harold K. Schneider already announces in the title of his book that he favors only one of the many perspectives used by social scientists to study the performance and dynamics of economic systems. Following Menger, who focused on individual units of production, Schneider examines how to resolve the unavoidable realities of competition, conflict of interests and scarcity of resources. He feels that this is the way to proceed if we are to decipher what and how much is produced, why some of these goods become commodities and under what terms and modes are they exchanged.

He was not being ironic and he was not alone amongst anthopologists in this venture. Though Malinowski maligned the concept of Economic Man, he also believed that social theories would emerge if we focused on the individual, his needs and limitations. This individualist perspective gained momentum during the sixties and seventies, revitalizing through the writings of Goodfellow and Firth the analysis of non-western economic systems. Firth transformed Malinowski's Emoting Man into a Reasoning Person who allocates resources and thinks twice about terms of exchange. Barth portrayed him as Competitive Man, allocating resources to outwit others. These conceptual frameworks served to guide the new generation of scholars whose writings are liberally quoted by Harold K. Schneider in his book.

Schneider, however, dared to trod where others feared. He valued the neat logical models of micro-economics and strongly believed that their potential to generate deductive hypothesis was extremely useful to anthropologists lacking time-series data. Furthermore, he strongly believed that the assumptions implied in these models fitted the realities of the non-western world as it did the realities of market economies. In an earlier publication jointly edited with LeClair, he brought together a number of field studies and controversial arguments in support of his contention. It was a generous attempt to present his case against the backdrop of opposing arguments. His committed presentation aimed to persuade anthropologists to examine carefully the paradigms they were using and to think through their data. Schneider's publication together with Polanyi's *Trade and Market in Early Empires* and Dalton's articles were the highlights of a controversy that was to rock the field of economic anthropology for two decades.

Six years later, with the publication of this book, Schneider offered anthropologists a review of micro-economic concepts (chapter 3) which he believed would help them understand and predict how non-western producers would allocate resources. *Economic Man* was born from his commitment to formalize the study of resource allocation and was inspired by the field research of Epstein, Barth and Salisbury. In turn, he encouraged a new generation of anthropologists and economists to rephrase their questions so that they not only could investigate how culture affects resource allocation but also how scarcity and conflicting needs determine what people do thus accounting for regional and seasonal variance.

Some anthropologists took on his challenge and provided excellent detailed case studies on how resources are allocated and/or how rates of exchange are set. Plattner, Moerman, Calavan, and Finkler operationalized micro-economic models. Bennett and Ortiz, instead, focused their research on the decision process itself rather than on the formal aspects of predictive models. Barlett, Chibnick, Moran and Cancian brought to light social, political, and ecological factors which affect the readiness to shoulder risks, the choice of strategies and the ecological viability of their choices. Gladwin, following Tversky, offered an alternative format to analyze decisions, portraying them as a protracted process of evaluating information about options. Yet, none of these anthropologists have proposed formal models able to generate predictions.

At best, they have offered explanations of preferred past strategies or have pointed out how social constraints and cultural modes of thought alter the grammar of micro-economic models. It has been left to economists (Barnum, Binswanger, Boussard, Anderson & Dillon Scandizzo and others) to revitalize their models by integrating some social variables in order to make them conform more closely to reality. However, their attempts have not yet convinced economic anthropologists who find assumption of undifferentiated units of production, single utility functions, maximization of utility, estimation of value and outcome expectations either unwarranted or too simplistic.

Decision analysis reached a temporary dead end in the late seventies and early eighties. The critiques leveled against it by culturologists, institutional economists, and political economists of various theoretical persuasions discouraged further research on how allocation decisions are made and how to model such decisions. Attention, instead, was turned to how power controls resources and terms of exchange and thus directs production and distribution of revenue. Economic Man disappeared under macro forces which ordered his environment and determined his options. Yet, as case studies sketched how these forces operated, once again it became evident that they act through a myriad of individualized ideologies, competencies and differing endowments. Not all peasants become capitalist farmers nor have they always been expelled from their realm. Each political and economic system may have its own internal set of pressures and contradictions but not everyone, so confronted, resolves the dilemma in the same manner.

It is thus time to refocus on micro processes and try to fathom how producers and consumers think through their alternatives. We should do so after a fresh reading of this book as well as the more recent vast literature about how individuals rank and evaluate options and formulate expectations. While we no longer can subscribe to the idea that African farming households are firms, we ought to reexamine the concept of indifference and marginal substitution, both of which may help formalize our general behavioral propositions avoiding further reliance on unrealistic equilibrating micro-economic models.

Economic Man may once again redirect descriptive research efforts about the behavior of producers along tighter analytical lines. Schneider's discussion of concepts may inspire new modes of depicting how decisions proceed and how we can operationallize our models so that they perform a predictive role. The book should also be read critically and together with more recent surveys on decision theory, the structure of domestic units, and the political economy of development.

Sutti Ortiz
September 1988

PREFACE

The term "economic man" has a long and disreputable history in anthropology. When I told a respected colleague what I intended to call this book he replied: "You're being ironic of course?" Malinowski, when he wrote his pioneer volume on cross-cultural economics, *The Argonauts of the Western Pacific,* took special pains to castigate that "dummy creature," and anthropologists since have had little use for a concept which, as they seem to have thought, described men as greedy, narrow, and essentially unattractive. In fact, it has almost been dogma in anthropology to think of non-Western men in opposite terms—as altruistic men, so to speak. Altruistic man is devoted to others, broad in his interests and in a sense noble.

I chose the title, this history of rejection notwithstanding, in order to express two related themes that underpin this book. The first is the book's orientation to one aspect of man. There is a long tradition in anthropology of viewing man from a special angle. Lucy Mair's *Primitive Government* could as well have been called *Political Man,* and Leopold Pospisil's *Anthropology of Law* could also be called *Legal Man.* This book singles out the economic perspective—broadly defined as a focus on how men relate their available resources to their desired ends—and explores human behavior cross-culturally from that stance including within the focus the production, exchange, and consumption not only of material means but also of more intangible values, such as honor and respect.

Additionally, the author seeks to challenge directly the prejudice against economic man. In stressing the logical, deductive role played by this concept, my intent is to suggest that anthropology can profit by opening its mind to analytic methods, not only in economic anthropology but more generally as well. Economic man is no more to be despised than esthetic man, religious man, or political man. He is in all of us, he is a part of all of us, but he is an abstraction from us and not the whole of any of us any more than the single-minded professional athlete is only what we see of him on the playing field, where he behaves as a sort of personified abstraction apparently motivated to do only one thing, win games.

Writing this book has brought me face to face with a problem broached several years ago by Gluckman, having to do with the limits of naiveté. It will be obvious in the text that I have had to acquaint myself with large areas of economics which are ordinarily irrelevant to anthropology. What has this experience said about whether the scholar ought to remain naive about boundary disciplines? In the first place, I tend to agree that there is a good case for staying in one's own pickle patch in order to grow better pickles. But I have also become aware in my dealings with theoretical, developmental, and agricultural economists that they do not see the value that a social anthropologist would see in a conjunction of economics and anthropology. Rather than a true integration, they tend to seek control of social data in order to plug it into their models as another parameter. One might think that students will make the cross-disciplinary connection, but for the most part students go where their teachers lead them, at least at first.

The fact is that in order to accomplish a cross-fertilization of anthropology and economics, some anthropologist has to learn both anthropology and economics and make the fusion. Maintaining the limits of naiveté becomes in this case staking out a new territory which can encompass economics, but only as much as and of the type that can be useful for answering essentially anthropological questions. That is, the pioneer must grope blindly into the adjacent field, steering clear of irrelevancies, recoiling from apparent blind alleys, and generally guarding his naiveté whenever he can identify it so that he remains, in the end, an anthropologist. There is always the danger that the anthropologist, beguiled by this virgin territory, will end up an economist. I hope this book is a beginning toward the real integration of social anthropology and economics despite the naiveté with regard to economics that it still displays.

I have dedicated this volume to Melville J. Herskovits and Edward E. LeClair, Jr., because I feel that they more than any others are responsible for laying the groundwork for the point of view expressed here. Ironically, probably neither would embrace it. Herskovits, although he was much more prone than anthropologists of his time to admit that there is virtue in comparing men for their similarities rather than their differences, nevertheless remained ambivalent until his death with regard to the sublimation of strange cultures under a general economic theory. LeClair, who like myself had trouble bringing Herskovits to a more generous cross-cultural view of economic theory, remained until his tragically early death in 1969 unconvinced of the value of social exchange, which is central to this volume.

The writing of this book was due originally to the stimulus of Stanley Holwitz who urged me to go ahead in late 1968. But the book was possible only because of the stimulating groundwork laid for it by such people as Scott Cook and Cyril Belshaw and numerous other students of economic anthropology whose works are heavily exploited in these pages. Thanks are also due to my students at Indiana University and Lawrence University, both undergraduate and graduate, who have demonstrated by the imagination with which they have employed for original research ideas expressed in this book that the approach developed here can have real value for achieving new depths of analysis in anthropology.

Harold K. Schneider

1 *The Meaning of Economy*

As behavioral sciences go, economics is ancient. Adam Smith's *Wealth of Nations* was published the year of the American Revolution, 1776, and to many it was merely an organization of knowledge that was already widely understood. But the fabric of economics has not gone unchanged, although a thread of continuity, represented in the theory of the competitive market, or microeconomics, runs through its history. Besides the modern growth of Keynesian and macroeconomic theory, which have challenged some of the most basic assumptions of the classical model, there has been a sometimes heated debate between the formal-theoretical and the institutional-descriptive economists (Bronfenbrenner 1966: 15).

Within economic anthropology a parallel energetic debate has occurred, and as the antiphony between opposed sides has risen in pitch some bystanders have pronounced a plague on both houses, believing that where there is so much heat there cannot be light. Yet wars about ideas and words are not necessarily merely the reflection of status fighting among scholars but may rather comprise the external rumblings of the search for truth. Profound new ideas are never accepted with equanimity into the established order. And, as in Parkinson's law of the perfection of planned layout (Parkinson 1957: 60), one suspects that it is when the conflict stops that the subject will be on the point of collapse, devoid of any new insights, and not when feelings are intense and divided.

In this chapter the two meanings of economics in anthropology, the substantive and formal, will be examined to prepare the ground for the main purpose of the book, which is the development of the idea of a formal economic anthropology.

SUBSTANTIVE ECONOMICS

The appelation *substantive,* which has come to be applied in connection with the views of Karl Polanyi and his followers, and which is an invention of Polanyi himself (Polanyi *et al.* 1957: 243 ff), designates a point of view which he developed in *The Great Transformation,* "Our Obsolete Market Mentality," and, most recently, *Trade and Market in the Early Empires.* From the latter work (Polanyi *et al.* 1957: 243):

> The substantive meaning of economic derives from man's dependence for his living upon nature and his fellows. It refers to the interchange with his natural and social environment, in so far as this results in supplying him with the means of material want satisfaction. . . . The two root meanings of "economic," the substantive and the formal, have nothing in common. The latter derives from logic, the former from fact. The formal meaning implies a set of rules referring to choice between alternative uses of insufficient means. The substantive meaning implies neither choice nor insufficiency of means. . . .

Since the meaning of these two uses of "economics" is outside most anthropologists' experience, it would be well at the outset to illustrate and contrast them.

Taking the substantive first, we may imagine a person buying groceries in a local store. While the economist of the formal variety views this as an exchange event in which the choice of groceries, price paid, inventory, and other such quantities are of prime importance because they are necessary to construct a supply-demand model, the substantivist focuses on the movement and flow of goods as they serve to maintain the buyer and seller and thereby, in some fashion which the substantivist would go on to explain, the society itself. Each actor plays roles that are essential to the system, and these roles must be supported. The material dimension in the transaction is of secondary interest, the focus being on people and how they relate and are supported. There is no perception of the actors as profit motivated; indeed, the existence of the profit motive outside Western industrial capitalism is denied. Whatever self-interested elements seem to appear in the exchange, such as the use of and attempt to aggrandize money or other goods, is seen as a gloss on an essentially altruistic relationship. The grocer gives the food to the customer because he is obligated to do so; it is a moral act. Any profiting from the transaction is a by-product.

While some of us may be acquainted with grocers like this, especially of the old corner-store variety, who seemed sometimes more interested in socializing with their customers than in making money, this illustration is defective in one important respect, in that it is drawn from Western, specifically American, society. Substantivists confine the use of the term to non-Western societies, explaining that exchange events in which there is a profit orientation are specifically Western capitalist and represent a dissociation of the economy from support of the social system. Dalton, Polanyi's economist spokesman to anthropology, has declared (Dalton 1961:7) that the formal method of economic analysis is suited only for Western capitalist societies, for which it was designed.

The formal meaning of economics also takes on freshness if illustrated in a novel way. Imagine a typical American college classroom in which students and teacher are engaged in discourse on some subject matter. In trying to understand why the two groups act the way they do, why students put varying amounts of time and attention into the course, why the professor gives

variable grades, we focus on the exchange between them of information and deference (or money, inasmuch as the professor
receives a salary and students pay the fees), rather than on how
their activities serve society, as a substantivist would do. The
amounts of the valued things that are exchanged must be re-
corded (a difficult thing to do when dealing with nonmaterial
goods), and all the relevant facts cast in a theoretical scheme
that assumes that the parties are individually trying to maximize
their *utility* (satisfaction, pleasure). Such an approach might
predict, from the logic of the model, that the C student performs
at that level because the marginal utility to him of a grade
higher than C in that course is less than that necessary to motivate him to work harder. This is his price for that commodity
(a C grade). Considerations of whether a student has the ability to earn more than a C, or of the value of the act for the
survival of the society, are ignored, in a single-minded attempt
to work out the logic of a limited set of variables under certain
assumptions, like the presumed desire to maximize utility, with
all other intrusive variables held constant. Although this method
is more usually applied to situations like that of our substantivist grocer and his customer, there is no theoretical reason why
it could not be applied to a situation such as that just described.
In fact, Peter Blau has pioneered in attempts to do this (Blau
1964).

Those readers familiar with functionalist thought in anthropology, whether of the diffuse American variety or of the more
precise structural-functional variety in British anthropology, will
detect a resemblance between functionalism and substantivism.
The view of societies from a static, self-supporting and closed
angle is characteristic of both. Both points of view focus sharply
on how societies maintain themselves, even to the extent of assuming a teleologic stance, that is, one in which the various
elements of the system are assumed to preserve the system and
have the purpose of preserving the system. Since the vast majority of anthropologists are functionalists to one degree or an-

other, Polanyi's economics came to have, for anthropologists, the aura of revealed truth.

George Dalton forcefully revealed Polanyi's views to anthropology in a pioneer article in the *American Anthropologist,* "Economic Theory and Primitive Society," in 1961. In this paper Dalton's aim was to show how closely fitted to 19th-century capitalist society economic theory is, and how unfitted it is, therefore, to the analysis of primitive economics. According to Dalton, economic theory originated in a society in which everyone derived his livelihood from selling something in the market and everyone was compelled to buy and sell to live. In this situation the logic of the free-competition model of society worked as long as the conditions of minimal government interference in the economy, unorganized labor forced to sell its services, and social decentralization of firms held. The mistake of economics, Dalton argued, was to conclude that a model fitted to a special society at a special time in history had universal applicability.

Contrasting this Western capitalist economy with primitive economies, Dalton argued that the substantive meaning of economy has universal validity, in that it refers to the fact that men everywhere need sustenance and the social system must see that it is provided. Thus Rome had an economy in the substantive but not in the formal sense, and the Omaha Indians might be said to have had an economy in the substantive but not the formal sense. Carrying his argument to a higher level, Dalton pointed out that primitive economies everywhere lack certain necessary elements for a market economy: they have special-purpose rather than all-purpose money, when they have money at all; they lack a combination of external and internal trade operating in the same market, a condition which is necessary to the maintenance of equilibrium in the economies of Western nations; they lack a division of labor integrated into the economy, which is another way of saying they lack a labor market; they lack a market for land.

In its most generalized sense, Dalton's critique reduced to the point that in Western industrial economy the balance of land in use, supply of labor, and supply of and demand for other goods is achieved by the market mechanism, which acts to feed information about variations in supply and demand from one part of the social system to the other. Without the market mechanism the balance is achieved in other, substantive ways. Economic theory is not designed to analyze the nonmarket substantive economy.

Paul Bohannan, who, unlike Dalton, is an anthropologist, has been instrumental in establishing substantive theory in anthropology. His special affinity for substantive thought seems related to the exceptional intensity of relativism that marks his social thought (Bohannan 1963: 10). To him the anthropologist is a translator of the life-view of his subjects to his own people, and in the course of arguing this Bohannan comes very close to denying the cross-cultural applicability of any conceptual scheme like formal economics. Speaking of the Tiv (Bohannan and Bohannan 1968), but generally seeming to refer to all Africans, he, with Laura Bohannan, denies the existence of ownership of land as we know it, believing that social relations dominate Tiv life and hence the transfer of land from one person to another follows social needs rather than individual desires to maximize utility. Tiv are not oriented to make money, and money is not a unitary symbol of value, as in our economy, but operates only to exchange certain types of goods. Therefore, the theme of *Markets in Africa* (1965), a volume of accounts of African indigenous economies produced for that book under the editorship of Bohannan and Dalton, is that African economies are to be understood substantively, a point underscored by careful attention to marketplaces, whose functions are shown to be noneconomic in the formal sense. People go to market for reasons other than making money, and exchanges in marketplaces link people together, thereby acting as an integrating mechanism.

Polanyi conceived of three types of economies: one formal type—Dalton's Western industrial capitalism—and two of the substantive type (Polanyi *et al.* 1957: 250ff). While Polanyi denied that any evolutionary significance could be attached to the three types, they do suggest evolutionary stages, and conform to the widely held band-tribe-civilization progression held by many evolutionary anthropologists (Sahlins 1968). In the simplest segmentary societies, *reciprocity,* motivated by such things as kinship obligations, serves to distribute goods from those who have to those who do not, and thereby achieves the necessary end of maintaining the system. At a higher level, *redistribution,* the second type of substantive economy, occurs where there is political or status centralization, as among the Northwest Coast Indians. In neither of these systems is there a market principle, as Bohannan calls it (Bohannan 1964: 217), operating. There are no prices, and supply and demand are not regulated by prices in a market. Decisions about production and distribution are made in terms of obligations (which has the effect of achieving the persistence of the society) and not in terms of profit.

To this whole scheme of thought Polanyi added another element, which was muted in publications subsequent to "Our Obsolete Market Mentality" (1947) and is not apparent in the writings of Dalton and Bohannan except by inference. This was the notion that the market system is "obsolete." While it may at one time have been necessary, he argued, it no longer is, and in fact works against the good of society and may even have the effect of destroying society because it is unrelated to social needs. The economy, in Polanyi's terms, seems naturally to be "embedded," i.e., to serve the maintenance of the system. When it does not it needs to be adjusted in order to avoid adverse effects on the social system.

It is this last theme, overt or muted, that has caught the attention of many critics of substantivism, who interpret it as a sign of the intrusion of normative considerations into what

should be a scientific enterprise. Reacting strongly to this nor-
mativism, Cook (1966) contrasted the substantive with the
formal approach, arguing that the relativistic and empirical orientation of the substantivists is inductive whereas formal technique is deductive, utilizing logic and laws of the mind—theory
in the proper sense. Inductivism glorifies the particular, and
Polanyi's claim that there are two meanings of economic—substantive and formal—merely confuses a science with its subject
matter. Cook charged the Romanticists (Cook 1966: 327) with
focusing:

> on situations limited in time and space, and who are prone to
> retrospection or are diachronically oriented; they are humanistic
> in outlook and nonmathematical in inclination, favor the inductive
> mode of inquiry, and are basically synthetic in methodology (i.e.,
> lean toward the belief that the whole determines its parts).

Although at first glance this critique might appear to be the
opposite of what it criticizes, i.e., glorification of the abstract
over particularity, its intent was merely to break through the
aura of "revealed truth" surrounding substantive thought in order to establish a claim for the legitimacy of formal or deductive thinking in economic anthropology.

Mathew Edel, whose own contribution to formal cross-cultural analysis will be reviewed later, has attempted an apprecia-
tive assessment of Polanyi's contribution (Edel 1970). As Edel
sees it, Polanyi caused us to focus on human values and incentives and away from profit orientation, which is trivial compared
to the problem of the high variability of values and incentives,
the study of which microanalysis or formal analysis is not prepared to undertake. Systems in general are highly variable with
respect to their values, the organization of their markets, and
the nature of their parameters, and this variability must be dealt
with before any formal analysis is possible.

To this I would add that however overstated or even un-
original Polanyi's thesis is (we shall discuss later its similarity
to the ideas of Mauss and other social anthropologists preceding

it), it has had the effect of turning our attention to the fact that the material sphere is not the only sphere of an economy, that economic analysis needs to take into account social behavior as a type of economic behavior. In one sense it may be said that when he speaks of the market economy as disembedded, Polanyi is suggesting this need to consider the relation of the market for material means and services to the social sphere. Personally I do not believe that Polanyi would have felt that social interaction could be treated as a type of exchange, but the effect of his writings and those of persons like Bohannan has been to raise that possibility, if only because in non-Western or in noncapitalist societies the exchange system is far more apparent in the social than in the material realm.

FORMALIST SOCIAL ANTHROPOLOGY

Placing a single label on formalists suggests that they are as united in their approach as substantivists. This is not true. In fact, in some ways certain formalists are further apart from each other than they are from substantivists. Three formalist approaches can be identified, although any one adherent has to a certain extent his own configuration. The unifying element among these formalists is, in contrast to substantivists, the partial or total acceptance of the cross-cultural applicability of formal theory.

Those formalists closest to the substantivists are *social anthropologists*. Manning Nash exemplifies this point of view in a paper he wrote about profit maximization among the Central American Amantenango (Nash 1961: 311):

> . . . the rationale of economic choice in peasant society follows the same general rule of maximization as economic activity does anywhere, at any time. What is distinctive about peasant and primitive societies are not the habits of mind about advantage,

nor an inability to calculate costs and benefits of a course of action, nor even an absence of a motive of gain; but rather the possession of a set of concrete social organizations which directly channel economic choice, on the one hand, and a set of sanctions which operate to keep economic deviants in physical as well as moral jeopardy on the other.

Although this seems merely to be giving us economizing with the one hand while taking it back with the other, whereas substantivists make no pretense of finding economizing in such situations, it does represent a concession to formal economic concepts and a step away from substantivism.

Fundamental to the social anthropological approach is the idea that economics is a type of behavior rather than a way of looking at all behavior, a type which is distinguishable from social behavior and is governed by the social. In Nash's terms, social organization channels choice and threatens with physical and moral sanctions those who attempt to allow maximizing motives to overcome their social responsibilities.

In a very real sense, the social anthropologist's bow to formalism stems not from a recognition of its value but from a desire to put it in its place as subordinate to social structure. In the course of doing this methodological errors are frequently committed, such as imputing empirical substance to the theoretical assumption of maximization, as in Nash's claim that maximization is a "habit of mind" which all people share. Formalists would exclaim that one might have trouble devising a way to measure such a habit of mind, but even if it could be done it would not matter. The validity of formal theory rests not on whether people really desire to maximize but rather on whether accurate predictions about behavior can be made by *assuming* that people desire to maximize utility (see Friedman 1953). Put another way, formalist social anthropologists are unsympathetic or insensitive to creation of assumptions and other elements of a theoretical-deductive approach (Leach 1961: 1ff).

The most notable exponent of the social anthropological view of economics is Raymond Firth, who is paralleled in sociology by Parsons and Smelser. Firth was trained as an economist and his teacher, Bronislaw Malinowski, is conventionally credited with the creation of economic anthropology, although Firth once described his ethnographic writings on the Kiriwina of the Trobriands as generally betraying a failure to understand or apply economic theory (Firth 1964: 212). Malinowski was, in Firth's terms (1964: 209), essentially a common-sense descriptive economist who failed to consider value in relation to price, concentrated primarily on factors of demand, failed to show how values are arrived at, and ignored the concept of scarcity, which is central to formal economic thought. *Argonauts of the Western Pacific,* Malinowski's most economically oriented book, published in 1922, scornfully rejects the economic man of classical theory, describing him as a "fanciful, dummy creature" (Malinowski 1961: 60).

Malinowski, therefore, appears not to go even as far as Nash, rejecting almost entirely the idea that formal economics has any cross-cultural relevance:

> Even *one* well established instance should show how preposterous is this assumption that man, and especially man on a low level of culture, should be actuated by pure economic motives of enlightened self-interest. (Malinowski 1961: 60)

But he refers to the Trobrianders as putting more time on activities than "utilitarian" ends require, working for its own sake and for prestige rather than for material advantage, suggesting that, like Nash, he equated "economic" with materialist pursuits and saw these pursuits among the Trobrianders as subordinate to social prestige.

Firth's position is also similar to Nash's (Firth and Yamey 1964: 22):

> It is sometimes thought that obedience to the social dictates of "custom" inhibits rational calculation. This is not at all the case. In some of the most primitive societies known, as in the Highlands of New Guinea or aboriginal Australia, there is the keenest

discussion of alternatives in any proposal for the use of resources, of the relative economic advantages of exchange with one party as against another, and the closest scrutiny of the quality of goods in exchanges between groups and taking a profit thereby either in material items or in that intangible good, reputation.

Although this statement seems to abandon the subordination of economic to social considerations, in the work from which it comes (*Capital Savings and Credit in Peasant Societies*) Firth continues, less emphatically, to assert this subordination: peasant and primitive economic considerations are "embedded in the social matrix" (Firth and Yamey 1964: 31). If Firth had urged development of a theory of what Homans (1958) has called social exchange, we might be able to say that in this book he finally embraced a true cross-cultural application of formal theory by perceiving the material and social spheres as one, but he expresses doubt that such a thing can even be done (Firth and Yamey 1964: 26), arguing that measuring and comparing "status tokens" is probably not worth the attempt.

In the landmark volume *Economy and Society* (1956), Parsons and Smelser express a point of view that relates them to Malinowski, Nash, and Firth (Parsons and Smelser 1956: 6):

> Economic theory . . . should, according to this view, be regarded as the theory of typical processes in the "economy," which is a sub-system of a society. The specifically economic aspects of the theory of social systems, therefore, is a special case of the general theory of the social system.

But lest we interpret this to mean that economics has autonomy somewhere in the system, we may quote Smelser to demonstrate that to Parsons and himself, just the reverse, in a Nash-Firth sense, is true (Smelser 1963: 32; see also Parsons and Smelser 1956: 307):

> Economic sociology is the application of the general frame of reference, variables, and explanatory models of *sociology* to that complex of activities concerned with the production, distribution, exchange, and consumption of scarce goods and services.

As an illustration of how economic sociology proceeds, Smelser (1963: 45) notes that as firms grow large their decisions are governed less and less by the state of the market and more and more by considerations of the attitude of the government, such as its trust-busting propensities. In other words, decision making takes into consideration to a very large degree the political atmosphere rather than being made simply in economic terms.

Characteristic of this general sociological orientation, then, is recognition of distinct social and economic spheres of life, whose processes are different and in which the self-serving propensities of men acting economically are controlled by society's needs. It differs from substantivism mainly in acknowledging that formal theory does have some cross-cultural applicability in the material realm, and in recognizing the continued subordination in Western society of the economy to the society.

As we leave this first and rather special type of formal approach, it would be well to keep in mind that although social anthropologists are really not interested in formal thinking, they are trying, like Polanyi, to express a truth that will be explored later under social exchange, namely, that economic relations involve prestige and social position as well as material exchange and these should be taken into account in both non-Western and Western societies.

If the substantivists have introduced into their conception of economic anthropology the ethic that a market economy is immoral, a feeling shared somewhat by social anthropologists, who tend to think of economic behavior as disruptive of social order (cf. Nash 1961), there is an inclination on the part of social anthropologists to introduce an assumed tendency for systems to maintain themselves in equilibrium, an assumption that, by virtue of its untestability, amounts to an assertion. In the formal theories to follow we shall encounter some strange assumptions, such as that men are perfectly rational, but the assumptions facilitate theory building and testing and do not stand as substitutes for theory building. Some (Friedman 1953) even believe that the assumptions of a positively tested theory are not thereby proved.

The question needs seriously to be considered whether claims of the inevitability of system maintenance, teleological claims that elements of systems have purposes to serve in maintaining systems, and normative claims that certain types of institutions are better than others are modes of thought that will serve to develop social theory, but in any case such assumptions are unnecessary to a true formal economic anthropology.

MATERIALISTIC ECONOMIC ANTHROPOLOGY

The second group of formalists may be labeled the *materialists*. These most closely parallel classical formal economic thinkers, except in their desire to apply economic theory cross-culturally. Economists seem to be of two minds on this question: either they believe that such an application is impossible, or they believe it to be comparatively uninteresting in light of the level of sophistication with which they can analyze Western economies. Like economists in general and social anthropologists, the materialists in economic anthropology accept that economics is a type of behavior contrasting, for example, with social behavior. That is to say, they see economics as a deductive, theoretical enterprise in which abstract variables are fitted to empirical reality. But also like economists in general, they confine their attentions largely to the realm of exchange of "material" goods and a few services, even though in theory they may accept that nonmaterial things and services may be treated economically (see Robbins 1962: 14).

Goodfellow, in his pioneering *Principles of Economic Sociology,* which applies economic theory to Bantu societies, exemplifies this approach. Discussing the problem of the cross-cultural application of abstract economics, he says (Goodfellow 1939: 8) that ". . . the difficulty of discovering the *forms* of modern economic life may well lead to a mistaken belief that the *functions* of that life are not to be discovered among our less advanced people." That is to say, the principles of economic theory are abstract and are tied, for purposes of analysis, to the specific forms of Western life. They may be applied elsewhere by fitting them to different forms. To illustrate this point, Goodfellow suggests (1939: 9) that the value of brides fluctuates with the supply of grain; i.e., women constitute in Bantu society a labor market, if one would only see this. Put another way, labor does not always come in overalls and punch time clocks.

Perhaps because he is primarily an economist or was extensively trained in economics before acquiring a cross-cultural interest, Goodfellow focuses on the realm of material goods and services, as economists do in reference to our own society. In fact, it may be generalized that this transporting of the economist's characteristic preoccupation with material goods and labor into the exotic realm is more likely to occur among economic anthropologists with extensive training in economics than among anthropologists who are more sensitive to the social realm and try to incorporate it into an economic theory. More about that presently.

Scott Cook also began as an economist and reflects this in his approach (Cook 1966: 335):

> Most members of every discrete human group have economically relevant wants that exceed the procurement means available to them. In band societies, simple tribal and peasant societies, these economically relevant wants lie predominantly, though not exclusively, in the subsistence realm. . . .

In the one analysis of an exotic market published by Cook to date (1970), concern is with the quern-making market of Oaxaca. Similarly, LeClair, who received a Ph.D. in economics before moving into anthropology, evidences in the way he con-

ceptualizes non-Western economics (LeClair 1962: 1197–
1200) a focus on material goods and services, even though his
theoretical view of economics is ostensibly not so limited but
encompasses anything of value, whether material or not (*ibid.*:
1189).

The difference between economic anthropologists trained in
economics and those without such training with respect to concentration on the material realm should not be exaggerated.
Cook and LeClair, at least, not only are well aware that economic analysis can be applied to social interaction and that it
can encompass such things as prestige, but they are also more
aware than conventional economists of the need to more fully
delineate the sociocultural parameters of any market proposed
for analysis. As Cook puts it (1970: 790):

> Economic anthropology . . . must achieve a working balance
> between its concern with economic quantities and economic per-
> formances and its concern with their articulation with a socio-
> cultural and ecological context.

Most anthropologists who have employed this materialist emphasis have done so naively, uncritically transporting this conventional orientation to their analyses of exotic systems, as I did
in my study of the Turu (Schneider 1970) and Pospisil did
with respect to the Kapauku Papuans (Pospisil 1963). Both
studies would serve to illustrate Burling's point in his seminal
essay on maximization theories and the study of economic
anthropology (Burling 1962) that economics in anthropology
should not merely do elsewhere what economists do in our own
society. Lest it be thought that there is no justification for a
materialist emphasis, I would point out that formal analysis is
easiest when it deals with values that are easily quantified and
obviously priced. Sophisticated economists in our own society
will cite this as justification for their concentration on commodities. The same justification could be applied in Oaxaca, Unya-
turu, and Kapauku Papua. When quantities of material goods

are being produced and exchanged in an obvious fashion, and especially when they are being exchanged by means of a medium of exchange, whether cattle, Western money, or some other object, the inclination to focus on that part of the economy and leave the harder, less naturally defined elements of the economy, such as prestige and status, to a later time, is irresistible.

SOCIAL EXCHANGE

Yet it is a fact much remarked by social anthropologists that in so-called primitive societies the social sphere dominates the material sphere more than in Western societies, and if we can establish that the social sphere is in large part one of social exchange serious steps should be taken to encompass this sphere in economic analysis, if only because the material sphere gives us too little to work with. The third group of formal economic anthropologists are those who are making this attempt to establish a theory of social exchange. Its leaders are Cyril Belshaw, Richard Salisbury, and Fredrik Barth.

Economists, as I have noted, have been well aware that economic analysis is not theoretically confined to the market for material goods and services. The definition of economics most favored by formal economic anthropologists and much of economic science itself, that of Lionel Robbins (Robbins 1962), says: "Economics is the science which studies human behavior as a relationship between ends and scarce means which have alternative uses." This does not confine economics to material goods and services. As LeClair asserts (1961: 1181):

. . . economists no longer believe, if they ever did, that human wants are confined, in market societies, to material wants, nor do they *assume* this to be true in any society. Nor is an assumption of the materialistic nature of human wants a necessary element in contemporary theory.

Or, as Firth puts it (Firth and Yamey 1964: 26): "It is possible to conceive of an economic system in which the items of productivity, of concern in maximization, are status tokens and symbolic ties."

Homans is usually given credit for raising the possibility of studying social behavior as exchange, which is the title of his paper on the subject (Homans 1958: 597). In his words: "I have come to think that the further development of small-group research would be furthered by our adopting the view that interaction between persons is an exchange of goods, material and non-material."

Homans seems to have leaned heavily for this idea on Blau, who until recently pushed this idea further than almost anyone (Blau 1955: 1964). In his *Exchange and Power in Social Life,* Blau specifies what social exchange consists of (Blau 1964: 17):

> An apparent 'altruism' pervades social life; people are anxious to benefit one another and to reciprocate for the benefits they receive. But beneath this seeming selflessness an underlying 'egotism' can be discovered; the tendency to help others is frequently motivated by the expectation that doing so will bring social rewards.

And Blau has also impressed Belshaw, who in developing his idea of *transaction* (Belshaw 1968: 30–32) views the classical microeconomic theory of the firm as only a special case of a more general theory of social organization based upon the fact that economy has to do with wealth and wealth occurs in all institutions. But here, reversing Parsons and Smelser (1956), "economics" governs "society" rather than the other way around.

A main task in the next two chapters will be to make clear the nature of microeconomic theory as it is applied to material exchange, after which we shall have a closer look at this notion of transaction or social exchange.

A BIRD'S-EYE VIEW

The similarities and differences between the various forms of economic anthropology can be summarized in a way that highlights the differences between them and prepares us for a discussion of philosophical issues, which occupies the next chapter.

Modern anthropology, which is not usually deductive in orientation (in contrast to formal economic anthropology), is characterized by what might be called a functionalist orientation, which consists of seeing societies or cultures as wholes whose parts serve to maintain the whole system. This static model has been attacked, particularly by social-change theorists, as being unrealistic. In fact, however, static models are profitably used in deductive science. In economics, for example, microeconomic analysis, the heart of formal method, is also called *statics*. Conceptualizing the world, or the aspect of it that one chooses to study, as static is not illegitimate but is rather a basic conceptual technique of all science. What makes functionalist orientations difficult to defend is that the stasis proposed is sterile, because the conditions under which the static theory holds are not specified, the variables which are being related are not carefully distinguished and delineated, and the different magnitudes which the variables can assume are not specified. Functionalism turns back on itself, so to speak, indulging in the circular logic that the system is functional because it is static, and static because it is functional. Paralleling this circular reasoning is a teleologic ascription of purpose to social structures, viz., the purpose of maintaining the system.

Formal theory is radically different from functionalism and essentially incompatible with it. Delineating limited static systems (never whole societies), it describes the conditions under which the system holds and the relevant parameters (e.g., amount of rainfall), makes certain assumptions about the conditions of actors in the system (e.g., that they are perfectly rational), and designates (usually symbolically, as mathematical functions) the variables whose relation is to be studied and the values of those variables (e.g., labor—symbolized as L—varies from one worker to 100, or whatever).

The differences between economic anthropologists in good part amount to differences of opinion about which of these approaches is appropriate and where to apply them. Formal economists claim that the formal theory is appliable to all human behavior, but in principle they confine its use to the area of so-called material production and consumption, bootlegging labor in on the side. Only the social-exchange theorists have now aggressively turned the application of the method to "nonmaterial" realms. The quotation marks around "nonmaterial" are meant to raise questions about the adequacy of this much-used term "material." Materialists are not really confining their analysis to material exchange as a special realm, since behavior itself is material in the sense of being measurable and quantifiable. Materialists are studying, for the most part, the economy for inanimate and animate nonhuman objects (e.g., cattle). Social-exchange theorists are including human animate values in their analysis. The difference, then, is between the economies of human and non-human values. Both of these groups would, I think, agree in rejecting functionalism as an inferior form of theory compared to formal theory, which is far more rigorous and therefore far more explanatory, although in a narrower sphere.

Substantivists agree among themselves that formal theory is suspect because, as Cook sees it (1966: 328), they romantically reject self-interest as an acceptable motivater of behavior. They believe rather that functional theory, with its emphasis on how actions serve the community rather than the self, more truly describes, at the least, primitive men, and even in Western societies, where the industrial revolution has given rise to institutionalized selfishness, they believe individualistic economic behavior is dysfunctional. It is noteworthy that in order to come to a conclusion like this, the science has to be confused with its subject matter (Cook 1966: 332). That is, a formal analytical way of looking at behavior must be infused with life and made to describe the characters of some men as if they were as single-minded and narrow-minded as the theory must make them in order to conduct its logical manipulations.

Social anthropologists of the Malinowski, Firth, Nash type, contrastingly, seem to be willing to accept the idea that in the area of material exchange primitive men are economic men, but they then retract it by asserting that the functional, community-serving propensities of the social sphere dominate and control material self-aggrandizing. This is truly a confusion of theory and reality that even the substantivists cannot be accused of, at least not to the same degree, because they mix the method and the data only in Western societies. Functionalism is a way of looking at all behavior in a given social setting. Formal economics is a different, incompatible way of doing the same thing. One can claim that behavior can be analyzed as being partially functional and partially selfish only if methods are inappropriately confused. Formal method only works if men are seen as entirely self-oriented, at least within the range of the field being analyzed. If one subjects their behavior to social constraints which subdue this supposedly innate impulse, the method no longer applies. In short, functionalism cannot have its economic cake and eat it too.

Substantivists, on the other hand, are faced with a simple problem. They need only decide whether functional or formal methods comprise the better way to describe all human economic behavior. This is a strategic, not a logical, question. But their claim that only Western men are self-serving and that formal methods apply only to them seems unlikely to hold up, especially as social-exchange theory, which is developing out of social anthropology, grows to challenge their claim of the essential altruism of human behavior.

2 The Philosophical Bases of Formal Economic Anthropology

The purpose of this chapter will be to develop the philosophical bases of formal analysis as it may be used in economic anthropology.

THE KNIGHT-HERSKOVITS EXCHANGE

The best place to start is the famous (to economic anthropologists) "debate" between Melville J. Herskovits, author of *The Economic Life of Primitive Peoples* (1940) and Frank Knight, a well-known economist of the University of Chicago who reviewed the book in the *Journal of Political Economy* (1940). Herkskovits thought the review and his rebuttal of it so significant that he published the two together as an appendix to his *Economic Anthropology* (a rewriting of the previous book), published in 1952 (Herskovits 1952: 508–531).

Knight's defense of formal economics against some of the charges leveled at it in Herskovits is of special interest because it places the formal economic point of view against an anthropological outlook even though the review was not intended for anthropologists and even though, as it turned out, most of what

Knight said went right by the anthropologists who read it—including Herskovits, to judge by the lack of influence Knight's views had on the second edition of his book.

The trend of Herskovits's critique of classical economics can be assessed from Knight's scornful accusations that Herskovits had misunderstood economics by maintaining that it is built upon a single case, Western societies, and had rejected the notion of economic man on specious grounds, namely that no such man exists. Defending economics, Knight's argument emphasized the *deductive* nature of economic analysis in contrast to the *inductive* orientation of Herskovits. In the nature of deductive reasoning the approach to the study of economic behavior is not through the ethnographic facts but by means of "universal principles," logico-mathematical in form, springing from the imagination. Generating the logical system necessary to deductive economics requires no cross-cultural data or facts from *any* system, except perhaps common-sense knowledge of the empirical realm to which the theory is to be applied. Knight was willing to apologize for attributing to primitive people types of behavior which do not exist, but his apology stemmed from a desire to be fair rather than from theoretical necessity. Economics is a theoretical, not a descriptive, science, Knight insisted. Herskovits's teaching of false principles, he declared, is worse than the teaching of false facts.

Knight's defense of formal economics is analogous to a theoretical physicist's claiming that to develop a theory of matter reference to mythical worlds and substances is legitimate. In fact, this would be a useful exercise, because it would allow one to develop areas of theory which are not verifiable in the known world (like antimatter). We might add, however, in agreement with Herskovits's chief rebuttal point, that it is well to be sure that the theory has some relation to the world it intends to explain and is not just a theoretical toy if one expects to use it to explain the real world. Accuracy about facts might ensure this hoped-for agreement between reality and theory. Knight felt that Herskovits's attack on economics was not merely epistemological but also ideological, because it accused economists of advocating politically conservative policies, such as creation of artificial scarcity in order to keep prices up. Knight's rejection of this charge rested on his claim that Herskovits did not understand deductive theory, although it is now plain to everyone that every "objective" analysis springs from a normative base. In fact, questions of the values that motivate the scientist need always to be considered when evaluating a scientific point of view. But, in defense of Knight, it is also true that the logic of ideas must be judged in terms of the rules of logic, and these can be conceptually separated from the normative nest in which they rest (a point that will be further explored in the final chapter of this book). The deductive philosophy must be judged for its adequacy as a research tool. Our concern in this book, like Knight's in his role as a scientist, is with the deductive methods as a means of increasing understanding of human behavior.

INDUCTION AND DEDUCTION

Knight's charge that Herskovits is an inductivist is echoed in the current debate between substantivism and formalism. Scott Cook's attack on substantivism (Cook 1966: 332) stressed the inductive nature of substantive thought as compared with the deductive nature of formal economics. Characterizing the two points of view, Cook presents the following table:

Substantive (Inductive) Method	Formal (Deductive) Method
1. derives from fact	1. derives from logic
2. implies neither choice nor insufficiency of means	2. set of rules referring to choice between alternative uses of insufficient means
3. power of gravity [as an empirical reality]	3. power of syllogism
4. laws of nature	4. laws of mind

The point of this exercise was to display Cook's conviction that substantivism deals with a different order of reality than formal economics. The substantive point of view is rooted in the empirical world, the formal in logic. Interestingly, E. R. Leach indulged himself in a similar exercise in his book *Rethinking Anthropology* (1961: 1–27). Leach thinks of Radcliffe-Brownian, structural-functional social anthropologists as equivalent to Knight's and Cook's inductivists, while equating deductive reasoning with the method of Levi-Strauss (although, strangely, Leach uses the terms inductive and deductive in a way precisely the opposite of that of these two authors and most other thinkers). We may generate the following table to parallel Cook's and Leach's discussions:

Radcliffe-Brown (Inductive) *Method*	*Levi-Strauss (Deductive)* *Method*
• classifying (butterfly-collecting)	• generalizing
• compares things	• compares variables
• uses organic analogy	• uses mathematical models
• treats whole systems	• treats variables in a system that can only be partial

To the person familiar with this debate this table and the one above are meaningful, but for one who is new to the dispute their meaning might be obscure, so it will be well for us to take a minute to illustrate from the works of Radcliffe-Brown and Levi-Strauss these differences in method.

Radcliffe-Brown's professed method, the comparative method, is one that characterizes most of anthropology. In *The Natural Science of Society,* Radcliffe-Brown puts his case as follows (Radcliffe-Brown 1957: 71):

The fundamental problem, then (in developing a science of society)—either in a logical sense or in a historical sense, but certainly logical—is "How many different kinds of societies are there, and in what respects do they differ from one another? What is the range of variation, and, more important, what common characteristics are there discoverable by analysis which are characteristic of all human societies? It is quite obvious that if we answer the last question, we get a series of natural laws.

That is to say, natural laws are derived and scientific analysis conducted by comparing human societies and seeing what characteristics they have in common. Finding such natural laws in Radliffe-Brown's writings is not easy, but what he meant is suggested by the opinion he puts forth in *The Natural Science of Society* that the "principle of justice" (Radcliffe-Brown 1957: 131) is the nearest thing he could think of to an "abstract structural principle." This is a principle of equivalent return (positive or negative). But while this is edging toward a kind of generalized economic theory, it still has more of the aura of induction, the seeking for least common denominators, than that of deduction.

Contrast this with the method of Levi-Strauss. His logical orientation is, in my opinion, most graphically displayed in his little-referred-to but widely known paper "The Family" (Levi-Strauss 1956: 261–285), where he presents the following argument. Why the incest taboo and the sexual division of labor? Both are found in most human societies. Attempts to explain them inductively which resort to biological determinants or other determinants in nature fail because, while the incest taboo and the sexual division of labor are universal, that which is tabooed is highly variable and the specific division of tasks between the sexes is frequently opposite in different societies. In one society men make the baskets and in another the women make them. In one society the men plow and in another society the women.

The answer to this enigma, Levi-Strauss might say, is to imaginatively create a deductive model, a logical system that will explain these things. Suppose the survival of society depends on cooperation among men, who are naturally uncooperative and self-centered. Men must stay together to protect the children, and also the mothers before and after the children are born, in order to ensure the birth and enculturation of the children. Different families must be linked to provide protection and mutual aid for warfare and production of material necessities. This can be accomplished by creating a system in which, to begin with, men are made dependent on women by the division of labor; men and women are prevented from doing some necessary jobs by simply outlawing them. It does not matter what is outlawed so long as the things banned to the men and the women are necessary to each (like cooking or cultivating for the man and hunting for the woman). In order to link the various families it is then necessary to prevent a man from having sexual relations with his own children, or mother and force him to seek sexual satisfaction outside the nuclear group. The particular form of the incest taboo in any specific society, then, is a function of the kinds of groups which exist in that society and the special ways that must be used to get them associated.

We can carry this comparison further by asking how these two approaches, the inductive and deductive, cope with the existence of marriage rules. Every society has some kind of marriage rule, as for example the prohibition, in America, against marrying a *linear* (in contrast with lineal or unilineal) relative. This means that mother, grandmother, etc., are forbidden to a man along with daughter, granddaughter, etc. In some societies the rules become quite complex in their manifestations (although simply stated), as for example the Kariera marriage system of some Australians, which, in a society divided into two moities and two cross-cutting sections (which may be designated Moiety A and Moiety B and Sections 1 and 2), advises a man that he must marry a woman of different M and S than his own (i.e., a man born into MaS1 must marry a woman who is MbS2).

Radcliffe-Brownians, faced with marriage rules, tend to deal with them by interpreting a particular rule in terms of how it serves the maintenance of the society of which it is a part, and to extend the same kind of ad hoc functional claim to any society having the same rule. The rules used by different societies are not compared in any systematic way, and rules which have not been observed are not imagined in order deductively to test their consequences.

Levi-Straussians take a different tack. Assuming that societies can be conceived of under given conditions as desiring to achieve maximum mixing of segments, they generate special, unknown rules as well as explain those that already exist. A notable example is Rodney Needham's attempt to explain why the rule of prescribed marriage to Father's Sister's Daughter (FZD) does not exist. (The fact that Needham's claim is disputed need not deter us, since our aim here is to illustrate methods and not to obtain results.) Needham purports to explain this by showing that the logical result of an FZD rule (Fig. 2-2) is nucleation rather than mixing (Fig. 2-1) (Needham 1926: p. 15); it thus runs counter to the direction societies are assumed to take (at least those of low population relative to industrial societies).

Mixing does not occur in the groups of Fig. 2-2, a marriage between two lines (A–B or B–C) at any level being turned back on itself in the next. Incidentally, this conclusion is possible only if we also assume that each of the lines (A, B, and C) constitutes a corporate decision-making group. If each generation (1, 2, and 3) were to make decisions independently, then the reciprocating effect of FZD marriage would not cause nucleation but would simply be a kind of alternating circulation.

Hence, based upon certain assumptions (the main ones in the above case being the pull toward mixing of segments and the corporateness of lines), it is possible to logically demonstrate, in a deductive system, how a certain outcome is *not* to be expected, which is logically the reverse of the ability to explain how, in certain circumstances, another outcome *is* to be expected. Granting that Levi-Strauss's approach is deductive (as per Leach's thesis), we must also admit that his theory differs from more sophisticated theories in theoretical economics in that the magnitudes of the variables are unclear, the assumptions are often not clearly stated, and the theory is, therefore, difficult to test and manipulate. But to the extent that it is deductive, his method is not dependent upon acquaintanceship with the total range of human practice with respect to incest and the division of labor;

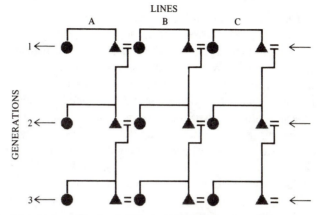

Fig. 2-1. Marriage to Mother's Brother's Daughter.

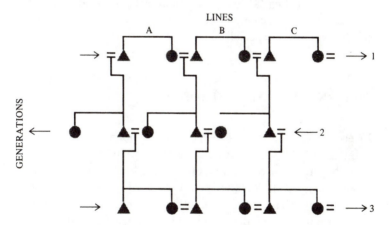

Fig. 2-2. Marriage to Father's Sister's Daughter.

the theory he generates is an exercise in logical completeness rather than in empirical comprehensiveness. Because of this, he is not afraid to make assumptions—such as that linkage of groups is a force working in history (whether for survival or whatever).

It might be argued, and with justification, that the two methods

of Levi-Strauss and Radcliffe-Brown in fact have something in
common, in the sense that, practically speaking, Levi-Strauss
cannot produce a theory which has much relevance to actual
human behavior without wide knowledge of how human beings
actually live (he has in fact demonstrated such wide knowledge;
see Levi-Strauss 1969, while on the other hand, Radcliffe-Brown's
wide acquaintance with the facts has pushed him in the direction
of theory, as previously noted. But, it seems to me, the resemblance stops there. The conventional wisdom that tells us that
induction and deduction are concomitants of each other should
not allow us to forget that despite the theoretically equal needs
for facts and theory in a natural science, anthropologists (like
most social scientists) have been long on facts and short on
theory. My feeling is that theory should be stressed, because it
is essential to the scientific method and is not likely to be forthcoming without a special effort.

THE ANALYTICAL METHOD

In economics, the deductive method has gone well beyond the
point reached by Levi-Strauss. In order to talk about that we
must begin our investigation of this method anew, at a more
sophisticated level. Anatole Rapoport (1968: xv–xvi) notes that
the heart of science is the *analytical method,* which consists of
". . . examination of the relationship between pairs of variables
at a time and construction of a mathematical theory in which the
causally interrelated factors are combined into a single equation."
This can be illustrated by reference to the most basic equation
occuring in economics, that supply is determined by demand and
vice versa. This generalization is derived in the following way.
We begin by taking two variables, Q_d, meaning "the quantity demanded," and P, meaning "price," and state a relationship between them, as $Q_d = f(P)$, or "The quantity of a good which will

be demanded by consumers is determined by (or, *is a function of*) its price." (It is important to be clear at this point that this is a theoretical assertion, not a statement of fact. We hope that this statement will fit some real situation, but at this stage we are simply building a logical world in which this relationship is assumed to be true.) This is a demand function. There is also a supply function, $Q_s = f(P)$, or "The quantity of goods supplied is a function of the price that consumers will pay for them."

In functional statements, the value of the left hand variable (the dependent variable) follows from the value given to the independent (right-hand) variable. An equation of the sort $Y = f(X)$ (Y is a function of X) is a so-called linear equation, having no exponents, whereas in an exponential equation the dependent variable appears with an exponent, as in $Y = f(X^2)$. Functional statements in economics are usually graphed, as any functional statement can be, and when graphed linear equations show up as straight lines while exponential equations appear as curves. In other words, if you plot on a graph every value of Y that follows from a given value of X, the coordinate dots, when all connected, will give a straight line. The coordinate dots of exponential equations will yield curves of various kinds.

Getting back to Rapoport's description of the analytical method, our pair of equations about demand, supply, and price can now be algebraically combined into a single equation, yielding $Q_d = f(Q_s)$.

Economics is widely known for its use of calculus in solving analytical problems. However, we should note that the algebraical technique that we have been discussing, which is more basic, is the only necessary method for determining price in static models like the ones we will be talking about. Nevertheless, calculus is a useful and necessary tool to augment algebra because it allows for analysis of movement, such as the movement of prices in response to changes in demand and supply. As Dinwiddy remarks (1967: 84):

Wherever it makes sense to express an economic relationship in functional form, the derivative (that is, the number expressing the slope of a curve representing movement, which is derived by calculus) can be used to measure the rate of change of the function as the independent variable(s) alter in value.

Calculus, the mathematics of things in motion, becomes essential for dynamic, macroeconomic analysis.

The fine points of the mathematical method need not concern us further. We are concerned rather with the fact that in this method variables *must* have magnitudes (we cannot talk about crops as such or prestige as such but must know the production or quantity of crops and the amount of prestige). With the functional relationships thus derived we can make deductive inferences.

The distance from Radcliffe-Brown and even Levi-Strauss to where we are here is worth noting. The analytical or algebraic method is not concerned with the quality of variables, as is so much structural-functional analysis, but rigorously quantifies them. Radcliffe-Brown's toying with the idea of a principle of justice can be seen to be a kind of elementary playing with functional notions, insofar as he implies that as one person does good or evil, he receives a return which is a function of what he gave. In the case of Levi-Strauss, while he has constructed a hypothetical system of functional relationships, the magnitudes of the variables are vague at best and the system is undeveloped.

ANALYTICAL ECONOMICS

The full-blown way in which theoretical economics employs the analytical method of science can be simply illustrated.

The oldest and deductively most sophisticated branch of economics is microeconomics, which deals with the individual and the individual firm in a perfectly competitive market. The method establishes first a functional relationship between demand and price, $D = f(P)$, or "Demand is a function of price." This can be graphed as a straight line when a linear equation, and, more typically, as a curved line if an exponential equation. Typically the demand curve is downward sloping, as illustrated in Fig. 2-3b. This means that as the price asked for a commodity increases (moves up on the verticle axis) the demand for it declines at an increasing rate (moves left on the horizontal axis) rather than at a constant rate, as in a linear equation (Fig. 2-3a), or at a decreasing rate, in which case the curve would slope concavely rather than convexly.

The supply of the commodity which is forthcoming at any named price is expressed in a second functional relationship, $S = f(P)$. These two equations or curves are now placed against each other, and the logic of the model (which includes all the assumptions about no monopoly, large number of buyers and sellers, actors being economic men desiring to maximize utility, etc.) predicts that the price of the commodity will be at the conjunction of the two curves (a solution derivable mathematically

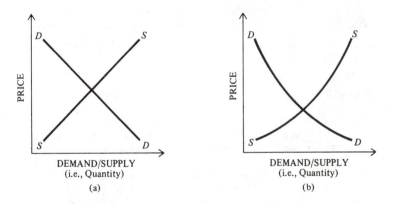

Fig. 2-3. Demand and Supply Curves.

by solving the system of simultaneous equations representing the functions and expressed as $Q_s = f(Q_d)$, or "The quantity supplied is a function of the quantity demanded"). This is the equilibrium price. In spite of its apparently narrow focus, the resultant predictability, if it works, is a very powerful technique in explaining an economic universe.

A great deal can be and is done within a deductive frame of thought in economics and anthropology without actually employing mathematics, but some attention to mathematics has been required to suggest the formal, logical underpinnings of the more verbal and less systematic way in which economics is more usually discussed and to support the claim of the proximity of this method to the analytical method of Rapoport. Mathematics is the language of the analytical method. Most of economics, however, and nearly all of economic anthropology are primarily concerned with establishing the parameters of the market, determining the magnitudes of the variables, and finding the correct functions, and seldom get to the relatively simple matter of calculating mathematically the logical implications of the knowns. Microeconomic theory is at all times a blueprint before the eyes of the researcher, who is busy trying to invest it with real-world dimensions but is always only partly succeeding. The same may be said to one degree or another about the relation of theory to the real world in any science.

Caroline Dinwiddy (1967: 29–31) has summarized the mathematical basis of economic method in a slightly different way:

> Most of the basic propositions of economic theory are concerned with functional relationships. . . . The problem is to find mathematical functions which would suitably describe supply and demand functions. . . . This type of approach which involves setting up a system of simultaneous equations and then solving to find the equilibrium values of the variables is one of the basic tools of the econometrician. . . . The chief problem does not usually lie in solving the system of simultaneous equations, but rather in finding functions which accurately describe the real world. . . .

THE MAXIMIZING ASSUMPTION

Accepting that the analytical method (or its subtype, economic analysis) is *the* method of deductive science, only half the story is told. Formal analysis in economics utilizes several much-debated assumptions, of which the primal one is that actors make decisions aiming to maximize their utility, or satisfaction. The famous and much-maligned economic man is a greedy fellow, seeking always to improve his position with respect to value taken in some general sense (utility). Is this assumption justified? Is it something peculiar to economics, a crutch upon which it leans in contrast to the harder sciences, which can do without it as they deal only with observable and measurable reality?

Not according to Krupp (1966:40), who contends that "maximization is to market equilibrium what gravity is to physical equilibrium." Similarly, Chomsky (1968:7) declares that the great success of physics has been based precisely on accepting the "occult" Newtonian postulate of an attracting force acting at a distance, namely gravity. Interestingly, according to Chomsky, Newton was scandalized by his idea, preferring a purely mechanical explanation for the motions of bodies, but he failed to find one. In the end the matter has been settled, pragmatically speaking, by the great success physics has enjoyed by utilizing this assumption, which, as with the maximizing assumption in economics, allows solution of equations and thereby prediction through establishing equilibrium points.

The scandal of the use of "mystical" forces in hard science is, of course, still with us. In psychology the behaviorists have rejected it, although Chomsky (1966:40) feels that the Descarteian concept of the mind is of the same order as the forces of gravity and utility and that its use would benefit psychology in its attempts to become more firmly established as a hard science. And

in economics the battle rages between those who would like to
dispense with mysticism and those who would not. As Krupp
(1966:43) puts it:

> . . . the attempt to identify theoretical terms with directly ob-
> servable phenomena has been extended by the more extreme
> empiricists to include the primary axioms as well. According to
> the more extreme applications of empirical methods advocated by
> some logical positivists, all the terms of a theory are required to
> be made operational. Theoretical issues are treated as though they
> can be resolved by empirical research, by the formulation of
> propositions in verifiable form. . . . Consequently, the validity of
> the axioms is judged by their amenability to operational empirical
> translation rather than by their logical form.

In other words, if man is assumed by the theory to be rational,
then rationality cannot be merely assumed but must be measurable, i.e., given concrete dimensions.

Probably the most famous essay on this issue is Friedman's
"The Methodology of Positive Economics" (1953), in which he
defends economic methodology from empiricist demands. He
points out that if we assume that actors are attempting to maximize utility, and if we make predictions logically derived from
this assumption, we *have not* proved that the assumption is
correct any more than we prove that leaves are motivated when
we make the assumption for purposes of prediction that they are
desirous of maximizing sunlight (Friedman 1953:24). That is
to say, an assumption cannot be tested by the truth of hypotheses
derived from it (Friedman 1958:16).

Assumptions such as maximization, deductivists and positivists
would argue, are necessary to theory, but their meaning is not
completely clear. When Malinowski speaks of the economic man
as a fanciful dummy (Malinowski 1961:60), or Herskovits
argues that people are not necessarily competitive (Herskovits
1952:526), they are asserting a position shared by others within
and outside economics who are intolerant of apparently airy assumptions. And, according to Krupp (1966:44), the problem
of the choice of axioms eludes any simple solution. Krupp goes

further and refers us for the source of the issue to a philosophical bias among the logical positivists toward empiricism and humanism, a charge similar to Cook's against substantivists (Cook 1966:327).

Whatever the eventual outcome of this debate, there is no question that for now such deductive methods as systems theory, with its concern with the continuity, feedback, equilibrium, goal seeking, regulation, and adaptation (Buckley 1968:xxiv), and game theory, with its central minimax assumption (players are assumed to desire to maximize payoffs at the same time as they minimize possible loss), are increasingly important in the social sciences (Buchler and Nutini 1969). Even archaeologists, such as Clarke (1973), are beginning to employ it.

THE STRUCTURE OF LOGICAL THOUGHT IN ECONOMICS

In the course of applying perfectly logical methods to the real world, a strange transformation takes place that gives the world as economists see it an eerie quality when viewed by noneconomists, especially inductively oriented persons. This is in fact probably the source of the contemptuous description of economics as the "dismal science." Conventional wisdom tells us that to do deductive science, one obtains a logical system such as a mathematical model, in which all the variables are perfectly defined and in which the relationship between all the variables is perfectly rational, and fit it to the world. But there is no one way of looking at the real world and no one way of constructing a logical system. So what in practice happens is that a complex interplay occurs between theory and reality such that the theory is continually being reshaped to fit the reality and the *reality is reshaped to fit the theory*. That is to say, those aspects of reality which best fit the theory are chosen for review, but reality is also manipu-

lated to fit the theory. On reflection we realize that this is exactly
what the laboratory scientist is doing, or an electronic engineer
when he pumps the air out of a vacuum tube in order to create a
transmitter or receiver. The justification for this, of course, is
that the understanding that grows out of examination of refined,
simplified, and controlled conditions can be extended to less
controlled situations. But it must be admitted that in economics
this reshaping of the world to fit the theory sometimes has taken
on normative aspects, so that practitioners have thought that the
reshaped world was the better or more natural state because it
fit the theory better (and served their social purposes, perhaps).
This is a subject about which more will be said shortly, but for
now, let us look at how the manipulation of theory and reality
has taken place.

In economics, as we have seen, mathematics is the tool that
has been employed to achieve logical control of the economy,
and it has been applied to the portion of the economy in which
goods and services are exchanged between households and firms.
This is microeconomics, the theory of the perfectly competitive
market, which relates supply and demand in terms of an assumed
desire on the part of individuals to maximize their individual
utility, which comprises some mixture of goods.

This view of the market, according to LeClair and Schneider
(1968: 457), reached its present form in the 1920s, but it had
its inception far before then, before Adam Smith, as previously
noted.

In the classical formulations of Adam Smith and Ricardo, the
economy was treated as a closed system, as theory demands, but
with little reference to political and other exogenous variables
in real life (*exogenous* variables are those outside the theory
being employed, which constitute the environment of the theory).
The value of having a closed real system for analysis with a
necessarily closed logical system has been made apparent, but
exogenous variables must be allowed for, if only to be held constant while the logic of the *endogenous* variables is worked out.

Contrary to the claims of Dalton (1961: 1) that this classical theory fit industrial capitalist society during its 19th century period of incubation, the theory, in fact, was only an approximation. Robin Williams has tried (1960: 152–53) to describe the kind of society and people the theory demanded in order to make its predictions. In this society the actors are rational in the way they put their resources to use, viz., most profitably, and they have perfect knowledge of the market situation, which, of course, they need in order to make rational decisions. There is free competition and hence production and consumption vary in response to prices, which, therefore, are determined by supply and demand. There are no very large producers, so that no producer commands more than a fraction of the market or can control the price. Factors of production (resources, chiefly land, as well as labor and capital), are perfectly mobile, shifting to the most profitable place as opportunity arises. (This does not mean that land literally shifts but that it may be bought and sold. Labor and capital, on the other hand, go where the advantage is.)

Commenting on this fully competitive society, Smelser (1963: 6) notes that it is constructed so that not only does no individual firm have the power to influence price or the total output of an industry, but power is ruled out entirely as a variable, so that no economic agent can at the same time be a political agent, no conspiracy is allowed between businessmen, and the state guarantees sales and contracts. In other words, the sphere of social exchange in which men vie for power and prestige is ignored as the market for goods and services is allowed to follow its dynamic, self-regulating course.

This self-regulating process is described by Williams (1960: 152–153) as follows: production responds to market demand as an indefinitely large number of individuals, each seeking to maximize his own utility, tries to sell as dearly and buy as cheaply as possible. This private vice is a public virtue, because by each person's acting selfishly the common good is served, as all manufactures are efficiently distributed and all demand satisfied. Every change in the supply-demand situation affects the decision makers (buyers and sellers) immediately, as the factors of production move to where the profit is to be made and money moves to that place in the market where the best buys are to be had. This shift in demand in turn feeds back on the production sphere, and so on in a perpetually equilibrating, negative feedback system (negative feedback being a kind of check-and-balance action).

To the economic theorist of the last century and early part of this one and to the businessman, the attraction of this theory must have been breathtaking. They certainly knew that society as it was did not conform to the society implied by the theory, because there were governmental barriers to trade, unions of laborers, and business cartels. But they must have felt that if these constraints could be eliminated, reality could be brought in line with theory and this in turn would serve the public welfare. Hence, the society prescribed by theory became a political goal centering on reduction of taxes, reduction of government interference in the market, and encouragement of freedom in the control of property.

Unfortunately, as is obvious now if it was not obvious then, one cannot hope to alter the whole world to fit a highly selective, closed theory, but only small parts of it and it does not follow that a free market also promotes the general good in every case. The social demands of economic conservatism are equivalent to those that might be made by what could be called a physical conservative, seeking some way to remove all the air from the atmosphere because without it the law of falling bodies would describe more accurately what happens in the real world and the law could then more efficiently be put to some normative use. The Keynesian revolution in economics amounted in essence to the facing of this fact and the abandonment of the hope that a free market would regulate itself and automatically accomplish the best for everybody.

While one must reject as impossible the ideal of altering a whole society to fit a closed model, one cannot reject the validity of attempts to reshape the world in some ways to fit the theory. One can imagine a so-called underdeveloped economy in which land holding is governed by lineages and land is not sold, in which the powers decree that the sale of land is to be allowed in order to make it mobile in the market and thereby make development more predictable and controllable. But for the most part, the decision-making process by economic men must remain very complicated, and a model isolating such a narrow dimension of it as does the microeconomic model must be content with limited predictions or must develop more complex theories.

Modern economists are more sophisticated in their understanding of how theory relates to reality, and modern theory shows the most recent results of the continuing process of fitting the model and reality to each other. In their discussion of the postulates of economics, Alchian and Allen (1968: chap. 3) draw a picture of the modern economic man. He is a far more uncertain man living in a far more variable habitat than his 19th-century cousin, who always knew what was right. He cannot see perfectly into the future in order to make a decision but is always prepared for changes in the value of things. He seeks a multitude of goods, but what he seeks is in some respects private to his value system. Scarcity is therefore in some respects more relative to him as an individual than was assumed in the past. He is willing to sacrifice some of one good to obtain more of other goods. And his valuation of any good depends on the amount he has, because the more he has of it the less he values any more of it. He is like his 19th-century predecessor in wanting less or more of a good in proportion to its price, but his preference patterns are not the same as those of other people. He continues to be rational but in some sense that is less obvious; that is, he acts rationally but not because he is psychologically rational. He seeks to maximize utility, but rather than being a definite, measurable quantity, this is rather a *quality* of valued things.

The explanation for this less certain, more relative man is twofold. In the first place, the theory, in response to attempts to make it more empirically useful for explanation, has come to pay more attention to the variability of its parameters. The economic actors don't have perfect knowledge; government as well as other elements not accounted for in the theory intrude in various ways in the market and can be coped with best by changing the theory to allow for the uncertainty they introduce.

Secondly, certain theoretical problems relating to treating satisfactions as absolute are avoided by introducing indifference analysis, which relates to Alchian and Allen's assumption that individuals' utilities are not the same, and the utility of any good is not a measurable quantity but a quality. As Curry and Wade (1968: 9) put it, "maximizing satisfaction no longer means achieving the largest sum total of satisfactions, but rather reaching a more preferred position." Our 20th-century economic man, in other words, is no longer trying to get the absolute most of the same things everyone else is trying to get, but rather is simply juggling his personal preferences to get the optimum combination of them as they suit him.

What then does microeconomic theory look like today? What is the form and logic of this model as it is currently structured and used to think about the economy for material goods and services? This is the subject of our next chapter.

3 *Elements of Microeconomics for Anthropologists*

Microeconomics or the theory of the competitive market, which is concerned with single goods or pairs of goods as they move in small segments of the market, is the classical segment of economic theory. Although it was central to economic analysis for most of the history of economics since the founders (Adam Smith, Ricardo, and others), its place has been taken in modern times by macroeconomics, which for the moment we may define as the study of the total economy from a more statistical, inductive point of view. Microeconomics is purely deductive and mathematical, not statistical (although statistics may be used in various ways in conjunction with the method).

If the concern of economists has shifted from purely deductive models of imaginary economies to more inductive concerns with real economies, why should anthropologists bother themselves with microeconomics? The answer is not simple but it includes at least these parts. First, in order to do macroeconomics large numbers of figures on all aspects of an economy are necessary, because the method requires aggregates rather than quantities of single things (e.g., aggregate prices). Only in modern industrial economies are such figures available. Secondly, whatever type of economics we choose to do, the logic and terminology of the micro model are fundamental, in the way that grammar is essential to writing. Finally and paradoxically, in many ways the micro model is better suited to some so-called primitive economies than it is to our own, where such things as monopolies and bureaucratic state structures have arisen to radically alter the conditions under which the micro model was supposed to be predictive, while making vastly more complicated the conceptual, methodological control of exogenous variables such as government.

Of these three reasons I would stress the second, that microeconomics is the "grammar" of economics. In order to acquire a working feeling for economic methods and to read economics, the micro model, whatever its predictive value, is essential.

The basic form of the model is simply stated. It conceives of an economic world as composed of two parts, one the household, consuming *goods* and supplying the *factors* of production (usually *land* and other immobile resources, *labor,* and *capital* or tools), and the other, the firm, utilizing the factors to produce goods for consumption by the first part. The reason for postulating the existence of two sectors is probably to be found in the nature of the social reality to which the model tries to be appropriate. On reflection it is obvious that the processes of production and consumption can occur within a single household or even, as with Robinson Crusoe, within a single person. But whether by a process of natural selection, as the French

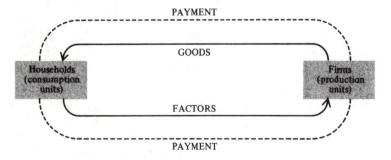

Fig. 3-1. Model of Competitive, Closed Economy.

sociologists might argue, or for some other reason, human societies are differentiated and made heterogeneous by divisions of labor of varying degrees of complexity. All societies have at least the division between men and women, and most also have differentiation of production and consumption activities in other ways. Think, for example, of the mutual dependence of such roles as father-son, teacher-student. Economics expresses this mutual interdependence or contingency in terms of differentiation of production and consumption: one party processes or manipulates the resources and another party consumes the finished product while producing the resources needed by the first to make the goods.

This division of the economy into two segments is conceptual rather than concrete. For example, in the society of the Turu of Tanzania (Schneider 1970: 61ff.) the homestead (*xaya*) both consumes and produces for the market, so that any homestead can be conceived of as a production unit to the extent that it is involved in production for the market (that is, someone else's consumption), and is a household to the extent that it is consuming products acquired from others.

The system as theoretically conceived is closed like an electrical circuit. This conforms to an essential characteristic of any static deductive model: viz., like an actual closed circuit or computer program, it must be complete unto itself; i.e., the variables in the system must be mutually causative and uncaused by anything else. It is this characteristic that sometimes bothers the noneconomist, who sees this theoretical conception as ignoring all kinds of exogenous variables. But a theoretical system can be designed to ignore such variables, so long as they are accounted for when the model is then related to reality. These exogenous variables can and must be held constant in order to concentrate on the logic of the relationship of the endogenous variables in the system chosen for study. Hence, any functional relationship stated for any endogenous economic variables contains explicitly the *ceteris paribus* condition, "all other things being equal." For example: $Q_s = f(P_x, I{-}O, P_n)$ c.p., or "the quantity of a good x which a firm will supply (i.e., Q_s) is a function of the price of the good (P_x), the input-output relationship of the capital tools $(I{-}O)$, and the prices of all other goods (P_n), all other things being equal (c.p.). (This production function, so-called, will be extensively discussed later.)

The closure of the system is illustrated by the *flow* of goods from firm to household, from which in turn factors (a kind of good) flow to the firm. Meanwhile there occurs a flow of payments from household to firm for goods, and a counterbalancing flow from firm to household for factors. The only thing left out of this model is some representation of the actual process of exchange of goods and factors for money or other payment during which the equilibrium price is established. But this equilibrium price, arrived at in these exchanges, is the heart of the model.

In any persisting social system, of course, there must be a high degree of balance of the flows and counterflows of goods and payments, because all social systems are to some degree in actual equilibrium. Understanding this alone might help us find less mysterious some ethnographic facts like the famous *kula* "decorations" of Malinowski's Trobriand Islanders that flowed against each other (Malinowski 1961: 82), or the flow and counterflow of marriages and prestations in Puram society remarked on by Needham (Needham 1962: 94) and the flow of people against things which Mauss felt characterized societies of "total prestations" (Mauss 1967: 45). Something akin to the economist's conception of the market seems obviously to be working in these instances as well as many others that could be mentioned, and will be discussed in the next chapter on social exchange.

In order to explain this flow, the microeconomic model conceives of the household as desiring to maximize *utility* (also sometimes called preferences, satisfaction, pleasure), a mysterious quantity that represents no given thing but is inherent in all desired things and equatable between them. Hence, the consumer may mix different quantities of goods to get the same quantity of utility (perhaps two pair of shoes and one pair of pants, or two pair of pants and one pair of shoes). For important theoretical reasons that will presently be explored, utilities can only be ordinally, not intervally, ranked. That is to say, the consumer is assumed to be able to tell whether one thing has more utility than another but not how much more.

In contrast to the household, the production unit or firm is assumed to desire to maximize *profit,* a more exact quantity defined as the difference between total revenue flowing into the company and total cost (i.e., revenue flowing out to finance production). This can be expressed as Profit = Total Revenue — Total Cost, or $P=TR-TC$. Of course, one recognizes that profit, like utility, is in a sense an essence rather than a thing because money only symbolizes the qualities and values of thought which it can buy (allowing for the fact that money may itself take on or have intrinsic value). The most abstract parts of microeconomic theory develop in working out the logic of what can theoretically be expected to happen at those points in the flow where decision makers with conflicting interests (i.e., the household and firm) meet. There are two of these areas. The first is between the household as supplier of factors and the firm as demander of factors. The second is on the opposite side of the flow system, where the household is the demander of goods and the firm the supplier of goods. In theory one analyzes this by first selecting one side of the flow for analysis, either the demand and supply of goods or the demand and supply of factors. Within the selected sphere one then first establishes a *curve,* i.e., a line on a graph showing the relation between two variables (always price and some kind of quantity when analyzing supply and demand), for each party (see Fig. 3-2). One curve shows the price the one party will pay for varying amounts of a value, and the other curve the price the other party will charge for supplying varying amounts of the value. These curves are such that the one showing demand (*DD*) for some value is always downward sloping and the one for supply (*SS*) always upward sloping. Finally, one matches the supply and demand curves to each area, and theoretically the equilibrium market price is at the juncture of the two curves (Fig. 3-2).

Demand and supply curves do not have to assume these shapes. For example, there could be a situation where supply of a good increased with decline in price, in which case the *SS* curve, like the *DD* curve, would be downward sloping. But the logic of microeconomic mathematical methods requires that the demand and supply curves assume something like the slopes indicated if predictions about price and other aspects of the system are to be made. Therefore, as we examine the logic of why the curves assume their shapes, we must be aware that there are different reasons for demand curves sloping downward in the two markets for goods and factors. In other words, as discussed in the last chapter, the real world must be seen in a way that conforms to the demands of a deductive theory.

The theory predicts that if all *ceteris paribus* conditions are met, the demand for a particular good will exactly equal supply

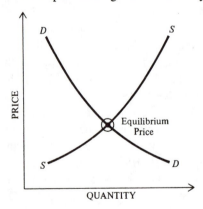

Fig. 3-2. Equilibrium Price.

and so all goods produced will be consumed without waste. When we look at the conditions that must hold in order for this to happen (see below), we must wonder about the usefulness of the theory for explaining any real situation, since the conditions seem so unrealistic. In fact, though, the "miracle" of a supply of goods approximately equal to the demand for them *is* achieved in real markets, leading us to believe that the theory is not utterly detached from reality. It was this "miracle" that in the first place generated interest among scholars of high caliber in explaining it.

In the last chapter (p. 41), we covered some of the conditions that must exist for the model to work. In addition there are the following, more formal conditions:

1. There must be only one homogeneous commodity sold in any given market. The point of this, of course, is that the logical system describing the *perfectly competitive market,* which is what we are describing, requires that all the units expressed in magnitudes be interchangeable. Apples and oranges cannot be equated with respect to demand and supply because people do not value them equally and the analysis won't work if one apple is not equal to another. Hence, for example, one might have to analyze the market for Jonathan apples separate from the market for Delicious apples.

2. There must be no obstruction to the free supply of goods, to the free expression of demand for goods, or to the free movement of prices. Again, the reason for this condition is that the logical model requires supply and demand to alter only in response to price, and price must be free to seek the level reflecting the supply-demand situation.

3. There must be a large number of firms and households. The reason for this is so that the actions of any one of these alone cannot affect price. Price must not respond to the decision of any one firm or household but must be determined by demand and supply of the whole of the market community. If

this condition is not met, as in monopoly, price will reflect not the supply-demand situation but rather the wishes of the firm with respect to the revenue it would like to have.

4. The total quantity and quality of resources must be constant. Again, the logic of the model is such that it can accommodate shifts not in the absolute amounts of the goods involved in supply and demand but only in the amount from the absolute stock offered at a certain price.

5. The value of consumer goods must be equal to the value of factors, so that the flow circuit can be balanced. Put in other words, the revenue accruing to the producing firms must equal the payments they make to households for the factors of production. As in the case with the other conditions, this one is built into the logic of the model as a closed circuit. A surprising implication of this is that profit cannot be seen as some quantity extracted from the economy but is rather a functioning, integral part of the economy.

To summarize, the conditions that are assumed to exist in order that the model be predictive are ones demanded by the logical structure of the model, in particular the need to simplify and hold constant most variables, both exogenous and endogenous. If necessary one could extend the above list to include other assumptions. Underlying all of them is the major assumption that the households desire to maximize utility and the firms profit.

Surprisingly, some so-called primitive economies may more closely approximate these conditions than our own economy, for which the theory was developed. For example, homogeneity is a very common element through many areas of tribal societies. Among the Turu of Tanzania, a stateless society whose basic structure is segmentary, being composed of homogeneous lineages, product homogeneity is usual in the sense of interchangeability of goods. In addition, market transactions are uninhibited by government intrusion. A combination of jural rules in the local segments and balanced opposition of force between segments ensures that market transactions will be conducted in terms of the values exchanged and not in terms of force. Furthermore, the rule of exogamy that forces men to obtain wives from outside their clans, far from interfering with the conditions necessary for free trade, creates mutual dependency (as previously noted when discussing Levi-Strauss' theory of marriage), since without this rule men might not bother to obtain wives elsewhere but would marry within the lineage and even marry their own sisters. Furthermore, in Turu society all homesteads act sometimes as households and sometimes as firms, all produce the same homogeneous things, and the number of homesteads is very large. Women constitute the labor market, for the most part, and the divorce rate is very high consonant with the mobility needed in this labor force, which must go to where the most value can be obtained for them.

This is not to say that there are no restrictions on the market that interfere with its acting entirely according to the model, but these restrictions—for example, on the mobility of land— have, in my opinion, been unduly emphasized at the expense of elements such as those noted above, which contribute to a highly competitive market system. Both Polly Hill (1970: 21), speaking of Akwapim farmers of Ghana who introduced cocoa growing to that country, and Leopold Pospisil (1963: 29), speaking of the Kapauku Papuans of New Guinea, have referred to their subjects as "capitalists," implying thereby a kind of economic activity that conforms well to the classical model. Pospisil is particularly straightforward in this claim. He insists that the Kapauku utilize barter only in a minor way (Pospisil 1963: 18), sales of goods through the use of a true cowrie shell money being the normal means of exchange for almost everything, including things for which Americans would never dream of using money. Even in the family, for example, food is in effect distributed through the market mechanism (Pospisil

1963: 30). [Incidentally, Kapauku money is clearly used by
them as both a medium of exchange and a unit of account (Pospisil 1963: 19–20), a distinction that will be explored later but
that, for now, may be explained as the difference between using
money to effect exchanges and using monetary units to calculate
the relations of the values of different things to each other. The
two kinds of "money" are independently variable (see Melitz
1970).] The Kapauku buy and sell land, goods, labor, and professional services such as midwifery. A foster son even pays for
the services of his foster father, and grief over the death of a
nonrelative is also compensated with money. Further (Pospisil
1963: 25):

> In one respect the Kapauku distribution of goods appears more
> capitalistic than our own. The natives do not have the institution
> of gift, by which ownership of an item is transferred to a re-
> cipient who is not legally obligated to reciprocate with an equiva-
> lent value. In other words, a Kapauku cannot forfeit, even by an
> explicit declaration, his legal right to request a return of something
> that has been given to another person.

Kapauku lease, rent, and loan capital and extend credit, so that
in 170 cases of loans involving 55 males as creditors and debt-
ors, the total value equaled 170,382 glass beads, which could
purchase 11,358 kilos of pork (Pospisil 1963: 26).

In short (Pospisil 1963: 28), Kapauku economy is marked
by such "capitalistic" features as true money (both as unit of
account and medium of exchange), savings, speculation, markets regulated by supply and demand, almost universal exchange
through sales, a paid labor market, lease contracts, and aggressive, competitive actions by Kapauku apparently motivated to
maximize wealth.

With this overview of the general structure of microtheory
completed, we may turn now to the more fundamental problem
of establishing the supply and demand curves for the goods and
factors markets.

HOUSEHOLD DEMAND CURVE

Taking first the demand for goods, i.e., that one of four sectors of the market which consists of households consuming goods, economics at one time employed cardinal utility theory exclusively to explain the downward-sloping demand curve demanded by the model. In this approach the *actor,* a term that we shall use, as economists do, to describe the decision-maker of the model, whether individual or group, is assumed to desire to obtain the *largest sum of satisfaction* or utility. In addition, the utility of each additional unit of a particular good which he desires is assumed to decline at the margin (the so-called *law of diminishing marginal utility*), so that the second unit obtained is of less utility than the first, the third less than the second, etc. In this method, establishing the maximizing path is simply a matter of comparing the utility (not the amount) of different goods desired by the actor at a given moment and taking into account change in utilities after a consumption act due to marginal decline in the value of the good chosen. As the utility of one good declines at the margin, the actor's preference turns to another good if its utility now exceeds that of the first good. He switches back to the first good when the utility of the second in turn declines to a level lower than that of the first. The pattern of desire for any good, or for the combination of goods desired by the actor, can therefore be expressed as a downward-sloping demand curve (Fig. 3-3), as the model requires.

As a prelude to graphs to follow, let us look carefully at the logic of this graph (Fig. 3-3), which shows the preference pattern for some good, say pork, for one of Pospisil's Kapauku. Point *a* shows that when the quantity of pork which our Kapauku is able to obtain is 2 (2 pounds, 2 tons, or whatever) its utility for him is high (5), but when he can get 5 units of pork (point *b*) its utility drops to 2. By connecting these two points

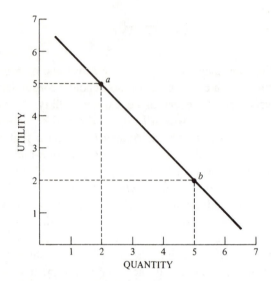

Fig. 3-3. Cardinal Utility.

and others that could be specified, we get a curve or line which expresses the whole preference pattern in one graphic picture. In the market for any one good, therefore, the utility-maximizing actor will always reduce his preference for a given product as the amount offered increases, because he can get more utility by switching to some other good in the market. Hence the demand curve for any product is downward sloping, showing a declining demand with increase in supply.

Unfortunately, while the cardinal utility theory of demand gives the kind of curve desired by the general theory and also seems to reflect reality in the sense that generally people desire more of a certain good in proportion to the amount they have of it and in relation to their desire for other things, the theory has the defect that it requires utility to be measurable and no way has been found to do this. Modern economics has gotten around this problem by developing a demand theory that gives the desired demand curve without having to do more than rank the utilities of various goods against each other, thus avoiding absolute measurement. That is to say, the utilities of different amounts of a good or of different goods are arranged hierarchically on an ordinal rather than an interval scale, the distance between the magnitudes of the utilities being indeterminate in the first but not in the second instance, as shown in Fig. 3-4.

This new method, called *indifference analysis,* assumes, to quote Curry and Wade (1968: 11):

> . . . that actors will allocate any fixed quantity of something among alternative uses in such a way as to maximize their aggregate utility as well as in such a way that their marginal valuation per units of cost of their various . . . reward units will be equal.

That is to say, as the actor seeks to maximize the utility of the aggregate of goods that he consumes, he balances different combinations of them so that at some point, say where he has a choice between obtaining with his resources two apples and five oranges, or five apples and two oranges, he will be indifferent to these combinations, taking one to be equal to the other

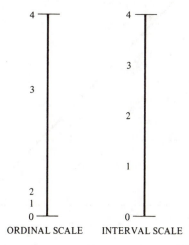

ORDINAL SCALE   INTERVAL SCALE

Fig. 3-4. Scaling.

with respect to the amount of utility it brings. But as he consumes one type of good, for example the apples, this affects his desire for the other, whose utility rises in proportion to its relative scarcity.

The value of this idea is so great that Edel uses it as the basis for his account of the usefulness of economic theory for anthropology (Edel 1969). Let's examine it, beginning with first principles. In indifference analysis one starts with certain goods, say A and B, that a consumer values, and establishes a curve that contains all the combinations of amounts of those goods that have the same utility for the actor. This would be as if in Fig. 3-5 three of A and two of B (point 1) are equivalent to two of A and three of B (point 2); the actor is indifferent to these two combinations. On the other hand, more of both of them is preferable to less of both of them. If the actor had the opportunity he would pick point 3, which gives him three of A and four of B, because this has more utility than the previous combinations (and therefore lies on a utility curve further

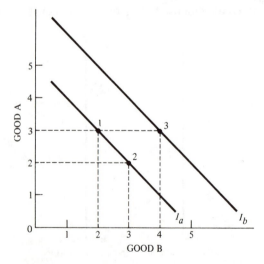

Fig. 3-5. Indifference Curves.

from O). In short, the actor will reduce somewhat consumption of one good to increase consumption of another if the utility of the different combinations is the same (points 1 and 2), and he will always prefer to increase his net consumption of all goods where utility is increased (i.e., shift to curve I^b) and resist any consumption combinations that reduce utility (i.e., shift from curve I^b to curve I^a).

Having established the notion of indifference, we must now take cognizance of the fact that the graph in Fig. 3-5 needs modification in order to show the indifference curve as bowed and convex to zero, which is necessary to the logic of the theory, rather than linear. This convexity is obtained by introducing the idea of the *diminishing rate of marginal substitution*. That is to say, while the actor may be willing to substitute one good for another of equal utility, the amount of utility each unit of the good represents varies along the curve in proportion to the consumption of the other good. If we think of one of the goods as being more essential to subsistence than another, we might call one a "staple" and the other a "luxury." The luxury item will have less utility per unit of valuation than the staple as the supply of staples possessed by an actor is diminished and subsistence is threatened. On the other hand, as his need for staples diminishes by his obtaining possession of them, he will give up more of the staples in order to consume some of the luxuries. We represent this situation in Fig. 3-6.

It will be noted here that the actor equates 5 S and 1 L (point *a*) with 5 L and 1 S (point *c*), showing that these two combinations have equal utility to him as well as representing equal numbers of total units (5 plus 1 equals 6). But note that both are also equal in utility to the combination 2 S and 2 L (point *b*), whose sum is only four units compared to the six units of the other preferences. Another way of putting this is to say that a consumer will be willing to substitute relatively more of a good of which he has much for a good of which he has little while keeping his utilities equated.

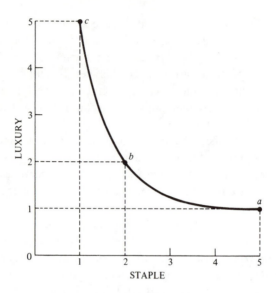

Fig. 3-6. Bowed Indifference Curve.

Throughout this discussion of indifference analysis we have been seeking a way to predict what the rational, maximizing consumer will do when faced with a choice. In cardinal utility analysis we found we had difficulty because prediction required measuring utility absolutely and that could not be done. In indifference analysis a prediction can be made by adding one more step to the theory, a *budget line.*

The analysis assumes that the actor has a given amount of resources which he can allocate to consumption. These resources can be employed to obtain various combinations of units of goods, as represented in Fig. 3-7 on the budget line *b.*

We can illustrate this by the case of an African farmer who could, with the same number of goats, pay for either twenty debes of grain and two dress cloths (point *a*) or five dress cloths and five debes of grain (point *b*). But note this essential fact: while he can obtain either of these combinations, he is not

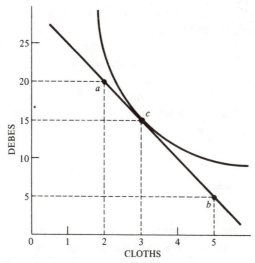

Fig. 3-7. The Budget Line.

indifferent to them. This is another way of saying that the budget line is straight but the indifference line is curved. In fact, as the tangent of the indifference curve to the budget line at point *c* in Fig. 3-7 shows, the actor can afford only one combination on the budget line to which he is indifferent, viz., fifteen debes and three cloths. All the other combinations that he can afford fall below his indifference curve and would be irrational, less desirable choices. Thus, our farmer might find that twenty debes of grain would feed his family during a critical period when their health is endangered, or, at another time, he might find that the happiness of his wives obtained by dressing them well is more essential to a home in equilibrium than more food reserves.

To summarize this sometimes intricate exposition of consumer demand theory, modern microeconomics tells us to look at consumer demand in a way that sees the consumer assigning utility to various combinations of goods as these combinations relate to his resources. His preference combinations form a convex curve relative to zero because of the diminishing rate of marginal substitution. The curve, when related to the various ways the consumer can mix his resources (expressed linearly), allows us to predict that the rational consumer will choose to apply his resources to the mixture of consumption goods on his indifference curve at the point where the budget line is tangent to the curve.

THE FIRM AND SUPPLY OF GOODS

The kind of reasoning involved in indifference analysis and marginal analysis, in which a variable such as utility is juxtaposed against a constant like the budget, can also be used revealingly in analyzing some aspects of the firm's activities. To begin with, we can look at what the firm chooses to produce (among those things which it knows how to produce) in terms of the *production possibilities curve*. The question before a firm such as an African farmer is which good, out of many possibilities, to produce. If he has a choice as between two goods like millet and maize, which should he pick? To begin with, one might postulate that if he has a fixed amount of land and labor the cost of producing 7 units of millet, or 3 of millet and 4 of maize, or 7 units of maize would always be the same and could therefore be represented by a straight cost line (Fig. 3-8). The producer could then ignore the question of the cost of production of the various combinations and concentrate on which combination would be most profitable (point *a*).

Practically speaking, however, the production possibilities cost line is curved, this time concavely to zero, as in Fig. 3-9.

The reason for this is that resources cannot be shifted from producing one thing to producing another without cost. The cost of producing an item increases as resources are shifted from it

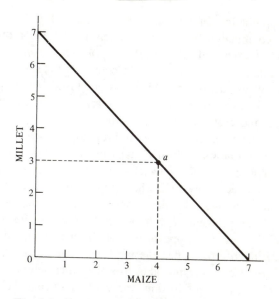

Fig. 3-8. Production Possibilities.

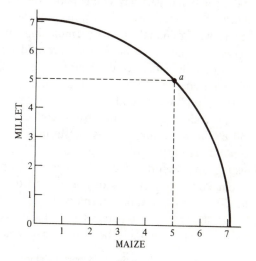

Fig. 3-9. Opportunity Cost.

to the production of another. Hence, as in Fig. 3-9, if one chooses combination *a,* the cost is ten (5 + 5), rather than seven as at each end. This is the *opportunity cost.* A tool or type of labor or other factor is to some degree specialized for the kind of production for which it is employed. As it is shifted from one kind of production to another, it is not as efficiently employed and cost for an equal output climbs.

The implications of this for anthropological work could be illustrated as follows.[1] When Chagga on Mt. Kilimanjaro began to grow coffee, a product which eventually came to dominate their internal economy and which represents one of the most successful examples of "development" in Africa, they were faced with the problem of shifting resources to this form of production. The problem appears to have been that although there was a desire to grow coffee the market was uncertain, so much so that producers were not able to satisfy themselves that shifting to this form of production was worth reducing the production of bananas.

Put in analytical language, they could make the shift only if the opportunity costs were low. The shift in fact appears to have been made with minimal costs by employing labor which was not otherwise employed in banana culture and by planting the coffee trees in the interstices of the banana trees, which space was otherwise unused. As the market for coffee grew in size and dependability, land and time devoted to bananas were gradually shifted to coffee, the income from coffee being large enough to offset the opportunity costs of shifting from banana culture and cattle raising to coffee culture.

An interesting and well-documented account of opportunity cost comes from Polly Hill's studies of the introduction of cocoa growing into Ghana by Akwapim farmers (Hill 1970: 21ff). Hill remarks on the naiveté of persons who have marveled at this event as if it were a miracle because it happened without

[1] For the following analysis I am in good part indebted to Mr. Julius Matiko.

European direction by farmers thought to be traditionalists. She notes that the Akwapim were already growing palm oil and exporting it in great amounts, although the palm-trees products are indigenous. On the other hand, Akwapim had also begun to grow rubber, certainly also a result of opportunity costs, since rubber had no indigenous uses. Beginning about 1897 (Hill 1970: 23), they began to migrate westward and buy land in Akim for the purpose of growing cocoa, and were exporting 40,000 tons a year in 1911. Hill clearly believes this stemmed from a changing cost situation in that (1) they had money from palm and rubber sales to finance the sale of land; (2) they could buy the land and move into strange areas because of the Pax Britannica; (3) there was a market for the cocoa; and (4) the labor of men was available for this new production. The production of palm oil did not decrease significantly until cocoa had been established for twenty years (Hill 1970: 24), which tellingly makes the point that opportunity costs relative to the production of palm products were low.

One may also analyze the question of *how* to produce[2] by

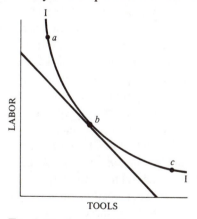

Fig. 3-10. Isoquant Curve.

[2] For the classification of production in terms of what, how, and how much (the latter yet to be explored), I am particularly indebted to Haveman & Knopf (1966) and Dorfman (1953).

means of the *isoquant curve,* which is similar to indifference analysis. Economists have found that when such factors as capital (machines or tools) and labor are mixed, the cost of the different mixes varies with the same level of output. The isoquant curve, representing a fixed output (see Fig. 3-10), is normally displayed as convex because the efficiency of production (measured by cost) declines as one shifts increasingly to labor intensive or capital intensive methods. At point *a,* where much labor is employed with few machines, the output is the same as at point *c,* where there is little labor and a great dependence on machines. However, note that at point *b,* which is a unique combination of machines and labor, the level of output is the same as at the other points but the cost is least. If one were to determine all the combinations of labor and tools possible for a producer, these would be represented by the *constant outlay line,* a linear curve like a budget line, and one could determine by the tangency of the isoquant curve to the constant outlay line what the rational mix of factors for a given level of output is. In fact, there seems no necessary reason why the isoquant curve could not be concave or even linear for some situations.

To illustrate, let us take an African farmer who wishes to obtain a certain level of production, say 500 lbs of millet, by spreading production over a wide area, such as 15 acres (land is his capital), and utilizing the services of one wife, or by putting two wives on five acres or three wives on three acres. If we assume that wives cost five cows apiece and land one cow per acre, the first of these solutions would cost him 20 cows, the second 15 cows, and the third 18 cows. The second of these combinations would be the rational one, if he has 15 cows, because it is the cheapest relative to output. With the same 15 cows he could obtain other combinations of wives and land but all would produce less than these.

In practical fact, this illustration is unrealistic, at least for the Turu. Among the Turu, the maximum amount of land which a single woman seems able to handle is two acres. Since this is the case, the first solution is impossible because no Turu woman could cope with 15 acres. The second solution is unlikely for the same reason. That is to say, why would a Turu farmer spend resources on five acres of land for two wives in order to obtain a certain amount of grain when he knows that each handle a maximum of two acres apiece? The third solution is unrealistic because it does not utilize the women's labor to the maximum. However, we should note that the unreality of the first solution is based on a physical impossibility. In the second and third cases, the mixes are possible and it could be that such solutions under certain circumstances would make sense regardless of the fact that land and labor are not fully utilized. In fact, the rational mix for Turu farmers seems to be one woman per two acres when combined with certain other factor proportions, such as an optimum number of cattle to produce the manure necessary to give the land its minimal fertility.

One useful idea that has cross-cultural applicability and relates to the question of factor proportions is the *economy of scale*. In some situations the return to be obtained with increase in the number of laborers or machines employed is such that it makes sense to incur increased costs in order to obtain the proportionally higher output. Economies of scale seem to be represented in a Turu village by work parties engaged in, for example cultivating crops, building houses, and threshing grain. When the time comes to hoe a millet field to prevent weeds, the job must be done quickly to avoid damage to the young plants. In order to get the job done in one day, the producer finds it economic to obligate his own future services and to pay the work party with beer and a slaughtered goat.

Turning now to the question of *how much* to produce, in the theory of supply of goods by a competitive firm, the amount of a good to be supplied is postulated to be a function of the price per unit of that good, the input-output relationship of the technique of production employed, and the prices of the tools or factors of production. This relationship may be expressed as

$S_g = f(P_g, I\text{--}O, P_f)$, where S_g is the supply of a good, P_g the price, $I\text{--}O$ the input-output relationship of the production machines, and P_f the price of factors of production.

Incidentally, the $I\text{--}O$ variable is of special interest to anthropologists. To economists this is the quality of the tool with respect to the spread between the first unit of a good it produces and the total number it is capable of producing without augmenting the machine. For example, in order to economically produce doughnuts with a doughnut-making machine, one must obtain a machine that can make innumerable doughnuts in order to produce the first. All the capacity of the machine beyond the amount actually produced by it (if short of its maximum productivity) is wasted. Hence, the machine is a fixed cost not varying with amount produced, a feature which is very important in the determination of rational prices. In anthropology we recognize something like this in the energy potential of a machine as witnessed in the evolution of human technology. Machines have a quality such that between different machines the same amount of energy input gives different energy outputs. For example, the introduction of steel axes among Salisbury's Siane in New Guinea increased the amount of time available for other activities because the steel tools were more "efficient" (Salisbury 1962: vi).

Turning back to our production function, the theory visualizes a firm as faced with the following problem: in a market situation where the amount that can be charged for a good is set by demand (which varies with supply rather than being conveniently constant), and in which some costs (like the machines used for production) are fixed but some (such as the amount of labor to be used) are variable (so that *total cost* [TC] is a mixture of fixed and varying costs), how does one decide how much to produce in order to maximize profits and avoid loss? As we shall see, the answer is not immediately obvious and certain common-sense answers are wrong, such as the answer that one should stop increasing production when the *average cost* (AC) of the products begins to increase. In fact, maximum profits are made where costs are increasing.

The answer starts with the specification that prediction can be made only for the short run, i.e., the period of time during which all the variables affecting production costs remain constant *except* the amount of labor used. Resources, tools, interest on capital, even the wage rate, but not the amount of labor, are held constant. Fortuitously, in the real world the supply of labor is most likely to be the variable cost in the short run, so the theory fits reality.

The answer then specifies that the firm is rational and will attempt to maximize profits. Profits are defined as total revenue minus total cost ($P = TR - TC$). So the problem becomes how to maximize the difference between TR and TC.

The logic involved in answering this question requires next

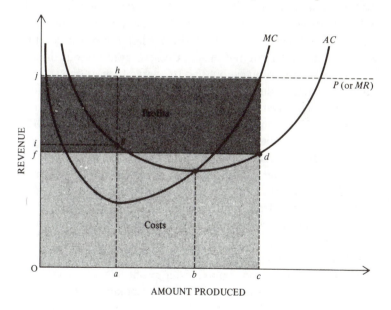

Fig. 3-11. Rational Output.

that we understand what is meant by *marginal cost* (*MC*) and *average cost* (*AC*). Average cost is total cost divided by the number of units produced by the firm. This is represented by the *AC* curve in Fig. 3-11. If we pick point *d*, average cost can be graphically represented at that stage in production as the diagonally shaded area to the left of *d*. In others words, if the number of units produced is divided by the total cost, we get a figure that can be plotted as *d* and *d* then can be used as a reference point to convert average cost into a graphical representation equal to the *area* of the graph covered by *f, o, c, d*.

Marginal cost, the theoretically more important concept, is the cost at any stage of production of producing one more unit of a good. That is, given the average cost at any point in production, the cost of producing one more unit will *not* be equal to the average cost (except where the two curves cross *a* at *b*). We need not concern ourselves extensively with the derivation of the MC curve, but will be content to simply note that the concept of marginal cost derives from the relative relationship between total cost and changes in output. The *AC* curve averages out the cost of each new unit produced but the *MC* curve focuses on each new unit, just as the concept of average speed (*AS*) averages out a change in the speed of a car which is accelerating from 0 to 70 miles an hour in ten seconds to give an average of say 35 MPH whereas the concept of marginal speed (*MS*) focuses on the rate of acceleration, which would probably take the form of an exponential curve and which could be expressed, through calculus, as a derivative. The *AC* and *MC* curves are related, of course, since both derive from total cost, but they are distinguished because both are necessary to the logic of price prediction. As we shall see, we need the *AC* curve to show the total cost at any point in production, and we need the *MC* curve to show when any point in production is maximizing profit.

Why do the curves assume a U shape? Looking at the marginal cost curve in Fig. 3-11, for each additional unit of goods produced after the first up to point *a* the capital investment of the firm is being increasingly more efficiently utilized because the production facilities are increasingly more nearly used to capacity, so marginal costs drop. If the cost of producing each additional unit drops, the average cost drops also, so the *AC* curve is going down. After point *a* marginal cost begins to rise while average costs do not because they are still drawing, so to speak, on a previous surplus of efficiency. The *MC* rises because capital is being used less efficiently, i.e., beyond its capacity. For example, there are too many workers for the number of machines available.

With this background we may turn to the final step in the logic of price prediction. In Fig. 3-11, the horizontal line *P* (which is also called *MR* or marginal revenue) represents the price consumers are willing to pay for the product. Price varies with scarcity, of course, but may be represented here as a constant in terms of which the variables of amount produced and revenue are allowed to vary. (This is another way of saying that *P* in this graph is equal to marginal revenue, the amount of revenue produced by each additional unit produced.)

What price should the producer charge? Since the price he can charge is determined by the consumers, the question really becomes, at what level should he produce given the price he can charge? Shall he produce at point *a*? This would be irrational, because although a profit could be made (that is to say, cost are *i, o, a, g,* leaving a considerable area of profit, *j, i, g, h*), if he continues to produce he can push the profit area to the right and downward as *AC* continues to decline. That is to say, if he continues to produce he can expand the area of profit both horizontally and vertically.

Should he produce at *b*? Here his marginal costs continue to rise (whereas they were only beginning to rise at *a*), but in addition his average costs are beginning an upturn. Common sense might dictate that where one's average and marginal costs are beginning to rise, that is the point where production should level off. Interestingly, however, this is also an irrational decision. The rational solution is best indicated by phrasing the situation slightly differently. How can we maximize on this graph the area which is vertically shaded (the profit area)? The answer is at point c. At point c the marginal cost line intersects the marginal revenue or price line, and we can demonstrate mathematically that this is the point at which the profit area is maximized. If one should produce at a higher level, the profit area would begin to shrink, as one can intuitively see by noting that the cost area is determined by where one is on the AC curve and from point d that curve moves up sharply. In short, at point c the profit area is shrinking horizontally but expanding vertically at a rate that makes up for the shrink.

All this is a way of saying that given a rational firm in a competitive market, the relationship between cost and revenue is such that where the relative positions of cost and revenue are such that marginal cost equals marginal revenue, that is the rational production level that will maximize profit. Any movement of production beyond that point will generate costs in excess of revenue, which will cause a reversion of production, and any movement below that point will generate forces in the shape of increased profits, which will cause an increase in production up to point $MC = MR$.

There is an interesting implication in this theory which should be underscored. What this theory says in effect is that you don't care about increasing costs of production (increasing MC and AC) but only about the difference between cost and price. You balance the cost of production against the revenue that can be earned, and you continue to produce at increased cost as long as prices can be increased to cover costs. Hence the reason for the peculiar real-life phenomenon, that when the costs to a firm rise, the firm, instead of cutting prices to keep up demand, increases prices. Its only theoretical alternative is to cut back on production and thereby decrease costs, which is an irrational course as long as profits are increasing.

In summary, the theory of the supply of goods by the firms

warns us to be aware of the variable nature of costs as they relate to revenue rather than be guided by common sense. One does not necessarily maximize by selling goods at the place where costs are lowest, but where costs are lowest proportional to price. In more practical terms, understanding the theory of supply familiarizes us with the concepts of profit, revenue, and cost (average and marginal) and the technical nature of the input-output relationship of factors of production.

Let us now briefly illustrate the use of this theory for field work through a review of the activities of Basseri Persian sheep raisers as described by Fredrick Barth (Barth 1964). Barth does not provide us with all the information we need in order to fully implement the theory, nor does he order his information in quite the way I shall, but there is enough information to go a long way toward operationalizing this model, and the reorganization of the material suggested by the model in fact improves on Barth's analysis.

These nomads, who are raising small animals, notably sheep, have certain fixed costs, consisting first of all of household goods such as a tent, bedding, saddle bags, ropes, and the like. Barth's way of presenting his data suggests that he thinks of these as the only fixed costs, but there are others. For example, in certain respects shepherding can be seen as a fixed cost. A shepherd must be provided whether there are two animals or 200, although, as we shall see, the marginal cost of herding increases with increase in the size of the herd over the maximum the herder can efficiently handle. And Barth says that 10% of the herd must be in rams in order to fertilize the ewes, leading one to suspect that in fact there are probably usually more rams than necessary at most times. Fixed costs would also apparently include the need to shift the herd at regular intervals no matter what the size, because only 30% survive if kept in the same locale for a year due to the fact that the strain of sheep raised is "less robust" than some other, meaning that they pick up diseases.

These would be the principal fixed costs. The price or marginal revenue line is represented by the fact that a live adult female sheep brings eighty *Tomans* on the market. We can treat this as an equivalent to the short-run price of our model, since Barth indicates no awareness of price fluctuation. However, in light of other things he says we must modify his claim on the suspicion that this value declines with age, since the animal's value derives in good part from her potential for the production of lambs, which stops after seven years. Other than that, the sheep produce approximately sixty Tomans of products each per year.

Most interesting is the marginal cost curve. Barth claims that one shepherd can care for 400 sheep, but the work is exacting and strenuous so that 200 is a more practical number, and he says also that the efficiency of care declines at the margin, reaching 0 at 200 or 400, whichever figure is appropriate since Barth seems undecided. One suspects that in fact this is a U-shaped curve and that efficiency *increases* with increments of sheep at the beginning but then begins to deline at some unknown point. This must be because of the fixed costs, which counter the small increase in inefficiency represented by the early growth of the herd. Among these marginal costs must be the need to maintain a ratio of 1:9 male–female, resulting in the need to carry larger and larger numbers of male animals at greater and greater cost because their care and the care of the females costs more and more at the margin. Furthermore, 15% of the females available for sale must in fact be kept aside to maintain the herd size at any given magnitude.

The most obvious fault in Barth's analysis that shows up under the microscope of our model is his failure to explain why shepherds do not utilize other labor hired under *dandune* and *nimei* contracts whenever the marginal value of sheep becomes zero, since these contracts allow the herder to fix his marginal costs. In the first kind of contract, the herder must return the flock he holds at the end of the contract period, less all its produce. In the second type, running for three to five years, he returns only half the flock and none of the produce.

In any case, Barth claims that when marginal costs exceed marginal revenue, a nomad sells out and moves into town, where he invests in land and a whole new ball game begins for him. How he does this is also unclear, since Barth claims that the market for sheep is slow. This must mean that the demand for the animals is not great and is inelastic. On the other hand, and more commonly, if the minimal balance necessary to keep a herd growing is violated, as for example by cutting into the 15% reserve necessary to reproduce the herd, a positive feedback cycle is instituted that causes a steady decline in capital and eventually forces the nomad into town as a destitute rather than as a rich winner.

Obviously sheep raising is only one sector of a larger Basseri economy in which sheep production as a road to riches is replaced at the right time by investment in land, and the process probably begins with poor peasants beginning a climb that in the early stages must be very profitable, since Barth claims that barring famine and great pestilence, a man can realize an increment on his capital of about 40% per year. Again, this must be balanced against the increasing costs as the herd grows.

Generally speaking, Barth's analysis fails, when it does so, because of inadequate sensitivity to the variablity of prices, costs, and returns in relation to each other. He tends to a mechanical view whereas analytical economics is highly sensitive to movement in the variables.

HOUSEHOLD SUPPLY OF FACTORS

Having matched the consumer demand sector with the firm supply sector, we have explained the logic of price in one half of the total market system. There remains the household supply of factors sector and the firm demand for factors sector, which must be integrated with each other and with the first half of the market in order for the system to balance out.

Members of a household earn the wherewithal to buy goods in the market by selling their services and capital possessions (factors). There is a curve for household supply of factors, which is laid over the firm demand curve to determine the equilibrium price for factors. The problem, so to speak, is again to get a firm demand curve that is downward sloping and a household supply curve that is upward sloping.

How do we obtain the household supply curve? As in the previous examination of the household, we are dealing with persons desiring to maximize utility (rather than profits), and just as in the previous instance we resort to indifference analysis, juxtaposing preference for two "goods," leisure and wages, to show how much leisure is equivalent in the mind of the consumer to how much wages.

Essentially, the supply of labor from the household is taken to be such that there is an upward-sloping curve because as the wages paid are increased the supply of labor increases, even though there is debate among economists about the adequacy of such an assumption (Haveman and Knopf 1966: 73ff.). They note that as a man's wages increase he becomes less and less inclined to give up more leisure for more wages, and more inclined to substitute some leisure for increase. The result is a backward-sloping curve (Fig. 3-12). In the first part of this curve, up to point *a,* the amount of labor offered increases with the amount of wages. But after this point the amount offered begins to decline (and the curve turns backward) with further increase in wages. There is, then, as Haveman and Knopf say, no law of upward-sloping supply of factors, but much may still be accomplished by focusing on the upward-sloping portion of the curve.

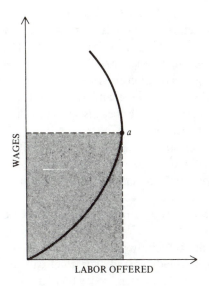

Fig. 3-12. Backward Sloping
Labor Curve.

THE FIRM DEMAND FOR FACTORS

Determining the demand for factors by the firm can be illustrated
by looking at the demand for labor, and the reasoning is identical
to that used in determining the firm's logic when supplying goods.
Instead of a total cost we have a *total revenue,* the average cost
curve becomes the *total revenue product curve* (*TRP*), and the
marginal cost curve becomes the *marginal revenue curve* (*MRC*).

The logic of the relationship of these entities leads to the conclusion that the rational firm will pay for factors that amount at
which the marginal revenue product equals the marginal factor
cost (*MRP = MFC*). This is exactly parallel to the conclusion
that the amount of a good which a firm will supply is determined
by the equation of marginal cost and marginal revenue. If the

firm pays a price in which *MRP* exceeds *MFC*, it is not obtaining as much of the factors as it needs to make the best profit, and if its *MRP* is less than *MFC* it is losing money. Hence it settles on the equilibrium factor price, $MRP = MFC$. Furthermore, the curve representing this relationship conforms to the needed downward slope of a demand curve and is therefore the reverse of the firm supply curve. This is because as the supply of factors increases, the cost declines.

There is an interesting problem connected with the place of labor in a market model, to which we allude here in order to illustrate a fundamental property of analytical economic thought. This problem can be illustrated by looking at Richard Salisbury's study of Siane economy in *From Stone to Steel* (1962). Salisbury's thesis was that these New Guinea people live in corporate groups whose members jointly produce subsistence goods (mainly food), which are mutually shared. The chief capital necessary to produce these goods is women, for whom marriages are contracted. In addition, Siane need to establish ties with persons with whom they have no obligatory kinship relations. These three spheres of exchange (within the corporate group, between corporate groups for women, and between unrelated people), are, according to Salisbury, "relatively independent" (Salisbury 1962: 106); he came to this conclusion by trying to hold everything else constant while observing the effects on Siane economy of the introduction of steel axes. But he managed to connect the different exchange spheres (as he felt he must, since some unitary system was necessary in order to make rational allocations) in terms of the amount of time given to each enterprise. He concluded that steel axes had the effect of causing a reduction of labor input into the subsistence sector and freeing it for other sectors, principally that of dealing with strangers through *gima* exchange, which is designed, through the giving of luxury gifts, to enhance the status of the giver. Salisbury came to this conclusion by observation of a sample of twelve men and how they used their time, seen in terms of half-day units.

The problem with Salisbury's conclusion, as Frankenberg has pointed out (Frankenberg 1967: 70), is that this amounts to a labor theory of value. We can draw upon Samuelson (1967: 27–29) for an explanation of this theory, which underlies Marxist economics. The labor theory of value was first expounded by the classical economists, such as Smith and Ricardo, and was retained by Marx although the classicists themselves dropped it. The labor theory of value says essentially that the value of a good and the price it brings are directly proportional to the amount of labor put into the product. Exploitation, in the Marxist sense, is reflected in the amount of revenue received by the capitalist which he keeps over and above what he pays labor. Morally he should pay the laborer the whole of what is received above costs of distribution and the like, since the value over these costs belongs to the worker, whose labor gave it its value. But, as Samuelson points out, attributing the value of a good solely to the labor time input ignores the cost of other factors of production. If these other factors were free goods (e.g., land), then the theory would make sense. But these factors are not free goods, and since the amount available decreases as labor input increases and more and more factors are needed, the cost of these other factors increases at the margin. The proportion of value in the finished product that derives from labor, therefore, declines at the margin as labor inputs increase.

Putting all this another way, as long as the elements needed to produce goods vary in supply, the cost and value of the inputs vary as the mix varies. This, as we have seen, gives us a bowed curve of production possibilities rather than a straight-line curve, as would be the case if only the labor input varied.

In the Siane case what this means is simply that the value of a certain activity in which a Siane chooses to engage (subsistence production, gima trade, or exchange of women) varies in proportion to the cost of other factors involved in production in addition to his time. Frankenberg suggests that the Siane material could be reanalyzed in two ways to avoid a labor theory of value: push the study of the relation of the value of product to labor inputs to the limit or use newly acquired money, which is now utilized between these sectors, to relate them as we do in our economy. Actually, after reviewing more recent studies of New Guinea (e.g., Epstein 1968) one wonders whether the Siane did not also have some system of accounting which did relate the various areas, so that they, like us, were able to calculate the value of putting labor into diverse areas in relation to the cost of doing so. Discovering this unit of account would allow us to see a unified economy without being driven to a labor theory of value.

THE COMPETITIVE MARKET:
GENERAL EQUILIBRIUM

Analysis of the various sectors of the market is called *partial equilibrium analysis*. When we combine together all these sectors and the market situation with respect to the demand and supply of all goods, we have *general equilibrium analysis*. The essentials of equilibrium analysis are illustrated in this passage (slightly altered to fit my graph) from Haveman and Knopf (1966: 41–42):

> With demanders competing freely among themselves to buy goods cheaply and suppliers competing freely among themselves to sell goods dearly, the market conflict is on. Resolution of this conflict will occur when one particular price is established in the market. This is the price which will equate the quantity that demanders are willing to buy with the amount suppliers are willing to sell. In Figure [3-13] this price is $2. It is the price that will clear the market. At any price higher than $2, businesses want to sell more of the product than households stand ready to buy. For example, at the price of $2.25 in Figure [3-13], suppliers desire to sell 9000 units [(b)] while demanders are willing to buy only [7500] units [(c)]. There is a surplus on the market which will tend to depress price. At a lower price than $2, for instance, $1.75, households

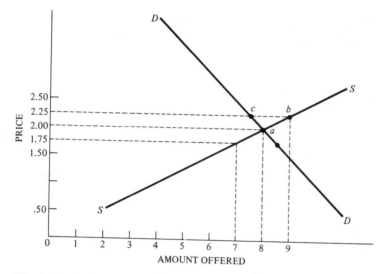

Fig. 3-13. General Equilibrium.

want to buy more [e.g., 8500 units)] than businesses are prepared [e.g., 7000] to sell. In this case, there is a shortage of goods and the price will be bid up. There is only one price in a market which will produce neither a *shortage* nor a *surplus*. This price will just clear the market. It is known as the *equilibrium price* [that is, equilibrium in the sense of a balancing of forces]. In Figure [3-13], the equilibrium price is $2, the equilibrium quantity is 8000 units, and the equilibrium itself is denoted by [*a*.]

The relationship between demand and supply is expressed in the following table, in which *S* means Supply, *D* means Demand, *Q* means Quantity, and *P* means price:

If *D* increases and *S* increases, the *Q* exchanged will increase and *P* will vary.
If *D* is stable and *S* increases, the *Q* exchanged will increase and *P* will decrease.
If *D* decreases and *S* increases, the *Q* exchanged will vary and *P* will decrease.
If *D* increases and *S* is stable, the *Q* exchanged will increase and *P* will increase.
If *D* is stable and *S* is stable, the *Q* exchanged will be stable and *P* will be stable.
If *D* decreases and *S* is stable, the *Q* exchanged will decrease and *P* will decrease.
If *D* increases and *S* decreases, the *Q* exchanged will vary and *P* will increase.
If *D* is stable and *S* decreases, the *Q* exchanged will decrease and *P* will increase.
If *D* decreases and *S* decreases, the *Q* exchanged will decrease and *P* will vary.

The term "vary" here means simply that, given the situation, the quantity or price may go up or down or remain constant depending on the magnitude of change in the variables.

Scott Cook has illustrated how a market can be discussed in terms of general equilibrium analysis in his report on the *metate*

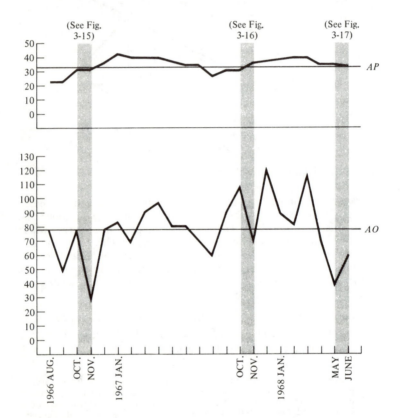

Fig. 3-14. Oaxaca Time-Series Data on Metate Prices and Output.

Cook's raw time-series data on prices and output of metates in Oaxaca City from Aug. 1966 to June 1968. His graphs 3-15 to 3-19 are derived from these data. The graphs 3-15 to 3-17, showing shifts in supply and demand, are based on the data indicated in this raw material by the vertical broken lines.

or quern market in Oaxaca, Mexico (Cook 1970). Cook found that the production of metates correlated closely with demand and price conditions and also with exogenous seasonal, ecological, and cultural variables. It should be emphasized that his use of general equilibrium analysis is for the purpose of describing how he thinks the system works, rather than how it actually works. The value of such an exercise is that it is a more economical and revealing way of communicating what Cook feels is the case in this market. Figure 3-14 shows output and price of metates for twenty-three months.

This material can be treated graphically to show (1) intraseasonal changes and (2) interseasonal changes in supply, demand, and price. Taking (1) first, intraseasonal changes from October to November 1966, October to November 1967, and May to June 1968 are shown in Figs. 3-15, 3-16, and 3-17. (The portions of Fig. 3-14 containing the raw material from which these graphs are derived are indicated by vertical broken lines).

In Fig. 3-15 a decrease in the supply of metates from October to November ($S_1S_1 \rightarrow S_2S_2$) with a proportionate decrease in demand ($D_1D_1 \rightarrow D_2D_2$) leaves price the same. Contrast that with Fig. 3-16, where the supply of metates offered in the market decreases as price increases, with the result that the October supply curve (SS) shifts to its November position while demand remains stable (i.e., conditions of demand are assumed to be constant, and hence the demand curve remains unchanged), so that prices increase from P_1 to P_2. In Fig. 3-17 the situation is the converse of that in Fig. 3-16; or as an increase in supply from May to June shifts the SS curve to yield a decrease in price (P_2). In Figs. 3-16 and 3-17 there is no change in the location of the demand curve, but simply movements along it.

Turning to situation (2), interseasonal movement, between January, the dry season, and August, the rainy season (Fig. 3-18), there is a decrease in demand with a decrease in supply and a consequent decline in price. Contrastingly (Fig. 3-19),

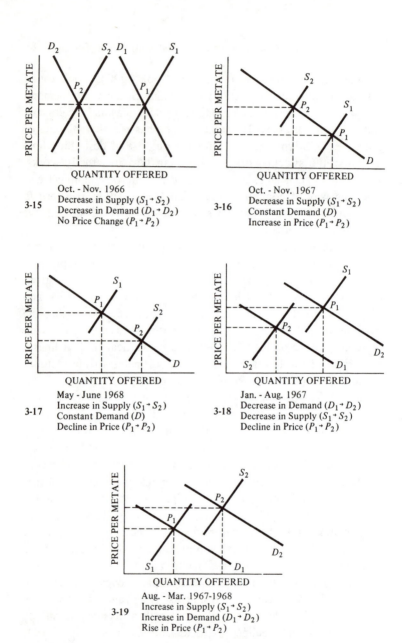

3-15 Oct. - Nov. 1966
Decrease in Supply ($S_1 \rightarrow S_2$)
Decrease in Demand ($D_1 \rightarrow D_2$)
No Price Change ($P_1 \rightarrow P_2$)

3-16 Oct. - Nov. 1967
Decrease in Supply ($S_1 \rightarrow S_2$)
Constant Demand (D)
Increase in Price ($P_1 \rightarrow P_2$)

3-17 May - June 1968
Increase in Supply ($S_1 \rightarrow S_2$)
Constant Demand (D)
Decline in Price ($P_1 \rightarrow P_2$)

3-18 Jan. - Aug. 1967
Decrease in Demand ($D_1 \rightarrow D_2$)
Decrease in Supply ($S_1 \rightarrow S_2$)
Decline in Price ($P_1 \rightarrow P_2$)

3-19 Aug. - Mar. 1967-1968
Increase in Supply ($S_1 \rightarrow S_2$)
Increase in Demand ($D_1 \rightarrow D_2$)
Rise in Price ($P_1 \rightarrow P_2$)

Figs. 3-15 - 3-19. Oaxaca Metate Equilibrium Prices.

between the August rainy season and the March dry season there is an increase in supply, increase in demand, and rise in price.

ELASTICITY

An additional important concept that will be of value to anthropologists is *elasticity*. This concept modifies the theoretically predictable outcomes listed in the chart of prices shifts in response of demand (p. 79). Elasticity refers to the fact that the response of demand and supply to price changes varies from reflecting them perfectly to not reflecting them at all. We can think of this as a relationship between units of price and quantity such that where there is maximum elasticity the maximum quantity is offered for a small change in price. For example, if the units of price were 100-ton gold bars and the quantity available was one pound of peanuts, a single bar of gold, when offered, would suck up the whole supply of peanuts. That is to say, the price unit is so large that the smallest change in the number of units offered would clear the market. Zero elasticity is the situation in which a change of price produces no change whatever in the quantity supplied. That is, the price unit is so small that a change can't equal the smallest unit of quantity. Thus, a one-cent change in the price offered for a diamond would have no effect on the supply of diamonds.

In between infinite and zero elasticity we can define three types:

Unit Elasticity: This is a relative notion but may be taken to refer to that degree of change in the quantity offered in relation to a small change in price that is theoretically expected in a competitive market in which elasticity is not a factor. To put it another way, under this condition quantities offered faithfully reflect price changes.

Inelasticity: Describes a situation wherein a given change in price
produces relatively little effect on demand. Cigarettes in our
economy have this characteristic. The demand for cigarettes is so
great among cigarette users that ordinary changes in price produce
little change in the demand.

Elasticity: Describes a situation wherein a given change in price produces a wild response in demand. Beer and wine have this characteristic in our economy. If the price is dropped a small amount
the increase in demand is out of proportion to the price change.

The importance of this concept can be seen by looking back
at the firm, wherein, it will be recalled, total revenue in its relation to total cost determines profit. Elasticity affects total revenue
as follows:

As price *decreases* total revenue *increases* if quantity demanded is
elastic.

As price *decreases* total revenue *decreases* if quantity demanded is
inelastic.

As price *decreases or increases* total revenue does not change if demand is *unit elastic.*

For the anthropologist the concept of elasticity takes on special
importance, because it is most useful in precisely that area of
production which is most prominent in tribal societies, namely,
subsistence goods. Food is a necessity, it has no real substitute,
the amount that can be consumed is limited, and it is not the
major portion of a consumer's budget. Given all these conditions,
the demand for food is inelastic. In America food is a small part
of the budget. It is worth considering the way this inelasticity
would affect an economy in which it is a much larger part of the
budget. The main effect would be simply that the demand for
food, as long as supplies are insufficient to feed the demander,
would not respond to changes in price and supply. The importance of the concept of elasticity in general is that it warns us
to not always expect an intimate equilibrium between supply and
demand. We should also be aware that the degree to which the
demand for any particular good is elastic or inelastic can be
established only by observation.

THE FLOW OF THE ECONOMY

Having completed the representation of the logic of microanalysis, we come full circle back to the flow diagram with which we began in order to see what the flow of an actual system looks like and to include in this account some consideration of input-output analysis, which may have an important place in future economic anthropology.

The total economy of a people will always be more complicated than the simple model presented at the beginning of this chapter, in which the flow is between the manufacturers of one kind of good and the consumers of that good. Attempting to show the flow of inputs and outputs in the Fur economy, Barth gives us the following diagram (Fig. 3-20) (Barth 1967: 158):

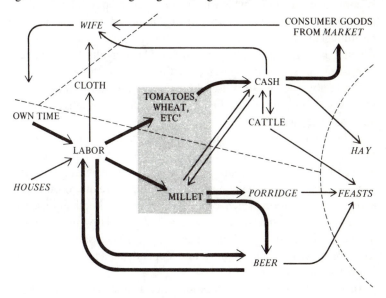

Fig. 3-20. The Pattern of Standard Alternative Choices for a Fur Management Unit.

This shows the pattern of "standard" alternative choices for a Fur management unit and is something like a game in the sense that the field is laid out to show the resources and various choices open to the players. The resultant diagram depicts all the main forms of goods and services in Mountain Fur economy, how they are produced, and how they are normally exchanged for each other. The diagram shows the system as seen by an ordinary villager rather than a craftsman or speculator, and for him it shows impressionistically that a certain balance of inputs and outputs is necessary to maintain the flow of the system. It also shows that inputs and outputs occur in various combinations rather than along a single line, in this case the three combinations of (1) labor-cash-crops-cash-wife-labor, (2) cash-cattle-cash, and (3) labor-millet-beer-labor. That is to say, taking (3) as our example, labor can be put into growing millet, which in turn is converted into beer, which in turn is used to pay labor, which in turn can be put back into growing millet, etc.; or labor can be funneled into another sector, namely growing cash crops, which takes us into a different circle. The magnitude of inputs into a certain sector is suggested by the width of the arrow.

While a flow diagram is useful for the preliminary outline of an economy, it is little more than a complicated descriptive device and has little analytical value.

A higher level of input-output analysis would be on the order of Lee's (1969) analysis of !Kung Bushman food production, where the inputs and outputs are measured and given magnitudes. This enables one to calculate exactly how inputs relate to outputs, a sort of calculation which can have interesting implications, as we shall see. The question that Lee asked was, How much work must a Bushman do (i.e., what energy input is necessary) in order to feed himself and his family and dependents (i.e., to get the output of life maintenance)?

In order to answer the question, Lee calculated the number of man-days devoted to food gathering in a !Kung camp, the number of persons who had to be fed, and the nutritional quality of the food consumed, particularly the staple mongongo nut. He reasoned that if all persons worked all of every day to feed themselves, a *subsistence effort index* (S) of 1.00 would denote this fact. That is to say, if ten people work ten days, 10 divided by 10 equals 1.00. On the other hand, if five people work ten days to feed ten, S equals .5. Lee calculated from the data he collected that for his camp, the S index was .23 for the period of most of July 1964, which means that one man working for one man-day can feed four people (or, e.g., two people working a half-day each can feed four). Whichever way one computes the implications, the fact is that the Bushmen must work far less than is usually thought in order to feed themselves.

Hence, even this elementary level of input-output analysis shows much more exactly what Barth was trying to show with his flow chart. For example, Lee's results show that Bushmen have a surplus of labor that could be applied to other forms of production, if they chose to do so and if the opportunity were available. It also shows that anything that would prevent them from achieving a subsistence effort index of at least .23 could be disastrous for Bushman subsistence.

Input-output analysis can be carried to much higher levels if one has the data and chooses to use it in this way. The possibilities can be suggested by reviewing briefly the theory of input-output analysis, which is a creation of Leontief (1963) (which must be carefully differentiated from the input-output variable mentioned in connection with the theory of the firm). The basic purpose of input-output analysis is to show logically how all the different sectors of an economy relate to each other, thus making it possible to determine with a high degree of accuracy what effect can be expected throughout an economy when input is changed in one sector. The method can be used, when augmented with computers, to analyze an economy of many sectors, but the logic can be displayed by imagining a simple economy of only three sectors: agriculture, manufacturing, and "households" (meaning, the area from which factors of production come).

Taking the agricultural sector first, suppose that in the economy we are studying the sector produces 100 units of goods (which can be anything one wishes: 100 bushels of potatoes, 100 tons of wheat, etc.), and these units are absorbed into the closed economy as follows: 25 units go to agriculture itself (i.e., it must use 25 units of its own product to continue the productive process), 20 units go to the manufacturing sector so that it can continue to produce, and 55 units go to consumers of various types. This can be tabulated as follows:

SECTOR	OUTPUT TO SELF (AGRICULTURE)	OUTPUT TO MANUFACTURING	OUTPUT TO CONSUMERS	TOTAL OUTPUT
Agriculture	25	20	55	100

In order to reveal how this economy is integrated it is necessary now to add a cross-cutting column showing the total of inputs to Agriculture from sectors other than Agriculture. This might look as follows:

AGRICULTURAL SECTOR	
Input from Self	25
Input from Manufacturing	14
Input from Households (Factors)	80

Put into words, the agricultural sector must obtain 25 inputs of whatever units are being measured from itself, 14 inputs from manufacturing, and 80 units from households in order that Agriculture can turn out 100 outputs to go to the various sectors as previously described.

After the agricultural sector input column is placed across the agricultural sector output row, the input and output rows and columns for the other sectors must be added, as follows:

INPUT

	Agriculture	Manufacturing	Consumers
Agriculture	$25_{(0.25)}$	$20_{(0.40)}$	$55_{(0.183)}$
Manufacture	$14_{(0.14)}$	$6_{(0.12)}$	$30_{(0.100)}$
Households	$80_{(0.80)}$	$180_{(3.60)}$	$40_{(0.133)}$

(OUTPUT)

If we ignore for the moment the decimal numbers in parentheses in the lower right-hand corner of each box, we can see that the Manufacturing row is simply a list of the outputs it makes and how they are distributed to other sectors and to itself. The same is true of Households. And the Manufacturing column as well as the Consumers column (which may be equated to Households in order to make the economy closed) are the inputs to each from all sectors including themselves, which make possible their output.

In order to make this data usable for calculations about how changes in one sector affect another, it is necessary to convert these input-output figures into comparable figures (that is, we must somehow equate 25 bushels of potatoes with 14 units of some manufactured good). This is done by changing these figures into ratios. Agriculture's inputs from the various sectors are divided by its total output so that, for example, Agriculture's 25 inputs to itself, when divided by its total output of 100, gives the ratio 0.25 (in parentheses). Or Agriculture's 14 inputs from Manufacturing, when divided by Agriculture's 100 outputs, gives a ratio of 0.14.

To our matrix with its ratios must now be added one other important fact (or is it an assumption?) about the relationship of sectors of an economy. Leontief tells us that there is a relatively invariant connection between inputs and outputs. This means that if inputs are changed the outputs of that sector will change, and, more importantly, since the sectors are interconnected a change in input in one sector will affect *all* the sectors, not just the one to which the input is directly connected. For example, if the Manufacturing input of 14 to Agriculture is altered, Agriculture's output will alter, but so will that of Manufacturing and Households.

Input-output analysis, then, improves on Barth's flow chart by showing all the connections in the economy and what the degree of connection is.

Leonard Joy (1967), in an article accompanying Barth's on Darfur (1967), points out that Barth's account of Fur economy would benefit from input-output analysis. In the course of his explanation he gives us examples from Darfur of what would constitute the rows and columns of the Darfur economy. Inputs would include the growing of various kinds of food as well as cattle raising and marketing. Outputs would again include agricultural products of various kinds, livestock, and even feasts. The fact is that in any economic system—that is, in any situation wherein one can detect a system closed to some degree—there are production activities of many kinds which are making outputs, and one needs to detect what is coming in to a sector from other identified sectors to enable it to produce. Having done so, one can construct a matrix like Leontief's.

Joy goes on to note that once a matrix is established the relationship between the sector can be manipulated mathematically with matrix algebra (or linear programming), as Dorfman (1953) explains in his paper on mathematical, or linear, programming.

The one example in the anthropological literature of which I have knowledge of a full-blown use of input-output analysis is Heyer's study of the Kamba (Heyer 1966). Joy remarks that her study throws light on such things as the influence of family and land-holding size on the choice of cropping systems, and, he feels could demonstrate the effects of population pressures, labor emigration for wages, and the opening of new consumer goods markets.

MACROECONOMICS

Our survey of the elements of microeconomics has been very brief and has left out much that would be considered essential in a strict development of the subject. But it does display the basic logic of the theory and introduces us to a whole range of terms and concepts that are useful to the economic anthropologist.

In this final section of the chapter I would like to discuss in a far briefer way macroeconomics, and particularly Keynesianism, which is so central to present economic science.

The theory of the competitive market in a *static* economy has been the subject of this chapter. This is the heart of classical economic analysis but it is no longer the main subject of much of economics, although all newer developments build on this base and are understandable only in terms of it. A second kind of analysis, essentially a variant of statics, is *comparative statics* (Berliner 1952: 55ff.). It is one of two theories of change; the other is *dynamics* (Berliner 1962: 55 ff.).

Comparative statics is essentially a type of statical analysis in which, however, focus is not on variations in the things ordinarily allowed to vary (labor supply, supply of goods, demand for goods, etc.) but on the *parameters,* the variables held constant in ordinary price theory. The aim is to determine in what way altering these variables affects the equilibrium price. This is what is done by the anthropologist who describes a society as a static system and then examines the effect on that system of *exogenous* variables such as contact with the Western world. It is sometimes said of structural-functional analysis that it cannot accommodate change. The meaning of this appears to be that its models of societies are static and change can occur in them only through the introduction of exogenous variables. Thus structural-functional analysis is both statical and comparative statical.

Dynamic analysis is importantly different from statics, and is, many claim, a superior type of analysis to comparative statics in the sense that it does all that comparative statics does and more. It is, furthermore, a center of attention in economics with the growth of macroeconomics out of the Keynesian "revolution." Dynamics is a kind of change analysis which finds the cause of the change *within* the system rather than introducing it from the outside. The change is a feedback reaction to the working of the variables and is not a result of tampering with the parameters. A dynamic model in economics might show that people's spending for consumption *now* depends on their income during the *preceding* period and not on present income. In anthropology such a truly dynamic analysis would be represented, perhaps paradoxically, by some of the 19th-century evolutionists, who, for example, argued that the growth of patrilineality stemmed from certain antithetical elements in the matrilineal stage that led to its destruction and directly to the creation of patrilineality (Evans-Pritchard 1952: 28ff.). That dynamics is at the center of modern economics can be illustrated by reference to current government policies having to do with the stemming of inflation. These policies, derived from economics, attempt to understand the dynamics that lead to growing instability in the economy, due to the fact that the economy is not necessarily self-equilibrating so that exogenous variables can be activated to reverse disequilibriating trends.

Macroeconomics, one might say, is not necessarily also dynamics, although it has worked out that way. Whereas statical analysis is concerned with the markets for individual commodities, macroeconomics is concerned with *aggregates:* aggregate employment (i.e., total employment), aggregate output, and aggregate prices (i.e., average prices). It is an attempt to create a model of the whole economy, rather than of sectors as in the partial equilibrium analysis of microeconomics. Its variables, therefore, are macrovariables dealing with macroquantities. The basic problem of macroeconomics is the flow of income (as opposed to micro-analysis's concern with determination of relative prices). But as mentioned above, this concern, in turn, grows out of Keynes and out of problems inherent in microanalysis when used to determine public policy.

The Keynesian revolution stemmed from Keynes's *The General Theory of Employment, Interest, and Money* (1936), a book whose fame was based upon the frantic search during the depression for an economic theory that could help stem unemployment. Many claim that Keynes said nothing new but that people were receptive at the time, a situation perhaps more understandable to the anthropologist than to most because he is used to thinking of innovation as fitting the times rather than the person. The essential feature of the Keynesian theory was the notion that the economy as a whole has elements in it which make it non-self-equilibrating. In particular, it showed, to paraphrase Joan Robinson (1963: 75), that contrary to classical theory, which made private vice a public virtue because attempting to maximize individual profit made for a stable economy, in fact private virtue is a public vice, in the sense that saving without investing creates a positive feedback effect which leads the economy into a deflationary spiral. To quote Dalton (1961: 16):

> The contribution of Keynes was to show why, *in a decentralized market economy* such as those of England and America in the early 1930's, the full employment rate of production is not automatically sustained. But rather that we experience sharp and deep output fluctuations. The basic reason is institutional: in a market economy, all incomes are derived from the sale of end-products to private households . . . , business firms . . . , government . . . , and foreigners . . . ; but there exists no automatic mechanism to assure that the total amount of such market purchases (effective demand) by [these demanders] will be sufficient to keep the labor and machine force fully employed. Moreover, the interdependence of the segments of market economy is such—each person acquires his livelihood by selling something to someone else—that a sharp reduction in one category of expenditure . . . inevitably induces

spending cutbacks in other effective demand sectors . . . : those who earn their wage and profit incomes in producing machinery will be forced by income cuts to spend less on household goods.

This positive-feedback situation (accelerating change as opposed to negative feedback or equilibrating, checked change) has associated with it two terms which are useful to know, the *multiplier* and the *accelerator*. To quote Krupp (1965: 75):

> The multiplier is derived from the *marginal propensity to consume;* that is, the small rise in consumption resulting from a small rise in income. If the multiplier is small, large change in investment will generate only modest changes in income. The accelerator refers to a relation between income and investment such that a change in income will generate changes in investment. If an initial change occurs in investment, income will rise. If the accelerator is positive and large, the increase in income will bring about a further increase in investment, and so on. The degree of instability depends upon the initial change in investment, the size of the multiplier and the accelerator, the level of income when the initial change was introduced and other factors. [Emphasis added.]

Edward LeClair was concerned with the question of why economic anthropologists were not concerned with Keynesian theory (i.e., macroeconomics) (LeClair and Schneider 1969: 464ff.), and offered the explanation that in simpler economies savings and investment decisions, which in our economy and in Keynesian theory are made by different people (on the one hand, by the head of the household and, on the other, by the head of a firm), are made by the same people because firms and households are not separate concrete entities but simply different aspects of the operation of any homestead. In this situation, LeClair thought, Keynesian theory would not apply.

In my opinion this explanation misses the mark. The reason for the lack of attention to modern, macro, Keynesian theory among anthropoligists is complex. For one thing, most anthropologists who have employed microeconomic theory do not realize that it is not the only theory available. They are not sophisticated about the fact that macroeconomics has captured the field and is different from micro theory. The assumptions and general conclusions of microeconomics have become part of the conventional knowledge of Amerian scholars and can be applied, in an approximate way, by Amerian anthropologists in the field if they happen to be convinced of the comparability of all human beings. Secondly, macro analysis requires statistical data of a volume never encountered in the field. It is difficult enough to obtain figures on the production of a few items, much less those on aggregate employment, production, and consumption. Thirdly, structural-functional anthropology has given most anthropologists a propensity to view situations in static terms, quite contrary to macro analysis, which is essentially dynamic.

No doubt other reasons could be assessed, but the exercise would be pointless. The question is, is Keynesian, dynamic analysis applicable in non-Western economies? As surely as is static analysis, must be the answer. No economy is safe from the operation of positive feedback mechanisms. And in all economies exogenous mechanisms, like our Federal Reserve Banks, are operative to adjust the feedback system, much as the mate on the bridge of a vessel monitors the gyroscope and occasionally adjusts it back to the proper course, where it is again allowed to automatically bring the course of the ship approximately back to the predestined path. Among the Turu of Tanzania, a very important equilibrating mechanism is natural rather than "manmade." Approximately every ten years a severe drought causes a redistribution of livestock and grain, countering a strong polarizing in the economy that causes cattle owners to become more and more wealthy while also causing them to reduce inputs into the agricultural sector. The nonowners of livestock choose to invest in surplus grain production. Hence, when the drought strikes, the farmers exchange their grain surpluses for cattle with the herders, who are caught short of food and do not find it sensible to eat their cattle.

The application of Keynesian analysis to anthropology must await far greater attention to the magnitudes of economic variables than has been paid up to now. Until then, micro theory may be the most effective technique available. Once micro analysis is mastered, macro analysis will inevitably follow as a method of extending our understanding of behavior of non-Western people the way it has enhanced our understanding of western economic behavior.

4 *Exchange and Society*

Robbins Burling, in his pioneer paper on formal economic anthropology (Burling 1962: 805ff.), made the point that we should not think of economics in anthropology as the study cross-culturally of what economists study in our own society. Up to this point this book has been essentially following this course. If economics in our society is a deductive enterprise focusing on production and consumption of goods and some services, there is much to be gained, as I have tried to show in the last chapter, by extending exactly the same study to other societies.

However, there is another area of human behavior that has engaged the attention of anthropologists since at least Malinowski's time and that has always seemed somehow to belong within the area of economics, although the reason why has not always been clear. I refer to the subject of reciprocity or gift giving. The ambivalence in the minds of many scholars about this is illustrated in *Argonauts of the Western Pacific,* Malinowski's most economically oriented book, which condemns conventional economic analysis but at the core of which is the vast reciprocity system of the *kula.*

Our task in this chapter is to show how recent conceptual developments have led to the startling conclusion that ambivalence about reciprocity probably derives from the fact that it is a kind of behavior that can be subjected to formal analysis and from the fact that when this is done the result displaces traditional functional analysis in sociology or social anthropology. Reciprocity turns out to be a species of *social exchange* (Blau's term, 1964: 88), a term which comprehends all forms of human interaction seen as forms of exchange, social structures being largely surface manifestations of this exchange or allocation process. The implication of this concept for understanding society are perhaps the reason for the emphasis given it by two prominent sociologists, A. W. Gouldner in "The Norm of Reciprocity" (1961) and Howard Becker in *Man in Reciprocity;* the latter has referred to human beings as *homo reciprocus* (Becker 1954:1).

SAHLINS AND SUBSTANTIVISM

As I explained at the beginning of this book, the differences of opinion between substantive and formal anthropology are to be set aside in favor of developing a formal approach. Insofar as substantive economic anthropology is a type of social anthropology, however, we must inevitably deal with some aspects of it as we look at society as a system of exchange.

In a recent paper by Sahlins (1965) on reciprocity, we can detect a point of view that comes very close to that which is emerging among formalists concerned with social exchange. In fact, an argument could be made that what substantivists have been saying to formalists all along is that the area of social interaction is economically as important or more important than the area of exchange of material values. I would not push this point too far, however, because along with their rejection of formal models of material markets in non-Western societies one detects among substantivists a real repulsion for the idea that social transactions are amenable to formal analysis. Many formalist-leaning sociologists, like Blau, seem to share this aversion to one degree or another (Blau 1964: 314ff.), but when we get to the forefront of formalist thinking about social transactions, as in the writings of Belshaw and Barth (Belshaw 1968, 1970; Barth 1967), aversion is gone and an aggressive reevaluation of social interaction with market models is well underway. Negativism on the part of functionalists with respect to formal treatment of social transactions is understandable because of the threat to functionalist theory that social exchange theory represents.

Sahlins (1965), as usual, is not conventional in his views, but behind his special treatment of reciprocity there is an area of congruence with substantive thinking. Sahlins casts his theory of reciprocity in the form of a model in which social alliances (friendships) are related to obligations to reciprocate material values in such a way that at one end of a continuum is *generalized reciprocity,* at the center is *balanced reciprocity,* and at the other end is *negative reciprocity* (Sahlins 1965: 152). Along this continuum one can state the relationship between friendship and obligation to return gifts as being such that as friendship decreases obligation increases. In generalized reciprocity of the most extreme form, altruism rules and no return for gifts is expected. At the "center" point of balanced reciprocity there is "mutuality"; that is, the feelings of the two parties are such that although they may be friendly toward each other, this friendship factor is balanced by self-interest. At the pole of negative reciprocity the parties are in effect enemies (i.e., not friends), and so the material aspect of their relationship dominates. Each will try to get from the other all he can without paying anything for it if possible.

The substantive dimension to Sahlin's idea of reciprocity lies in his implied claim that amounts and qualities of "friendship" cannot be calculated, although, strangely, his theory implies such calculation. That is to say, if demand for equivalent material return increases with decline of friendship, then magnitudes of friendship are implicit and one could restate Sahlin's proposition as "the degree to which reciprocation of material values is expected varies exactly and inversely with the degree to which people are friends." Knowing the material values, one could deduce magnitudes of friendship. But it is clear from Sahlins's discussion of his model that he does not think of friendship as "economic," and in fact he claims at the end of the article (*ibid.*: 186) to have shown that an exogenous variable (friendship) governs the forms of exchange of material values.

Put another way, Sahlins's theory is typically functionalist and substantivist in refusing to consider the possibility that "friendship," social subordination, "prestige," or whatever one wishes to call it can be dealt with as a value and manipulated formally. Society and social processes are, to him, "noneconomic" and not subject to economic laws. In Sahlins's conception, for one person to expect of another a return proportionate to the value given is unfriendly.

MARCEL MAUSS AND THE GIFT

In the opinion of many, Mauss's classic study of reciprocity, *The Gift* (1967), is simply another substantivist argument, though cast in the more conventional evolutionary form of Polanyi rather than in Sahlin's novel spatial terms. In his introduction to the 1954 edition of Mauss's work Evans-Pritchard says that Mauss stressed how much we have lost by the replacement of the moral transactions found in primitive societies with rational, mechanical economic systems (Mauss 1954: ix), and Levi-Strauss, in the 1969 English-language edition of his famous book on the elementary forms of kinship (Levi-Strauss 1969: 52), claims that Mauss sought to show that exchange in primitive societies is a "total social fact" rather than an economic act. Or, in Sahlins's terms, primitive men are friendly but as they evolve friendship is gradually replaced by mechanical, non-friendly relations.

Actually, Mauss's book is ambiguous, so much so that in a recent article Panoff (1970: 60) claims that Mauss has been completely misrepresented and is not a substantivist at all, nor an evolutionist. One can read Mauss either way. His book is called *Essai sur le don, former archaïque de l'échange,* suggesting that he is talking about a kind of exchange that, as Evans-Pritchard and Levi-Strauss say, has disappeared in modern society. Mauss differentiates social from economic activity in much the same way as Sahlins and social anthropologists do. And he is ambiguous about the important characteristics of his three exchange systems.

On the other hand, we can also agree with Panoff that the book can be seen as an essay in which a kind of exchange found in all societies (Panoff 1970: 60) is analyzed in a way that agrees well with formal economic theory.

According to Mauss, gift giving is an apparently altruistic act which, in fact, is self-interested (Mauss 1969: 1). That is, gift giving is a form of social deception designed to gain some advantage under the guise of good will. This proviso should not be taken merely as an ethnographic observation but rather is crucial to the logic of Mauss's theory. To Mauss all men are economic men, who must sometimes work through gift giving rather than direct exchange of material means. The apparent contradiction in his thinking, reflected in confusion over whether he is a formalist or a substantivist, is resolved if we note additionally that he thought of gift giving as a kind of exchange necessarily more frequent in so-called primitive societies than in our own (Mauss 1969: 2). Mauss does seem to sentimentally prefer gift giving as a form of exchange, but this personal preference should not disguise his clear representation of it as an economic act. That he does not in fact call this an economic act but reserves that term for material exchange is merely a matter of taxonomy. He clearly thought of it as a kind of optimizing behavior.

Mauss explains that among primitive people gift giving takes a form which he calls *total prestation* (Mauss 1969: 4), in which giving a gift puts the receiver under obligation to return either material or nonmaterial values, such as "courtesies, entertainments, rituals, military assistance, women, children, dances, feasts and fairs" (Mauss 1969: 3). It is a system of goods and people circulating side by side. Borrowing from modern alliance theory (Fox 1967), we may say that a system of total gift giving is one which exchanges all values, material and nonmaterial, by means of gifts and thereby creates a vast system of alliances based upon the fact that inherent in the giving of gifts is a persisting social dependence between the interacting parties based on the obligation to repay and on an equilibrium of mutual obligations. Gift giving, therefore, is different in primitive societies than in our own in that in the former it is total whereas in our society it is more selective and juxtaposed with direct exchanges. For example, in the hiring of labor for manufacturing the laborer and employer may have no feeling of continuing interpersonal obligation in addition to the contract to do the work for a certain wage in a certain time. Total prestation, we should be clear, is not Sahlins's generalized reciprocity, because repayment must be made. But the concept is like generalized reciprocity in that repayment is with "friendliness."

Potlach was Mauss's term for the pattern of gift giving that appears in societies like that of the Northwest Coast Indians, where there is an especially marked hostility between the giver and receiver and gift giving is used to subordinate others. Thus, a system of total prestation is one of friendly interdependency while a potlach system is one of hostile interdependency. One gets the impression that to Mauss there is friendliness in the total prestation system because obligations are equally balanced, whereas in the potlach system they are not balanced and one party is under obligations to the other disproportionately greater than are due him. The obligation is in fact so great that the subordinate party is angered by his subservience and aggressively desires to relieve himself of it.

While it is implicit in Mauss that exchange imbalances create social differentiation (as among the Kwakiutl) and that society, contrary to Sahlins, is an economic structure, the idea is not well developed. Are there grounds for accepting Mauss's view? In order to determine this we shall have to reexamine the Kwakiutl case.

THE POTLACH

The potlach phenomenon has become the focus of theoretical attention by many schools, and as a result several competing interpretations of it exist, most notably the functionalist interpretations of Barnett (1938) and Drucker and Heizer (1967), and the ecological views of Piddocke (1965), Vayda (1961), and Suttles (1960), all of which are essentially substantive; and the more formal views of Codere (1950) and Boas (particularly as "summarized" in a recent volume of *Kwakiutl Ethnography* [Boas/Codere 1966], an attempt by Codere to represent Kwakiutl ethnography through editing of Boas's works), and the thoroughly formalist view of Belshaw.

The functionalist view, which because of its similarity to substantive theory can be related to Sahlins's, is expressed first by Barnett (1938), who, say Drucker & Heizer (1967: 8), designated the function of the potlaches as: "the identification of an individual as a member of a certain social unit and the defining of his social position within that unit." These authors, in their recent book *To Make My Name Good* (1967), support Barnett but attempt also to combat what they consider to be a misinterpretation of the potlach that has grown up over the years and that consists, essentially, of an economic approach (Drucker and Heizer 1967: 133):

> The potlach did not give, or create, social status. Present data make abundantly clear that this was as true of the Southern Kwakiutl as it was of other northwest coast groups. No matter how many potlaches a chief gave, he did not alter his formal rank one whit beyond that to which he was legally entitled through heredity or acquisition of rights in marriage.

Like other substantivist views, the functionalism of Drucker and Heizer is not relevant to the approach used in this book, and this brief reference to it is merely to make plain that there is some question about what was varying with the giving of goods in the potlach. If, as Drucker and Heizer say, social status was not affected by the potlaches a chief gave, then it is difficult to see how Mauss's view that potlaching served to vary the ranks of chiefs and clans (Mauss 1967: 4) can be supported.

If Drucker and Heizer take a noneconomic view of the potlach, the ecological theorists, particularly Suttles, approach an economic interpretation. In a sense the views of Piddocke and Vayda are merely a revised functionalism, adding some attention to the habitat of the social system but still interpreting all events as serving the maintenance of the social system. But in order to construct a logical interpretation, they must vary a value called "prestige" against food and other material values. In Vayda's words (1961: 623):

> . . . as the effectiveness of food production was varying from time to time and from place to place, there were movements and countermovements of food, wealth, and prestige from person to person and from group to group in such a way as to minimize the adverse effects . . . of any local and temporary lack of success in food production. In more general terms, the hypothesis is that the self-regulating economic systems served to distribute goods in a way that contributed to the survival and well-being of the people.

To which I would add, prestige was reciprocally bestowed on the givers.

Although Suttles's views on the potlach are often placed alongside those of Vayda and others of the ecological school, they are in fact more sophisticated. Suttles sees the potlach as something more than just a device for redistributing food from the haves to the have-nots in return for prestige (Suttles 1960: 303):

> . . . with this total socio-economic system, its most important function is to be found neither in the expression of the individual's drive for high status nor in the fulfillment of the society's need for solidarity, neither in competition nor in cooperation, but simply in the redistribution of wealth.

That is to say, Suttles perceives that if one ignores the ecological approach and simply looks at the economic system as such, any mechanism that would lead to polarization of wealth must be equaled by a mechanism that would redistribute it or the system would be demolished in an exponential positive-feedback explosion. However, it is not clear whether Suttles realizes that such a mechanism could operate without also distributing food from the haves to the have-nots. That is to say, an effectively balanced economic system is not necessarily a "just" one, so long as not everyone is killed off.

To summarize to this point, the views of Mauss on how the potlach functions have little support from functionalist writers like Drucker and Heizer, but the ecological anthropologists accept the idea that prestige, which they never really define, is being exchanged for goods for the purpose of stabilizing food distribution and to preserve the system. Suttles has gone a step beyond this to a view close to that which a microeconomist would hold, saying that the potlach is a device for redistributing wealth within the micro system so that the economy remains in balance. There is a remnant of an ecological view in his failure to dissociate the idea of a stable economic system from that of a just system (i.e., one which feeds everybody).

In accordance with his theory of the purpose of ethnographic work Boas, from whom facts and ideas about the potlach originally came, makes few attempts to interpret this institution. However, he does make the significant remark (Boas/Codere 1966: 77), that the potlach's "underlying principle is that of the interest-bearing investment of property," suggesting that he saw the potlach as a kind of economic activity. Codere, elaborating on this, declares (1950: 80):

> [The potlach's] "objective" features are an economy many stages removed from ordinary subsistence activities, an elaborate hierarchy of social positions possessing scarcity value, and the development of so complex a scheme of credit, investment and interest that it is accurately descriptive to term it "finance."

But while Codere accepts that the potlach was a "financial" institution, she does not claim that rank was exchanged for goods (Codere 1950: 63):

> The Kwakiutl potlach is the ostentatious and dramatic distribution of property by the holder of fixed, ranked and named social position, to other position holders. The purpose is to validate the hereditary claim to the position and to live up to it by maintaining its relative glory and rank against the rivalrous claims of the others.

Anyone who has followed my review of the literature on the potlach up to this point may by this time be hopelessly confused. Is rank or prestige exchanged for goods? If so, what is this prestige? If, however, position is merely validated, what is gained by giving so much wealth away? What was the effect of the distribution: did it get people fed or was it merely a regulator on the closed economic system?

Anyone can play the game of trying to guess what is the proper interpretation of the potlach. As Belshaw remarks (1965: 21), Boas was writing at a time when theory was not sufficiently developed to guide field work, so that despite the great volume of Boas's writings on the potlach and the Kwakiutl, his data are often not of the kind necessary to settle these theoretical issues. However, Belshaw's interpretation of the potlach is one which we may borrow as resolving in a reasonable way the questions raised above.

Belshaw feels (1965, 20–29) that the basic Kwakiutl group, the *numaym,* was a patrilineal group with some corporate functions. Within the numaym there was a complex system of titles that indicated a man's position and prerogatives. These titles were a kind of property, with attached social power. The problem of how rank could be varied in the light of the putative fixing of the ranked positions, the problem on which Drucker and Heizer have laid great emphasis, is solved by noting that in the first place ascribed positions, in this case inherited patrilineal titles, are in fact always subject to achievement under certain circumstances. Strangers could be accepted into the numaym and given fictive status, and, as in many other patrilineal systems, maternal links could be used for entrance. Entrance to a patrilineage could also be obtained by manipulating marriage ties. To this I would add that though a person could not buy a title, the prestige of the title could fluctuate.

Given this situation, a man had to play this status game by giving gifts, chiefly blankets, a currency that could not be refused and that *had to be returned on demand.* This alone "validated" power by putting the receivers in a position of obligation and dependence, but to this was added the fact that interest was charged amounting to about 100% over a twelve-month period. Belshaw gives the following illustration (1965: 25):

This [i.e., high interest rates] made it possible for a man to enter a potlach in a very short space of time, or to build up the quantity of goods involved to a fantastic peak. A young man, for example, borrows, let us say, one hundred blankets from ranking persons in the *numaym* of the tribal subdivision of the Kwakiutl to which his own *numaym* belonged. He lends these to other persons, who, knowing of his plans to enter the potlach, [must] repay them in a month at the 100 per cent rate of interest plus an additional premium of 100%. He now has control over 300 blankets. He then makes a further loan, repaid in the same manner, and further added to by outright gifts from such close kinsmen as his father. By these methods, at the end of one year he is likely to have control of over 400 blankets. This quantity is sufficient for him to engage in a formal potlach, though of minor quantity. He can repay most of his loans during the potlach and with a small surplus make the essential potlach gifts to numaym other than his own.

The system was, of course, inflationary in the extreme. Probably because of this, pieces of copper of great value, representing accumulated value from different potlaches, were used to give simultaneously status to their holders while bringing the system back into some kind of equilibrium through their destruction to achieve this status. Veblen might have called this conspicuous destruction. Belshaw feels (1965: 27) that this equilibrating device was not entirely successful and that the 19th-century potlach as we know it and the great material wealth of the Kwakiutl were results of inflation (1965: 27).

To this we need merely add that the system of absolute rank of tribes and numayms that characterized the Kwakiutl must therefore in fact be an epiphenomenon of the allocation process involved in potlaching, even though, as the functionalists emphasize, the ranking system appears fixed.

Something like the dynamic process Belshaw describes must have been occurring, if only because there is no other way to explain the frantic entrepreneurship of the Kwakiutl. Codere (1950: 23) passes on a traditional story about the Kwakiutl in which an inspector of the facilities at Fort Rupert once asked why the cannon were in such a state of disrepair. He was told they had been used only once and then ignored, because on the one occasion that one was fired to impress the people, the Kwakiutl had chased the cannon ball into the forest and returned it in an attempt to sell it back to the fort.

TOLAI

In light of the inadequacy of the data from the aboriginal Northwest Coast there is no reason to spend more time on its system, whose structure will never be discernible now except by deduction from principles developed elsewhere with contemporary data. The famous *kula* system of the Trobriands, which Malinowski describes in *Argonauts of the Western Pacific,* is similarly lost to us.

Scarlett Epstein, economically attuned as one must be to uncover the kind of data needed to test our theories, provides us with a contemporary "potlach" system whose rationale can be made plain.

In Tolai (Epstein 1968: chap. 2) money in the form of small shells called *tambu* is used as a medium of exchange for all kinds of goods and services. Furthermore, there is an extensive trade system based on regional specialization of food production. However, the industriousness of the people with respect to the production of goods is explained not by the need to obtain food but rather by a burning desire to become wealthy and powerful. Money, as it is accumulated, can be stored with an elder of one's matrilineage who is not only powerful (that is, has established a reputation for fierceness and business acumen) and therefore the best protector, but is also the rallying point of the lineage during times of warfare. Loaning out stored money at a rate of 20% is permitted to this elder for financing his own activities as long as he returns it, so that altogether he acts somewhat like a bank.

Given these conditions, a Tolai could make money not only by manufactures but also by distributing presents of crops, spears, clubs, and ornaments to kin and neighbors who had to repay the gifts with money in an amount exceeding the value of the gift. Returns of 30% in such transactions were apparently common. Rich men could do this relatively easily, so there was a tendency for wealth to polarize with the rich. But on their death, all the goods of wealthy men were distributed (much like the Kwakiutl coppers). Epstein summarizes the system as follows (Epstein 1968: 31–32):

> The traditional economic and political system was carried on in the same way as a card game played for chips, with periodic re-

distributions of the chips among the participants. Absence of inheritance of accumulated tambu wealth ensured flexibility in the
social system. The Tolai had not 'social classes', yet they were
obviously conscious of the existence at any one time of a few
self-made economic and political leaders, each of whom had a large
following of people who helped in production and sale as well as
of men acting as warriors. Drive, thrift, and the managerial ability
of potential 'big men' accounted for their ultimate recognition as
ngala [rich heads of lineages].

The Tolai system is, of course, not literally the same as the
Kwakiutl, but the systems are alike in essentials. In both cases,
men seem motivated far more by the desire for power and prestige than by the need to fill their bellies. That is to say, in neither
case do men live by bread alone. In both cases, there exists a
system of finance—that is, a system whereby credit and loans
operating through a system of money make possible amplifica-
tion of economic power and provide the leverage necessary to
rise. And in both cases, perhaps, physical force appears as a
factor, a balancing factor one might say, in the system. In both
cases the particular form taken by the rank structure and financial system is conditioned by the particulars of the habitat (opportunities for production, the form of the money, etc.). In
both cases social differentiation is a reflex of the financial activity. As is generally true of societies at this level of production, in both cases there is kinship-based corporate activity,
which acts to provide credit and mutual aid for members of
minimal groups. Finally, there is a system of redistribution to
counter the inevitable polarization of wealth that must occur in
a dynamic system, where positive-feedback effects are inevitable.
In fact, this positive-feedback, cyclical effect is the basis for
social differentiation.

Paula Brown, in connection with an analysis of Chimbu transactions (Brown 1970: 115), generalizes the economic situation
found among the Tolai and Chimbu to all of Melanesia and
Polynesia. Brown says that among the Chimbu of New Guinea
giving of gifts between individuals or groups, which she calls

transactions, results in continuing relationships, which, however, are dissolved when one party fails to reciprocate. Barter, trade, or commerce consisting of direct exchange are rarely part of Chimbu life. These transactions are a complex system of (Brown 1970: 113):

> food and pig production, manufacture, payment, feast, kin and affinal exchange, "Big Man" rivalry and exchange, and ties to distant friends where scarce goods can be obtained. The transactions include subsistence and special foods, manufactures and valuables, and range from reciprocal assistance among close kinsmen to payments, feasts, to occasional exchange and barter. It is possible partly to distinguish realms, but it is really one system— every social relationship is transactional. Relationships lapse and are forgotten without transactions, and new relationships are set up with a transaction. This tends to stress the immediacy of the relationship rather than its traditional character and is correlated with changes in membership and allegiance, and the ready incorporation of participant residents in quasi-kinship groups.

This, of course, reminds us of Pospisil's description of the capitalistic Kapauku (Pospisil 1963) as discussed in the last chapter.

ZINACANTAN

One of the most interesting status-ranking systems in the world is the cargo, fiesta, or *mayordomia* system employed by many Latin American people. Frank Cancian's account of the system employed in Zinacantan (Cancian 1965), a Maya community, demonstrates another aspect of the economic variability that can occur in such systems in contrast to the inflation we saw among the Northwest Coast Indians. In the Northwest Coast more and more goods were apparently exchanged for fewer and fewer ranks because of the decline of population. In Zinacantan we have more and more people vying for an apparently static number of positions. Almost all Zinacanteco adults participate in the cargo system (Cancian 1965: 126), but the growth of the Mexican economy has raised the level of income of the Zinacantecos, resulting in increased demand for higher positions. The system requires of its adherents that they incur costs proportional to the rank of the cargo, so that the positions act somewhat like the Kwakiutl coppers or the Tolai death dispersals of money to reverse the polarization of wealth that inevitably occurs and to help maintain the equilibrium and therefore the playableness of the system. But Cancian claims that despite the increase in the number of "rich" people, except for the low-prestige, lowest level of the four levels the number of positions is not expanding.

What is happening is perhaps better illustrated by putting it in terms of a Lorenz curve (Haveman and Knopf 1966: 31ff.), an economist's device for showing the distribution of income in a community (Fig. 4-1).

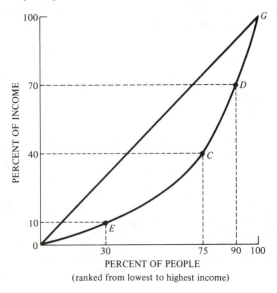

Fig. 4-1. Lorenz Curve.

If all the people in a sample had equal percentages of the total income, the "curve" would be the straight line running from *O* to *G*. As income becomes increasingly unequal in distribution, the curve bows toward the "people" axis. If we take point *C*, 75% of the people receive 40% of the income and (it follows) the remaining 25% receive 60%. At point *D* 90% of the people get 70% of the income, while 30% get 10% at point *E*.

Using a Lorenz curve, we can illustrate what appears to be happening in Zinacantan. If we rank the cargos as a form of "income," arbitrarily differentiating them in terms of value so that the Fourth and highest level is worth four times as much as the first level, and if we plot on the horizontal axis the percentage of cargo holders holding cargos at each level (Cancian 1965: 28ff.), we get a Lorenz social-wealth curve as illustrated in Fig. 4-2.

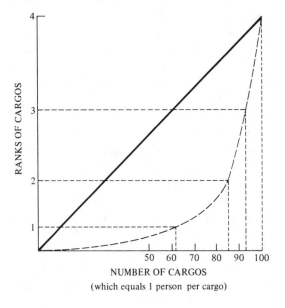

Fig. 4-2. Zinacantan Social Lorenz Curve.

If we could be sure that the amount of value placed on the various ranks is correct, we could say from this graph that about 7% of the men holding cargos control about 40% of the social wealth.

Cancian's point is that with the rise in wealth in this community the demand for all cargos and in particular the demand for upper-level cargos by lower-level holders has increased, which means there is pressure to flatten the Lorenz curve. The number of first-level cargos has been increased, and since most people never get beyond this level, this is an important modification. Other than this, waiting lists have been created that allow a person to sign up for a position when it is vacated. This may involve years of waiting, but to a certain extent a person can trade on his position in the waiting list and the position on the waiting list can be otherwise "finagled."

Other than these observations, which derive unsystematically from formal economic theory, Cancian is unclear about the cost of the cargo, suggesting alternately that it varies with ability to pay (Cancian 1965: 98) and that the cost is fixed (Cancian 1965: 100). How can this contradiction be resolved? Obviously the cost of the cargos cannot remain constant as income rises, or their value deflates (they cost proportionately less and less) and they are eventually rendered useless as a rank indicator. But the cost of the ranks can't have increased proportionately to income, because Cancian says that there is an increasing "surplus" of wealth (Cancian 1965: 190). Is it possible that the cost is increasing but more slowly than the general rise in income? If so, the system could continue for some time, but in the end deflation would again result. Obviously something about this situation is unknown, namely why the cost of cargos, if they are in fact in great demand, does not rise to clear the market of the "surplus" wealth as it apparently once did.

Whatever the facts turn out to be in the Zinacantan case, it seems obvious that systematic use of formal economic theory will help resolve the unknowns in the situation. Cancian is more of a substantivist than a formalist, yet even he sees the applicability of formal analysis to this situation, particularly in his chapter 16 on "Disequilibrium and the Future," where he refers to the increase in population and increase in the number of First-level positions as disequilibrating and equilibrating, respectively (Cancian 1965: 187).

GOULDNER AND OBLIGATIONS

Gift giving, then, seems to be amenable to formal analysis because it is a type of exchange, even though it deals with an unusual type of value, social power. Although his emphasis is still functional in the sense of trying to understand how societies persist, A. W. Gouldner is one of those who in the last decade has contributed importantly to the development of the theory of gift giving.

To Gouldner there is a norm of reciprocity that is universal among men (Gouldner 1960: 171), which consists of the idea that people should help those who help them, and should not injure those who help them. Gouldner's norm has interesting parallels with Radcliffe-Brown's "principle of justice" (Radcliffe-Brown 1957: 132), derived from Kant's, "A person who does evil should suffer evil, and one who does good should receive benefits." I don't think that this is accidental. All functional thinkers, like Radcliffe-Brown and Gouldner, are very much conscious of balanced exchange as basic to society. For example, Gouldner quotes Simmel (1950) to the effect that "all contacts among men rest on the scheme of giving and returning the equivalence" (Gouldner 1960: 161–162).

To Gouldner this norm of reciprocity is the very foundation of society because it activates people to exchanging and interacting behavior before there is personal benefit in doing so [it is a "starting mechanism" (Gouldner 1960: 176ff.)]. In this notion can again be seen the substantive or functionalist idea of the primacy of norms and obligations over "economic" benefits that we have not so much rejected as decided to relegate to substantivists while we focus on self-interested exchange. In this respect it is interesting that Blau (1964: 92) turns Gouldner's notion around, arguing that human societies begin with people exchanging because it is self-serving to do so, and then, in time, norms are generated to govern the mutually satisfying exchanges in order to keep them going during those periods when there is an imbalance in the beneficiality of the interaction. In other words, for both Gouldner and Blau, a norm keeps people interacting even when there is no benefit to be gained. The difference between them is over which comes first, the norm or self-interest.

In the development of an economic theory of social exchange Gouldner's thesis is interesting because he suggests that exchange of values may proceed from one end of a continuum, where the exchange of material or nonmaterial values incurs no obligations (i.e., the exchange values are equal), to the other end, where the value given by one party is returned only in obligations. In the middle of the continuum are situations wherein one party gives more than he receives and repays the difference in obligations. By obligations Gouldner means certain role actions that are satisfying to the partner in the status-role dyad (Gouldner 1960: 169). This thesis has no relation to that of Sahlins (friends give gifts), because it asserts an equivalence of values in exchange, some of the value lying in "obligations."

Because Gouldner feels that obligations constitute a value, he also feels that the amount of obligation given is contingent on the benefits received, so that obligations vary with (1) the intensity of the need for them by the receiver, (2) the resources of the donor, (3) the motives of the donor, (4) the variable statuses of the participants in the exchange, (5) the value of the gift, and (6) the cultural setting. As far as I can see, Gouldner is merely stating that obligations are payments that are subject to the laws of supply and demand, so that the amount given depends on how much the receiver needs the benefits and on the cost to the supplier. That the market situation varys between cultures goes without saying.

There is one important respect in which Gouldner seems to differ from Mauss, namely in his view that gift giving almost always results in an inequality and thus in a subordination-super-ordination relationship. Mauss seems to see the relations between segmentary lineages as conferring equal benefits upon both parties.

This small difference has radical implications. Gouldner, in contrast to Mauss and other evolutionists, is saying that competition and economic activity are universal, not merely characteristic of Western societies.

If obligations or titles (or whatever other term one chooses to label differential power relations) are values which operate in the market like any other values, a question naturally arises about the completeness of accounts of the economic activities of people like the Kwakiutl, when their financial activity is described without reference to marginal variations in social values. Potlaches and credit relationships among the Kwakiutl must have been affected by supply and demand of money. And the values of titles must have varied at the margin both among the Kwakiutl and Zinacantan.

HOMANS AND BLAU: SOCIAL EXCHANGE

However much we may read into Mauss and Gouldner and the analysis of the Kwakiutl and Tolai a theory of society as exchange, real elaboration of such a theory is relatively recent, being associated prominently with Homans and Blau in sociology and Belshaw and Barth in social anthropology.

Blau's work in this area begins most notably with his *Dynam-*

ics of Bureaucracy in 1955, but George Homans must be said to be responsible for popularizing the idea in his paper on "Social Behavior as Exchange" (1958). The great virtue of Homans's contribution is its attempt to delineate more clearly what it is about another's behavior that is valuable. The answer to this will help us to determine how people assign value to behavior in all societies. Homans's basic thesis is as follows (Homans 1958: 598–599):

> Suppose we are dealing with two men. Each is emitting behavior reinforced to some degree by the behavior of the other. How it was in the past that each learned the behavior he emits and how he learned to find the other's behavior reinforcing we are not concerned with. It is enough that each does find the other's behavior reinforcing, and I shall call the reinforcers . . . *values,* for this, I think, is what we mean by this term. As he emits behavior, each man may incur costs, and each man has more than one course of behavior open to him.

That is to say, people, as they interact with each other, have various alternative ways of expressing themselves, each alternative having different costs, and so an economic choice can be made in terms of the equation Profit = Reward − Cost (Homans, 1958: 603), which reminds us of the equation for the firm's supply of goods, $P = TR - TC$ (Profit = Total Revenue − Total Cost). Homans develops this argument most extensively by reinterpreting the results of group experiments done by H. B. Gerard and reported in "The Anchorage of Opinions in Face-to-Face Groups" (Gerard: 1954). These experiments showed that persons who are members of groups whose members like each other very much will tend to change their opinions on some important subject to conform to those of the group, whereas in groups whose members don't like each other very much disagreements on some important subject will not dissolve so easily.

Homans's reinterpretation postulated that the members of the group have a value which he called *personal integrity,* meaning holding to an opinion, and that agreement with the group gives them another value, *acceptance,* a value which, however, varies with the prestige of the group. He then argued that in instances where a member of a group could be accepted by a prestigeful group and also maintain his integrity he would do so. That is, he maximizes his utility by achieving both acceptance and personal integrity. His integrity is in this case compatible with acceptance, because his strongly held personal opinion about some matter is in conformity with the opinions of other members of the group; he does not have to change his opinion in order to be accepted. On the other hand, those people who were members of groups having little prestige gave up little by holding to an opinion that differed from that of other members of the group. In other words, in these two instances the utility to the subjects of taking the positions they took was higher than that deriving from other alternatives.

Compare these two situations with two others: (1) the disagreeing member of the highly attractive group was likely to shift (i.e., change his opinion) in order to be accepted, as the cost of maintaining his disagreement was high; (2) the people who were not in disagreement but who belonged to unattractive groups were, as in (1) above, getting little satisfaction, and were likely to disagree in order to increase integrity.

Homans's analysis, in truth, is economic only to a very superficial degree. For example, since he is talking about profit and cost he is apparently modeling his analysis on the theory of the firm's supply. What is the firm producing? Apparently opinions of an agreeable or disagreeable nature. And what is the profit to the firm? Apparently acceptance by members of the group. What is the role in this analysis of the variable of group attractiveness or unattractiveness? This could be equivalent to demand price or total revenue. Hence, restating the case, if the revenue (acceptance) that a firm (the individual) can obtain for the supply of goods (agreeable opinions) rises, the output of the good will rise. But notice the kind of question left unanswered: where there is a low prestige group whose members are producing divergent opinions in order to enhance their individual prestige through display of integrity, what governs the level of production of divergence? In other words, what is the marginal cost situation and price that would cause the individual to produce singular opinions up to and only to the point of the equation of marginal cost and marginal revenue or an equilibrium price?

The main problem with Homans's analysis might be summarized as being the lack of quantification of the variables (either intervally or ordinally), which in turn prevents the use of marginal analysis, which, as we have seen, is at the heart of the logic necessary to determine rational behavior on the part of the firm. Nevertheless, Homans does broach the possibility that things like group attractiveness, personal integrity, and the like are values, obtaining them incurs costs, and the behavior of people involved in these social exchanges is potentially amenable to economic analysis.

Although Homans himself did not employ economic reasoning of a very high order, he was aware of and reported in his paper the work of Peter Blau on the dynamics of bureaucracy, which considerably improved on Homans.

Blau's field work was among agents in a federal law enforcement agency. He discovered that, contrary to common sense, inexperienced agents, whose pay and promotions depended on the quality of their reports, tended to consult other inexperienced agents for help rather than go to experienced agents. In Blau's terms, agents liked being consulted, but the value to any one of them of very many consultations declined with their frequency, so that the experts raised the price by frequent interruptions in the consultations, which had the effect of demeaning the consultor. Commenting on this, Homans concluded (1958: 291):

> This implies that, the more prestige an agent received, the less was the increment of value of that prestige; the more advice an agent gave, the greater was the increment of cost of that advice, the cost

lying precisely in the foregone value of time to do his own work. Blau suggests that something of the same sort was true of an agent who went to a more competent colleague for advice: the more often he went, the more costly to him, in feelings of inferiority, became any further requests.

A serious problem with this conclusion parallels the problem we had with the potlach. What is this prestige? Blau, in a second edition of *The Dynamics of Bureaucracy,* the work from which Homans drew his material on him, clears up the matter as follows (Blau 1963: 139ff.):

> Agents who regularly consult an expert colleague do not merely pay him respect by asking for his advice, but also become obligated to him for having received help from him, and these obligations are the basic source of the informally generated status differences in the group. Transforming this social exchange into an economic exchange would, in effect, be a way of escaping from these obligations. A man who pays a consultant a fee for his services has discharged his obligations to him.

Note how Blau here uses the term "economic" to mean material exchange while "obligation" appears to have a meaning for him similar to Gouldner's.

In his general work on social exchange (*Exchange and Power in Social Life:* 1964), which succeeded *The Dynamics of Bureaucracy,* Blau carried his analysis further than the simple notions of cardinal utility or marginal analysis that governed his earlier thoughts, and subjected the actions of his agents to indifference analysis (Blau 1964: 172–173), borrowing the graph in Fig. 4-3 from Stigler (1942: 73).

The O-X axis represents increasing amounts of "relaxation and sociability," the O-Y axis status enhancement that comes from advising others, using time that could otherwise be used for relaxation. The line B-A, of course, is the agent's budget line, representing in this instance the time he has available. Hence P is the rational allocation between X and Y. The various I . . . I lines simply represent the idea that this indifference curve, like others, can be shifted in and out relative to O as

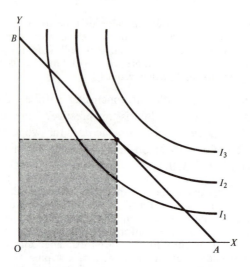

Fig. 4-3. Indifference Analysis of Blau's
Secret Agents.

resources in time change and opportunity to both enhance status
and relax varies.

Blau adds to this analysis another dimension that can be
employed in indifference analysis when he points out that:

> The average slope of the indifference curves would reveal . . .
> [an agent's] status consciousness, specifically, how significant it is
> for him to achieve superior status among colleagues relative to
> the significance that relaxation and sociability have for him. If X
> represents the benefits a man receives from devoting time to per-
> forming his own work (rather than from his leisure time), the
> average slope of the indifference curves would indicate the degree
> to which he is oriented to colleagues as a reference group rather
> than to his instrumental tasks and the superiors who evaluate his
> performance. One would expect, for example, that social co-
> hesion makes these indifference curves less steep, indicating the
> increased significance of colleague approval and informal status
> (Y).

While indifference analysis may therefore be used to represent an agent as a consumer of "sociability" and "status enhance-

ment" in a market consisting of a number of other agents, the fact is that an important condition of a competitive market, numerous suppliers and numerous consumers, is violated. Blau, in fact, seems more truly to view this situation as one of *bilateral monopoly,* a market consisting of only one supplier and one consumer, the experienced and the junior agent. How, in such a market, can one determine the rational outcome of exchanges?

Blau finds the solution in the use of the Edgeworth Box (Mansfield 1970: 41ff.). In this method of analyzing bilateral monopoly, a box (Fig. 4-4) represents the total supply of two goods available to two competitors, which may be designated Good X and Good Y, and the indifference curves of each party are represented as facing each other.

At the beginning of the encounter the goods, we will suppose, are distributed between the two persons as at point *P* (i.e., Person 1 has less of Good X than Person 2 but has more of

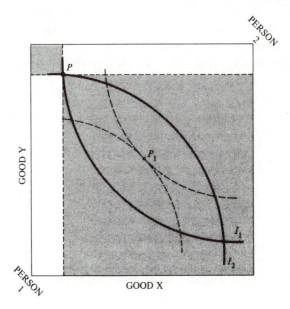

Fig. 4-4. Edgeworth Box.

Good Y). Point P is assumed to be on an indifference curve of each party (I_1 being 1's indifference curve and I_2 Person 2's). Person 1 would be willing to move from point P to any point on his indifference curve without feeling that he had decreased his utility (or increased it), because, as we know, he is indifferent between the various points on this curve. Person 2 feels the same about his curve. However, unlike as in indifference analysis there is no budget line. How then can we derive the maximizing solution? The answer is that, in effect, each party treats the other's indifference curve as a budget line. Unlike the usual budget line, however, this one does not represent a fixed amount of means that can be applied as a constant, but is a variable line whose position depends on considerations extraneous to the model. The parties negotiate with each other about the position each desires (i.e., how to divide up the available utility). In this case, we will presume that the parties have refused to reduce utility lower than point P, leaving the area between I_1 and I_2 still up for negotiation. When that is settled by further negotiations or some other decision-making means, we will find that although the model can not predict at what point the curve will settle, it can predict that it will be a point at which the utility curves of the two parties are tangent. This point of tangency (P_1) is the *Pareto optimum*. The two curves must be tangent because if they are not, either party may not be obtaining the optimum utility available to him or may be forcing the other party to reduce his utility.

In short, bilateral monopoly analysis predicts the particular mix of goods that will satisfy Persons 1 and 2 on a given indifference curve, but it cannot say what proportion of total utility each party will get, because that is negotiated or otherwise decided outside the model.

Blau utilized an Edgeworth box from Boulding (1955) that is reproduced in Fig. 4-5. The "goods" that are being competed for are:

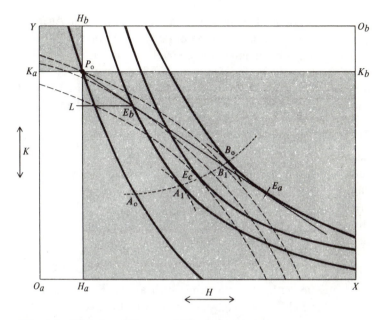

Fig. 4-5. Edgeworth Box and Blau's Secret Agents.

K (the vertical axis): the time devoted to problem solving (weighted for difference in competence). Person O_a, the experienced agent, has more problem-solving ability (more competence) and so he has more time remaining to devote to other activities (O_aK_a). The inexperienced agent, O_b, has less competence and less time (O_bK_b).

H (the horizontal axis): the degree of "compliance" (presumably Gouldner's obligatory behavior) each is willing to express, which raises the other status. Agent O_a is willing to display only a relatively small degree of compliance (O_aH_a), while Agent O_b, the inexperienced agent, is willing to express much compliance (O_bH_b).

As in the foregoing explanation of bilateral monopoly, if we start with point P_o as a given (this is the coordinate defining the area open for negotiation as far as the experienced agent is concerned and the point below which he refuses to go—that is, he won't give more time to others than K_aY and this is the minimum amount of compliance he will expect from Agent O_b because of his prior status in the organization), we see Agent O_a receiving much compliance for a small amount of his time. But each agent would be indifferent to moving along his curve into the area $P_oH_aXK_b$. If the experienced agent did this, he would change his mix toward a reduction in the time given to his own problem solving in return for more compliance from O_b (i.e., to a point where the inexperienced agent would give him more deference in return for more help). The inexperienced agent, in turn, would be indifferent to a shift along his curve, in which case he would increase his problem-solving ability for an increase in compliance. Of course both the agents will move into this area from P_o because we assume they are maximizers and neither is in the optimum position at P_o.

The no-man's land between the curves of O_a and O_b, defined by point P_o, will be negotiated somehow, and the two agents will agree to settle at some point, such as A_1, E_c, or B_o. But in contrast to indifference analysis, the mix of the two goods (time and deference) will be determined by the Pareto optimum, which is the point at which the curves of the two agents are tangent, and not by a budget line. If we connect A_1, E_c, and B_o they form a curve of Pareto optima which is called the contract curve. The final negotiated position of the mix of goods will always be on that contract curve because that is always where the curves will be tangent and to deviate from the tangent point would be to reduce the utility of the opposite party. In other words, the model can not tell us whether A_1, E_c, or B_1 (or any particular point between A_o and B_o) will be the solution, but can predict that it will be somewhere on that line.

In this graph, Blau has added another element, the fair rate of exchange or exchange opportunity line ($P_oE_bE_a$), which may be considered to be a rule parameter of the exchange. That is to say, this rule says that exchanges can occur only along this line. Although the agents are maximizers, they are also law abiding so the best they can do is to come as close to the Pareto optimum as possible, namely point E_b, which moves the I curves of both forward from P but leaves the inexperienced agent possibly worse off than he would have been if the two had been able to negotiate a better position in the area indexed by E_b. This is Blau's way of pointing up the strain that may be put on rules by the maximizing realities of a situation. As he says (Blau 1964: 174ff.):

> As long as an increase in the volume of consultation, at whatever exchange rate, is possible that moves both parties to higher indifference curves, it is to the advantage of both to expand their exchange relation. But once a point of tangency of the indifference curves of the two parties is reached, as it is at point E_c, no further movement can be made which will benefit both parties, no matter what the price.

What is the nature of these negotiations that establish the point on the contract curve which is optimum? Quoting Blau again (1964: 176):

> The point . . . is influenced by the personal relation between the consultant and the consulting colleague, the skills of each in concealing how much he would be willing to return for the benefits obtained if he had to, and in particular the other benefits that one or both derive from their social interaction. The man who reveals his great need for advice may have to pay more compliance for it than the one who successfully conceals it. The consultant who expresses a supportive interest in helping colleagues tends to earn more appreciation and willing compliance than the one who extends assistance only grudgingly. The man afraid to go to the supervisor for advice may have to pay a higher price for advice from colleagues than the one known sometimes to avail himself of this alternative resource. Generally, available alternatives strengthen a man's bargaining power, and the major alternatives accessible in work groups are other colleagues.

Bilateral monopoly analysis seems to appeal to social scientists other than Blau. Recently indifference analysis and analysis of bilateral monopoly have been utilized by Curry and Wade (1968), who quantify policy (e.g., the policy of a political authority who can get social security payments at different lev-

els) and juxtapose various mixes of policy in relation to resources in order to explain why the poor put up with poorer
police protection and other politically undesirable conditions
(Curry and Wade 1968: 22).

To sum up, Blau feels that the exchange, between agents, of
information and understanding (which takes time) and deference (which implies deferential, attentive actions, such as, perhaps, the use of status-enhancing terms like Mr. and Sir) can
be treated by economic analysis.

Uriel Foa has recently proposed a classification of valued resources that is apparently exhaustive and that augments Blau by
making explicit what "social" resources consist of. Foa's scheme
(Foa 1971: 347) is represented in Fig. 4-6.

For his own purposes, Foa felt that the cross-cutting continua
of less to more concrete and less to more particular were revealing. We may set this aside and attend rather to the interesting fact that movement from general to particular is movement
from what we usually think of as "material" to what we usually
think of as "social." Furthermore, the most particular of these
values is equivalent to Blau's *intrinsic rewards,* which are, in

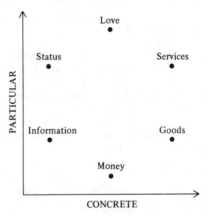

Fig. 4-6. Foa's Classification of
Valued Resources.

his terms, noneconomic and noncalculable, in contrast to his *extrinsic rewards,* which include all the other values in Foa's scheme. Foa's scheme, revised and compared to Blau's, is as follows:

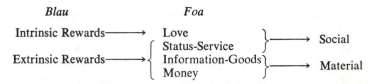

Blau's position on intrinsic and extrinsic rewards is confusing because it seems to intrude a foreign point of view (basically humanistic) into economic analysis. Since Blau so aggressively applies economic analysis to the exchange of extrinsic rewards, as in his use of bilateral monopoly analysis, one gets the impression that his notion of intrinsic rewards is an evasion of the path he has chosen. What role do intrinsic rewards play in his theory except to hedge predictability in the analysis of extrinsic and material exchanges? As in the case of Sahlins with his idea of friendship, do people who like each other refuse to charge each other rational prices? Intrinsic rewards are apparently not even equivalent to the norm of reciprocity that Blau has allowed as an exogenous noneconomic variable which stabilizes economic exchanges (Blau 1964: 92).

My inclination is to try to divide Blau's intrinsic rewards into two elements, one economic and the other not. On the one hand, the category includes acts of affection which are exchangeable and therefore subject to economic analysis; on the other hand it contains a T factor, as I will call it, which expresses trust and which I would relate to the norm of reciprocity by making the extension of credit to another person due either to a sanctioned norm or to experience. This T factor would then be exogenous to the market system and equivalent to Sahlins's friendship, except that it would not obviate economic analysis. More will be said about the T factor shortly. For the present we will find it useful to try to look at love as an economic good.

In the first place, the fact that love, like the exchange of information between agents, is particular in Foa's sense does not make it unamenable to economic analysis. If bilateral monopoly analysis can be applied to the relations of agents, it can be applied to the relations of lovers. Love itself is not a unitary thing. That it has gradations can be made clear by asking the question, will a man kill himself for the love of a woman (regardless of what love songs say)? And if some men will, will all men? And if not all, will the remainder give their lovers expensive gifts? Some will but not all. And if some will not give them expensive gifts, will they give them inexpensive gifts? And so forth. What a man will give for a woman's love is variable on a scale from everything (his life) to scarcely anything (a little kiss).

On the other side, what is a woman's love? If a man offers to kill himself for a woman, will she let him sleep with her? And if not that, will she kiss him? And if not that, will she let him pat her on the hand?

Can we not conceive quantitatively of a man desiring to obtain from a woman the greatest expression of affection consonant with the smallest expenditure of his time? And can we not put this on an indifference curve and subject it to bilateral monopoly analysis and arrive at a Pareto optimum? I think we can, as surely as Blau could analyze his agents' relationships. In short "love," as defined here, is a marketable commodity.

Love, or friendship, as a noneconomic element can be best illustrated in a strange setting by reference to the Turu institution of *waighembe* (Schneider 1970: 101ff.), which is paralleled in much of Africa. It is a parameter of the economy which relates to the honorableness, trustworthiness, and general responsibility of one person as perceived by another. In waighembe a Turu estimates this quality, which I call the T factor, in another person and if he thinks it is high, he tests that person by initiating with him a reciprocal relationship, beginning with a small gift for which a return of equal quality or value is expected within a year. If the gift is received on time, the value of goods exchanged is escalated, culminating eventually in the exchange of cattle. At this point a virtually open-credit relationship occurs, as a function, one might say, of the exponential growth of the perceived value of the T factor. If, when the relationship is inaugurated, the person chosen by another to be waighembe cannot afford to give the inaugurator the thing requested, the inaugurator gives what he attempted to borrow to his chosen partner! To Turu, the waighembe relationship is equivalent to that existing among members of the same lineage; that is, it is the same as the norm of reciprocity.

I do not mean to imply that this T factor cannot be given value (in a sense it is like our credit ratings), but only that there may be value in making it a parameter of the system rather than incorporating it into analysis. Whatever the case, it is an important element in every society and certainly does not, as Sahlins suggests, preclude economic analysis. And Blau's introduction of this supposedly noneconomic, intrinsic reward dimension into his theory does not seem to serve the development of a theory of social exchange.

BENNETT AND THE JASPARESE

John Bennett (1968), utilizing ideas about the economic analyzability of reciprocal relations among Westerners, namely Saskatchewan farmers, does two things for us. In the first place he transfers Blau's type of analysis out of the associational organization into a larger, communal social setting, more familiar to traditional anthropological analysis, and hence allows us to see social exchange in larger dimensions. But he also extends the analysis of reciprocity beyond systems of subordination-superordination to alliance systems and so brings reciprocity into the core area of social anthropology.

Bennett's Jasparese are farmers and ranchers in the upper great plains of Saskatchewan. The *ranchers* engage in reciprocal exchanges of *labor,* including branding cattle, haying, cattle transportation, machinery repair, corral construction, and road work, and the *farmers* exchange *labor* and *machines* for harvesting, planting, roundups and branding, grazing, fencing, field operations, and minor chores.

The exchanges among these "operators" are represented by them as spontaneous, altruistic, and egalitarian but, Bennett explains, they are in fact a massive and important part of the economic system. In fact, he feels, the system of reciprocity is an attempt at economy of scale in which the different producers obtain the use of a variety of equipment by loaning the equipment they own and their labor in return for what they borrow.

In this system of reciprocity, the tendency is for most exchanges to be carried out by people of equivalent specialization and scale, between whom, therefore, a balance can be maintained. Dyads and "rings" of reciprocators develop at this level. Exchanges between people on different economic scales are less favored because since the lower-scale operator cannot reciprocate labor and machinery sufficient to keep the balance, a relation of "paternalism" (Bennett 1968: 290) develops. That is, the subordinate pays for what he has received by being attentive and deferential to the demands of the superordinate. Finally, the large-scale farmers create their own rings and dyads, so that the community, as we can see, evolves into a set of ranked rings connected by paternalistic associations.

Despite his emphasis on the economic component of these reciprocal relations, Bennett is preoccupied in this account of Jasper with the reason why the operators feel that selfish motives should be hidden or even denied. Bennett's explanation for this is that due to the desire to implement community (Bennett 1968: 302):

The all-absorbing business of farming and ranching, its hard work and long hours, and the pecuniary values that have come to characterize it, have undoubtedly removed many of the old stimuli and satisfactions and motivations for social intercourse. Jaspar people . . . need to use economic activities to provide them with the sense and function of community.

In the nature of functionalist statements this cannot be denied because it cannot be tested. But insofar as friendliness is a part of the reciprocity system, one wonders again whether it cannot be explained, as in Turu waighembe, as a necessary component of credit relationships. Bennett's two points, that community is necessary to human beings and that among all-out entrepreneurs such as Americans community declines as entrepreneurship rises, need not be denied in order to recognize that such expressions of community in reciprocity may have an economic interpretation. One is reminded of Robin Williams's phrase, pseudogemeinschaft, used to describe the behavior of used-car salesmen toward their customers. Here the purpose of such behavior is not to satisfy the salesman's need for community but to establish in the customer a feeling of trust in preparation for the salesman's attempt to "sock it to him." The Jasparese are not necessarily exploiting each other, but they *are* establishing their *bona fides*.

BELSHAW, BARTH, AND EPIPHENOMENA

Bennett's analysis of Jaspar, like Mauss's original study of the gift and Blau's study of social exchange, suggests an intimate and inexorable relationship between gift giving and social structure which may be summed up in the proposition that where there is an inequality of means (whether material or less concrete, such as information) allocation decisions generate a system of subordination and superordination, which is a subtype of general social structure, which is itself a product of allocation decisions

made in other circumstances. This thesis is most closely associated with the names of Cyril Belshaw and Frederick Barth.
The most significant difference between Belshaw and Barth
on the one hand and such people as Homans, Gouldner, and Blau
on the other is that the former are by training social anthropologists rather than sociologists, which explains their focus on
general social structure rather than on class or ranking. Belshaw's view may be summarized as follows (Belshaw 1968: 95):
the division of labor in human society (of which the relations of
producer and consumer is just one example) is not merely one
dimension of society but the whole of it. Recognizing this, we
also immediately recognize that all interactions between people
who have interdependent needs constitute *social transactions*.
The flow of these transactions throughout an integrated system
creates the family structure and other regular social patterns. The
study of society becomes, therefore, the study of the flow of
transactions, which makes obsolete simplistic teleological formulations such as "the family exists to provide sexual fulfillment,
procreation, and socialization." None of these "functions" of the
family prevents it from splitting, but changes in the supply-
demand situation can do just that. The theory of the firm can
then be seen as a special case of a more general theory of transaction that comprehends the exchange of all values, material and
nonmaterial.

Continuing, and quoting Belshaw (1968: 40):

> It is I think quite possible for economic anthropology to develop
> along lines which would enable it to make a contribution to these
> questions (about how societies work), asked of a politically
> identified society. Such a society will operate through transactions
> between roles and between role-playing corporate institutions. The
> formation of a model of social structure can thus be carried out in
> a manner consistent with the kind of transactional analysis which
> has been referred to earlier. Furthermore, the social model can be
> built up through the identification of roles, which should place
> heavy emphasis upon the roles played by corporate institutions.
> Rather than beginning with an *a priori* functional sub-system, as
> does Talcott Parsons, it would be possible to ask what roles are in

fact played by corporate institutions in given societies, and what transactions lie between them. This might well be closer to empirical reality, yet not prevent abstract argument and reasoning, and would at the same time be closer to anthropological methodology.

Barth's position is close to that of Belshaw. Contrasting his recommended approach to the study of social structure with that of structural-functional anthropology, he says that (Barth 1967: 662):

> what we see as a social form is, concretely, a pattern of distribution of behavior by different persons and on different occasions. I would argue that it is not useful to assume that this empirical pattern is a sought-for condition, which all members of the community equally value and willfully maintain. Rather, it must be regarded as an *epiphenomenon* of a great variety of processes in combination. . . (italics mine).

The empirical pattern, then, is an epiphenomenon of *allocation* decisions or transactions (Barth 1966: 4). To Barth (1967: 667) all behavior is new in that it consists of allocations of time and resources made or renewed at the moment of action. Thus households persist in any society because their forms are re-created by behavior each day, behavior based on allocations and not simply on positive valuation of the form.

Illustrating his point, Barth (1967: 663) notes that if there is status differentiation in a community, one need not view this as a given, socially dictated structure. Observation of the pattern of gift giving may demonstrate that an imbalance of gift giving raises the giver's status and lowers the receiver's, thereby creating social stratification.

Looking backward from Belshaw and Barth, we can see that their thesis is implicit in most of our reciprocity theorists. Reciprocity is a delayed system of exchange, the delay being accompanied by feelings of friendship or normative obligations to repay, making systems of subordination—Kwakiutl ranking, Tolai incipient class, Middle American cargos, American "classes," or Indian castes—epiphenomena of allocations. But Bennett's study of the Jasparese suggests a second type of basic structure, one perceived by Mauss, namely the alliance dyad or ring, which is an epiphenomenon of economies of scale among those who are relative equals in terms of the control of material means. It is this balanced control of resources and mutual extension of credit that prevents the emergence of class differentiation, leaving only the economy of scale and the unstratified social system. Or, to put it another way, in those areas of society where obligations are equally divided one observes alliance rather than stratification.

Alliance theory, as such, in anthropology generally has a kind of quasi-economic look about it, resulting from the fact that it deals with exchanges, particularly marriage exchanges (recall our earlier discussion of Levi-Strauss, the leading alliance theorist, in chapter 2). In fact, though, this theory is merely a recast of structural-functionalism in the sense that the aim of the analysis is not to do economic analysis of the exchange events but to show how the exchanges operate to maintain the system. At the heart of alliance theory is the idea that in the sweep of evolutionary history human beings have better survival value if they ally rather than go it alone. Alliance theory focuses mainly on the linkage of lineages. Marriage rules, a center of attention, are seen to evolve to fit different types of lineage arrangements and different size populations in order to optimize survival (Fox 1967: 176, 219).

Hence in some societies, particularly small-scale ones, cross-cousin marriage, which tightly binds two moieties together and (along with more complicated variants on rules) thoroughly mixes the members, serves the purpose of maximizing chances of survival, which is equally served in large-scale societies by an almost total lack of marriage rules due to the fact that chance meeting will statistically achieve the optimum mixing.

Alliance theorists, like descent theorists, have been notable for avoiding economic modes of explanation or even rejecting them. Radcliffe-Brown, the greatest of modern descent theorists, generally rejected economic interpretations of marriage, choosing instead to describe marriage, in typical structural-functional language, as a unifying process (Radcliffe-Brown 1950: 51):

> In so-called primitive societies the exchange of valuables is a common method of establishing or maintaining a friendly relation between separate groups or between individuals belonging to separate groups. Where material goods are exchanged it is common to speak of gift-exchange. But the exchange may be of services, particularly those of a ritual character.

And he goes on to say (Radcliffe-Brown 1950: 52) that:

> there are societies in some parts of the world in which the marriage payment and the counter-payment are equal or approximately equal in value. We may regard this as an exchange of gifts to establish friendship between two families, of which the son of one is to marry a daughter of the other.

Radcliffe-Brown's intent in making these statements seems to have been to show that the establishing of alliances was more important than the "economic" element in the transaction. But since he does not specify what was exchanged or the conditions of the exchange, there is no way to decide whether the exchanges were in fact "noneconomic" in the sense of being economically irrational. And one wonders what he could have meant by the claim that the goods exchanged were equal in value. The economist would not be surprised if the goods exchanged are equal in value to one party in the transaction. He would be surprised rather if a person gave up a good for one of less value to him.

Marriage systems can, however, be understood in economic terms, in contrast to functionalist alliance theory. In some systems, like that of the Puram described by Needham (1962: 78ff.), lineages are differentiated between the wife-taking and wife-giving lineages, the wife-giving lineages providing the women to the others in return for which there counterflows rice beer and pig meat. If the wife-giving unit is seen as the production unit for women and the wife-takers the consumers, the rice and meat are payment for women. But rather than thinking of these as producing and consuming units, one should think of them simply as differentiated "role-playing" institutional groups in Belshaw's sense. In order to operate as an economic unit, each lineage, or each household, must obtain a proper mix of production resources including women, and women must be gotten from elsewhere because of the rule of exogamy (which, like the norm of reciprocity, is an exogenous variable), which does not permit a man to marry a woman of his own lineage. If a man wishes to obtain the "economy of consolidation," so to speak, in which the same woman acts as a production worker and child-bearer, he must marry a foreign woman.

That the rule of exogamy serves to mix and create alliances is what occupies Needham's attention. My attention, in contrast, is riveted on the fact that if one reviews the rings or circles of alliances created by this marriage rule, one notes that they are irregular (Needham 1962: 80–81). That is to say, they resemble Fig. 4-8 rather than Fig. 4-7.

What Fig. 4-8 is meant to suggest is that although wife-giving cannot be reciprocal but must be indirect, paths or rings previously established may be altered so that at any given time the actual rings reflect market arrangements between the wife-giving and -receiving lineages.

Why these arrangements cannot be reciprocal is another question. In some societies which utilize corporate lineages and rules of exogamy, including a large number of African societies, reciprocation is allowed. The answer to this question could be arrived at, in all probability, by aggressive cross-cultural economic studies. A possible answer might be, as suggested by Fox (1967: 223 ff), that where reciprocation is not allowed the lineage as a whole is truly acting as a corporate decision-making body, in contrast to societies where reciprocation between lineages is allowed but not between individual families within the two lineages who have previous ties. Other than that, the more pressing question of why one lineage is superordinate to another must be answered. Here we may approach an answer by means of the model developed previously, which indicates that

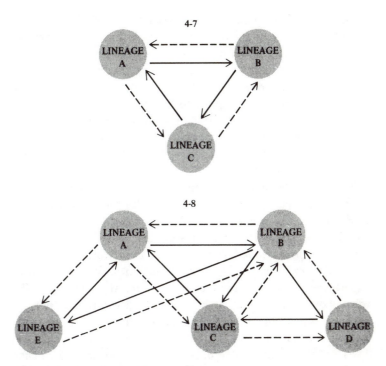

Figs. 4-7 - 4-8. Puram Marriage Rings.

paternalism results from imbalance. Put in other terms, where the value of a woman exceeds the ability of the wife-receiving group to reciprocate in material values or labor, paternalism arises in varying degrees. This is what Leach seems to be suggesting in his discussion of degrees of filiation in *Rethinking Anthropology* (1961: 19ff.).

E. R. Leach has tried to define some aspects of this paternalism by noting that in some Southeast Asian societies, such as Kachin, men actually try to utilize this phenomenon to advantage within a system of ranked lineages by marrying the daughter of a man of higher status than themselves (Leach 1961: 81ff.). While the son-in-law thereby becomes a client of the father-in-law, he also raises his own status. Leach has also demonstrated (Leach 1961: 116ff.) that the amount of brideprice paid for a girl varies not only with the value of a woman as a wife but also with her status value, so that, in instances where a man's wife is of a higher status than he, he pays extra for that. Dowry systems, in which a woman's family gives a price to her husband, are the reverse. Leach summarizes (1961: 102) by saying that where Kachin-type marriage, by which he means marriage in which differential status exists, occurs, the marriage is part of the political structure. In other words, it is "paternalistic."

The extent to which marriage systems can be viewed in economic terms has probably best been illustrated by Hart and Pilling (1961) in their essay on Tiwi marriage. The Tiwi live on an island off the north coast of Australia, from which they are protected from surrounding peoples but from which they cannot flee. Adult men are the decision-makers in an economic sense, and women, who are food collectors, are their chattels. The rules allow all women to be betrothed (i.e., contracted for), including women not yet born. The authors think of this as a rule that all women must be married at all times (Hart & Pilling 1961: 10). I think it more likely that this is an epiphenomenon of the great demand for women. The owner of a woman also has the right to make a contract to dispose of any of her female children. Controlling women is very important, probably because of the ability thereby to increase production of food through the economy of scale, by which food was used to develop reciprocal paternalistic relations with other men. Men make contracts with other men from whom they can obtain women in return, but because few men below the age of twenty-five have control of a woman trading tends to be confined to older men, and the wealth in females polarizes to such an extent that in fact men under thirty-five are unlikely to be married while many older men have many wives (one had twenty-one wives) (Hart and Pilling 1961: 64). To quote Hart and Pilling (1961: 25):

To get a start in life as a household head and thus to get his foot on the first rung of the prestige ladder, a Tiwi man in his thirties had first of all to get himself married to an elderly widow, preferably one with married daughters. This was the beginning of his career as a responsible adult. The widow did several things for him. She became his food provider and housekeeper. She served as a link to ally him with her sons. As her husband, he acquired some rights in the future remarriages of her daughters when they became widowed.

(The reasons he began with an elderly widow are too complex to go into here. See Hart and Pilling 1961: chapter 3.)

The role of women in the production of food and the intricacies of the process of production are not as clear in Hart and Pilling's account as is the wheeling and dealing for women. But it seems reasonable to infer that Tiwi women are unusually profitable and therefore in great demand, enough so to lead to what amounts to a monopoly of them by senior adult men against the great pressure from young men to acquire them.

This pressure is so great that Hart and Pilling believe it has lead to systematic evasion of the Kariera marriage rule (Hart and Pilling 1961: 28), which is this society demands that each man marry a cross-cousin of a certain class, as in Fig. 4-9.

Put another way, there is moiety and section exogamy in the society; since there are only two moieties (I and II) and two sections (A and B) in the Kariera system this prohibition in effect dictates his marriage into one square of a 2 × 2 matrix:

That is, a man of IA had to marry a IIB. Considering that the populations of Australian societies that follow such rules are

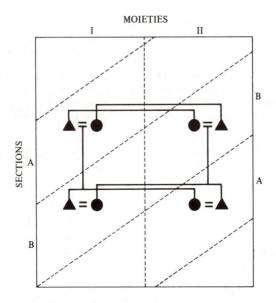

Fig. 4-9. Kariera Two Section Marriage System.

small (e.g., 1062 Tiwi in 1928–29, according to Hart and Pilling [1961: 6]), the rule does not leave much room for maneuvering, one would think, and Hart and Pilling seem to agree. But Australian peoples have been widely alleged to violate their own marriage rules, and one wonders what all this can mean (Berndt and Berndt 1964: 76). I would like to suggest that cross-cousin marriage systems in these societies are the result not of rules but of maximizing choices, and that the systems in fact may be simply epiphenomena of the wheeling and dealing. The idea at least deserves examination if there are grounds for believing Belshaw and Barth that the beautifully balanced systems of circulating connubia are understandable as epiphenomena.

Alliance theorists have only hinted at the economic dimension of alliance systems. It is an unplowed field, and we can say little more about it here than to suggest that many of the unsolved questions about rules and social structures would benefit from economic analysis. Such an analysis is likely to show that problems of allocation of resources for valued things, including women, children, men, livestock, inanimate objects, and obligations, generate many of the surface structures that occupy descent theorists and alliance theorists at the expense of the underlying processes.

A study of African social systems and economies that I did a few years ago (Schneider 1964) will serve to illustrate how the Barth-Belshaw approach can explain surface structures or epiphenomena.

In traditional anthropology African societies are described almost exclusively in terms of structure, as if these surface manifestations are hard, enduring, object-like entities linked together in functional systems. I chose to examine several of these structures as they related to the allocation process with respect to women, livestock, and land. The chosen structures were (1) locality of family after marriage, (2) divorce rate, (3) disposal of wife on death of husband, and (4) type of descent. In terms of these categories a particular society might be described as, for example, being (1) patrilocal, (2) having high divorce rate, (3) having the levirate or inheritance of dead man's wife by his brother, and (5) having patrilineality. The study showed that in fact these variables change with the magnitude of brideprice supporting Radcliffe-Brown's well-known claim (1950) that no society is altogether patrilineal or matrilineal. Specifically, my investigation showed that as the brideprice becomes significant and then grows in magnitude, the place of residence chosen by the married couple shifts from matrilocal, to avunculocal, to patrilocal; descent shifts from matrilineal to patrilineal, the patrilineal form increasing in intensity; and the wife returns home to her family at the death of the husband only up to a certain level of brideprice magnitude, after which she increasingly tends to remain with his family and to marry one of his brothers (which is the levirate). This model assumes that all the African societies studied have essentially the same system, so that differing forms of these societies are equivalent to one society in various phases of change. I believe that such an assumption of parallel basic systems is workable but recognize that there are variants of it that might produce different surface manifestations from those detected. I have compensated for this by striking a statistical average in working out the model, and have tested the conclusions with a large sample of African societies in an as yet unpublished manuscript (Schneider n.d.).

What is the nature of the allocation system that generates these epiphenomenal social forms? The basic fact about these economies is that a classificatory group of brothers acting corporately to control land extend reciprocity to each other and thereby achieve economies of scale. Women are legally without status and constitute the labor market for the production of food and children. A rule of exogamy, which forbids any man from having children by his own sister, extends over the whole of the classificatory group, and demands that although he may require his sister to perform productive labor for the growing of crops, a man may not impregnate her but must bring a man in from the outside to do so. There is a clear tendency in these systems for men to optimize control of production and minimize costs by combining the two main production activities within a single woman, which forces one to marry a woman from another group and send one's own sister out to be married. This, however, cannot be accomplished unless compensation in some form can be provided. Furthermore, it appears that the value of a particular woman is uncertain enough and potentially great enough that exchanges cannot be accomplished on a quitclaim basis except for very high payments. Therefore the exchanges in fact consist in most cases of a mutual exchange of self-productive capital held by each party for the term during which the other party keeps his share of the items exchanged. Hence when a wife dies or is divorced, the capital given for her is returned with some adjustments, as among the Turu, where payments for depreciation of the wife are made out of the brideprice cattle.

In Africa the most thoroughgoing patrilineal societies seem to be those in which livestock, particularly cattle, are an important asset—that is, where the number of cattle per person is about one or more. Where there is no asset that can be transferred for compensation, we find matrilineal-matrilocal systems. As compensation increases the husband is allowed to remove his wife to his father's home, so that the system becomes matrilineal-patrilocal, but with the male children moving to live with their mother's brother when they marry (avunculocal residence), since mother's brother owns them despite the patrilocality of the marriage. As compensation reaches a higher level the system shifts to patrilineal-patrilocal, and this increases in intensity as the amount paid increases until at the other extreme one gets patrilineal-patrilocal systems in which there is no divorce. That is to say, the amount paid for the woman (e.g., fifty head among the Turkana) appears to purchase full rights in her and there is no divorce because there cannot be. A kind of verification of this is that when amounts paid for bloodwealth are examined, one finds that in any given African society the price charged a person for killing another (i.e., taking full rights in that person's person) seems to equal the amount that would be charged in brideprice for full rights in a woman.

This African situation raises some interesting economic questions which I shall mention here only in passing. Why is the amount of control a man gets in his wife apparently about the same for about the same absolute amounts over much of the sub-Saharan continent, at least in the cattle-raising areas? This suggests a high stability in the supply-demand, means-ends situation both for women and for livestock and crops, and perhaps reflects some kind of fine ecological tuning. It also suggests the possibility of widespread intertribal trade links. Why are cattle, particularly heifers, so highly prized in comparison to other goods? The answer may simply be that, as Keynes said of money (1936: 239), they have high liquidity proportional to carrying costs—that high liquidity, I might add, lying, as with women, not only in the value of the products they produce (here including milk, meat, hides, and manure) but also in the calves they produce. In this connection we should remember that our own important economic concepts of chattel and capital derive from early terms for cattle. The situation in Africa reminds one of the thesis put forth by Eggan about the Plains Indians (Eggan 1955). Eggan remarked that these Plains tribes, notably the Cheyenne and Arapaho, despite varying cultural and social backgrounds, tended when they moved onto the Plains and became buffalo hunters to assume similar social structures, apparently in response to the demands of this new kind of economy (Eggan 1955: 93). While the allocation model that would explain the social system on the Plains is not as apparent as the African one, some things seem clear. Plains social structure tended to bilaterality, extended families, and bands (Eggan 1955: 89ff.). These features suggest small, highly mobile groups composed of whomever could be pulled into the organization, through emphasizing kinship of any kind, as they followed the buffalo herds. An additional element may have been one pointed out by Ewers (1955: 216ff.) with respect to the Blackfoot, namely that buffalo hunting was for the purpose of producing buffalo robes to be sold to an external, non-Indian market, as well as an Indian market. The wealth so obtained and wealth in general were reposed in horses, which, like Eastern African cattle, served not only as instruments of warfare and production but as repositories of wealth—and perhaps even as money—as well.

Similarly, in an essay on the social structure and economy of the Dry Zone Sinhalese, Leach (1960) demonstrates how the social structure is derived from the allocation system. The Dry Zone Sinhalese have a rule of bilateral inheritance that allows both men and women to inherit land. The land is severely restricted in amount by the fact that it must be irrigated by holding tanks. When women marry they may go to live with their husbands or their husbands may come to live with them, depending on economic opportunities. This situation seems to suggest the inevitable development of extreme fragmentation and inefficient use of land, since people who leave their own compounds and villages leave unexploited land behind.

In fact, each village tends to have several dominant compounds that have some characteristics of patrilineages. How is this possible where bilaterality is the rule? The strategy of the leading adjacent compounds is simply to establish exchange marriages with each other. By this means the land of the husband is combined with his wife's land for a more economical operation, because their lands are side by side. Hence, although technically when a wife marries she goes to join her husband because he is in a neighboring compound, the fragmentation process is defeated through an allocation process that produces patrilineality as an epiphenomenon.

A THEORY OF SOCIAL EXCHANGE

Having completed this review of some of the more important papers and books on the subject, we are prepared to attempt a preliminary theory of social exchange. To begin with, a distinction, already embedded explicitly and implicitly in the literature, must be made between two kinds of "goods," material and social wealth. Social anthropology has insisted on the value of this distinction by asserting the existence of a material sphere of exchange called "economy" and a social sphere that dominates the former. As has been noted and as will be argued further below, this dual classification is somewhat unsatisfactory because it implies that there is something insubstantial about actions and interactions in contrast to the "hard" reality of material things, but we will find it useful to work with these primitive categories for the time being.

Utilizing Foa's scheme, I suggested that the material sphere contains money, goods, and information while the social contains service, "status," and "love." It is time now to refine these notions by taking account of the ambiguity in this scheme, in that not only is service, in the sense of hired labor, traditionally dealt with by economics as if it were a material good, but information is rather unconcrete to be called a material good. A more profound characteristic of so-called material resources than supposed concreteness is that in contrast to love and status they are exchanged or can be exchanged for each other in terms of their instrumental value without any personal involvement. That is to say, a lady who sells her love in a brothel is not involving herself with her client in the same way as lovers in the social sense. Status and love relationships are personal in the sense that they involve continuing interaction between two persons over a more or less lengthy period of time (i.e., the interactors play roles such as father-son, student-teacher). The idea intended here is expressed by Radcliffe-Brown (1952: 32ff.) in his differentiation between rights *in rem* and *in personam,* or rights in a person as a thing and as a person. To illustrate, among the Turu (Schneider 1970: 104ff.) when a woman is being dealt with as a social being, she is a wife, a mother, a daughter, or whatever, but when she is being dealt with as a potential wife whose services are being traded she is referred to as a cow. This distinction is most familiar to us with respect to people seen as fellow human beings and as slaves.

Social exchange may now be defined as that kind of exchange in which in return for some "material" or "social" value the recipient returns obligations (satisfying role actions, as Gouldner calls them) that are expressive of subordination to the giver and which are called by many different names, e.g., subservience, serfdom, deference, clientship, respect. In Levi-Strauss's terms this is a *transitive* system (Levi-Strauss 1963: 311). But social exchanges can off-set each other, in which case an alliance is created that is manifested by expressions of respect and friendliness between the parties involved. This is Levi-Strauss's intransitive system.

Having stated the matter so simply, we may wonder what all

the difficulty has been in putting a finger on it. The answer is probably that it cannot be so simply stated unless conceived of in economic terms, as traditionally it has not been. That is to say, traditionally economy and society have been treated as opposed rather than as related.

In all the cases of reciprocity that have been reviewed in this chapter this equation of the material with the social is either explicit or implicit. For example, when Homans speaks of a member of a group reducing his personal integrity in exchange for acceptance, he is saying, translated into my terms, that the subject is increasing the amount of deference given to the members of the group (by changing his opinions to one degree or another to fit theirs). Blau, on the other hand, puts his equation in a direct form. A junior agent gives deference in exchange for the time/ competence of a senior. Interestingly, Blau suggests that this outcome could be avoided if the junior chose to pay the senior for his time, which would convert the relationship from one of social exchange to one of material exchange and, presumably, would also prevent the rise of a class or status system within the office.

Bennett's Jaspar situation is a more complex development of the equation. Farmers who give without receiving immediate return get from others friendliness, but only when each is obligated to the others on the basis of specialization of skills or kinds of machinery owned. That is to say, friendliness is an attentiveness to others that does not involve subordination. When there is no reciprocation paternalism results. Among Kachins, similarly, while the son-in-law who marries up the class system pays livestock for his bride the payment is presumably insufficient to cover the value received, so he became a client of the father-in-law. If marriage is made with a family within one's class an alliance relationship occurs, which implies counterbalancing material-social exchanges. But note also that the Kachin classes may be epiphenomena of the material-social exchange, which is to say that, as with Bennett's Jasparese, the quantity and utility of the resources possessed by a people who exchange will decide whether there will be classes as well as alliances and how many. The nature of the Kachin economy generates three levels. Jasparese economy seems to generate only two, and in America the situation is complex due to the affluence of our economy, so that while our folk model gives us three classes, in fact the number of rings and levels is indeterminate.

To conclude this survey of illustrative cases, potlach and the Tolai case (as well as Melanesia in general) are classic examples of status systems supported or generated by gift giving. The nature of these economies may be simply put: property owners and decision makers engage in acts of production of material wealth not only for the purpose of feeding themselves and for the pleasure derived from these goods, but also in order to give gifts that will obligate others to them and thereby increase their social power. That which the economic man seeks in order to maximize his profit and utility is a balance of material and social wealth.

One element which remains unexplained in all this I mention merely to display the whole picture. This is the matter of interest payments and other material payments that sometimes occur in these exchanges. If, among the Kwakiutl, a giver of gifts receives deferential obligations from others, why must the recipient of gifts return the gifts and also pay interest? In this case the answer seems to be, so that he can reverse the relationship and become the superordinate. Is this the case also in Tolai and other systems in which social exchange involves interest? A related problem is to be found in many African brideprice-paying societies and also among the Puram (Needham 1962: 92ff.), where although each side of the marriage exchange gives material wealth to the other (e.g., cattle for the bride), the recipients of the bride occupy a status inferior to that of the wife-givers. Is it possible that the inferior position is proportional to the difference in value between the wife's service and the number of livestock the husband can afford to pay? That something like this is involved is suggested by such facts as that a Turu bridegroom is required to do service for his future father-in-law unless he chooses to cancel that obligation by paying an extra heifer. If my suspicion is correct, we cannot think of social exchange as necessarily always of the extreme type, wherein one party gives material gifts and the other returns only deference.

Taking this distinction between the material and the social as legitimate, Maurice Godelier (1971), after analyzing the economy for salt currency among the Baruya of New Guinea, argues that formal economic methods can be used to analyze the market for material wealth in primitive societies, but specifically excludes the area of gift exchanges and the acquisition of social power, feeling that the economic anthropologist's legitimate role is the study of the economy of material means. But many formal economic anthropologists seem by their actions to be suggesting otherwise. Orans's study of Indian castes (Orans 1968: 889), the studies by Blau on the structure of bureaucracies, Epstein on the Tolai, and Leach on the Kachins and Sinhalese, and those by Belshaw, Salisbury, and Barth are examples.

I feel that the matter is not one that can be decided by fiat. That the two spheres, the material and the social, must be studied together seems inevitable. This can be illustrated by reference to a controversy between Fortes and Worsley (Fortes 1969: 220; Worsley 1956) over the proper interpretation of Tallensi kinship. Fortes argues that what he calls the kinship system of the Tallensi is given and not determined by the "economy." Worsley attempts to argue that the existence of valuable productive resources which are used to maximize consumption of food "is a pre-condition" of kinship (Worsley 1956: 69). Fortes's refutation of Worsley would have been more difficult, I believe, if Worsley had included social exchange as a dimension of Tallensi economy, because Fortes's theory sees kinship status as given and fixed, whereas social exchange analysis would have shown it to vary in ways that I have demonstrated above. This debate, I think, is complicated by a typical social anthropological confusion of rules and strategies. If this were resolved, we would probably find that within a given set of rules (of which portions of what Fortes means by kinship would be part) much of the structure of Tallensi society would be seen as an epiphenomenon of the general economy.

Alchian and Allen (1968: 6) make the point about the intimate relation of society and economy in, for me, a different way. Whereas there are extensive free-market systems in some societies, such as our own, there are other societies, such as the socialist countries, where the supply, price, and even demand of material goods are controlled politically, i.e., by the social exchange system. As these authors conclude: "If we were to devote primary attention to socialist systems, we would investigate much more fully political exchange and political decision making." The point may be further underscored by reference to the case of the introduction of steel axes among the Yir Yoront of Australia (which is developed more fully in the final chapter), in which almost the only important dimension of the economy was the system of subordination-superordination based on control and loaning of axes by men to women and children. When the supply of axes was increased and ownership dispersed by the missionaries, who handed out the axes indiscriminately, the society dissolved.

These illustrations make the point that even if it is possible in some cases to study the market for material means alone, anthropologists would be missing the most interesting part of their subjects' societies, a part that is traditionally within the sphere of social anthropology, by making a practice of this. If Godelier means to say that the social area should not be studied formally because it cannot be studied that way, that matter remains to be settled by attempts to do so. I think the evidence is to the contrary, and that in the end we may even find that the distinction between material and social can be replaced by a more general idea, that of the exchange of property. If we define property as rights in things, rather than as things, a distinction going far back in the history of sociology, then economics would be definable as the study of allocation of property. This concept would imagine economic man using whatever resources he has, social and material, to accomplish his ends, and it would ask why material means should be distinguished from social means in this process.[1]

Now that we have established the nature of social exchange and argued that it is closely intertwined with the material sphere, several interesting issues in economic social anthropology remain to be investigated. Many sociological writers have made a distinction between systems of reciprocity existing at one level of human evolution and market systems existing at a more "developed" level. This is Polanyi's distinction except that he has two primitive levels, reciprocity at the lower and redistribution at the higher. The same historical model seems to be present in Mauss's thought, with his progression from total prestation through potlach to market. Paralleling this is Levi-Strauss's idea of progression from elementary through medial to complex marriage systems, in which the earliest system (elementary) controls choice making through rules which insure social survival while the latter achieves this by "statistical" processes, that is, by free-market activity.

The question posed by these evolutionary schemes is whether to look at them as describing various degrees of development of economies, from a predominance of social exchange to a predominance of material exchange, or whether to see them as simply confusing models with reality. There is a strong tendency in sociological thought to see strange people in terms of the rules they use to govern their lives, while seeing our own lives as dynamic, and filled with choice. So much is this the case that when patterns *are* observed in strange societies, they are converted into rules. That is to say, if there is a pattern of matrilineality, as among the Kariera of Australia, we interpret this as a "submerged rule" of matrilineality (because the people themselves don't recognize the "rule") rather than as an epiphenomenon of the

[1] Demsetz (1967) explores some of the implications of this idea in his "toward a theory of property rights."

decision-making process. We see our own classes as statistical results of economic processes, but we see Indian castes as normative and ideological.

My point can be further developed by reference to Sahlin's model of reciprocity, which is a kind of evolutionary scheme phrased in spatial terms. I feel that what he is trying to say with his delineation of three spheres of exchange—generalized, balanced, and negative—is simply that in the first there is a norm (as in the family) that dictates that all wealth must be shared without resort to rationalistic calculations by the individual members of the group. In the balanced situation, norms of reciprocity exist as parameters of economic activity that ensure peaceful and honorable behavior in the transactions. The third, negative reciprocity, is a situation in which exchanges can occur but there are no governing norms. Raw power and mutual need are the only regulators of the market. I feel that if Gouldner is right, the latter situation, if sufficiently enduring, will tend to convert to the balanced situation through an initial development of trust between the exchangers, which is then institutionalized into a norm. On the other hand, I don't think generalized reciprocity as such exists anywhere, although corporation decision-making by the family or business firms resembles this condition.

To put it another way, social exchange is pervasive in any kind of interactional system we normally describe as a society. The exchange of material means is directly or indirectly influenced by an intertwined system of obligations. In fact, what we mean by society *is* social exchange. The implication of this is that an economy as such, taken as a system of interdependent people who are individually striving to relate means and ends, is transcendent of any particular society insofar as there is trade with persons outside the sphere that encompasses social exchange. But where such exchanges with outsiders are extensive and important, there is a tendency to extend social exchange into that realm and thereby broaden society to become coterminous with the whole of the important economic sphere.

Another issue has to do with status systems. Bennett, among others, gives us good reason to believe that status systems can occur in any social situation. Gouldner, in fact, argues that *all* exchanges have some element of subordination-superordination in them (i.e., there are no pure alliances). When we see only alliances in primitive systems (Mauss's total prestations; Levi-Strauss's elementary systems; Polanyi's reciprocity), are we imposing this on them because we cannot see the dynamics of status formation among them? Or are these systems, in accord with the classic picture of segmentary, unilineal descent groups, really pure alliance systems without centralization or status differentiation, which evolve into politically centralized systems when some imbalance occurs in the homogeneous state (Mair 1962: 107ff.)?

An additional issue has to do with the mode of analysis. Traditional social anthropology has utilized a *static* approach (see chapter 2), in which the system is seen as closed. We may ignore the fact that anthropology tends to differentiate poorly between the reality and the model and concentrate on the fact that such a mode is not sensitive to positive and negative feedback processes. As a result, anthropologists are ill-equipped to understand the *dynamics* of inflating potlach systems and, similarly, are insensitive to equilibrating or negative feedback processes such as the Tolai redistribution of wealth at the death of a big man, or the Kwakiutl destruction of coppers and other goods. It seems particularly important when studying social exchange to look at the power-aggrandizing activities of subjects in a way that allows first of all for the fact that status striving (a kind of positive feedback activity compared to balanced, segmentary alliance) can occur and then for the fact that in order for a system to survive, this polarization process must be controlled by some equilibrating device.

The final issue to be raised here has to do with the form of formal analysis to be used to study social exchange. We have seen that Blau and others, notably Curry and Wade (1968) and Buchanan and Tullock (1969), have found indifference analysis and bilateral monopoly analysis useful. Game theory, which grew out of economics and which is another way of analyzing behavior as the process of relating means to ends, is another possible avenue, which we have not explored but which has been used by Riker (1962), Barth (1959), Moench (1971), and others. The fact is that the methods to be employed are presently unclear and will evolve with increasing attention to social exchange. As suggested above, there is a possibility that dynamic analysis will be necessary to do justice to this area, because statics is too limited to comprehend certain important aspects of status dynamics. On the other hand, in these situations, it may prove useful to treat the giver of gifts as equivalent to the firm and the receiver as a consumer, in which case the theory of the firm would be used to analyze the actions of the giver and indifference analysis of the receiver. Whatever develops, the starting point is obvious, namely a view of behavior as relating available means to desired ends. The social exchanger desires to obtain the highest profit or utility from social and material means. In order to do so he must relate whatever means he has to that end, whether we choose to conceptualize that process in terms of the firm maximizing the difference between cost and revenue, or in terms of the consumer maximizing utility.

5 *Money*

The concept of money is deceptively simple. However, a close examination reveals various vexing problems concerning what it is and also the same controversy about how to define it that marks the substantivist-formalist debate with respect to economics in general. Money has been chosen for special treatment in this book because it has been a focus of attention in economic anthropology. Such people as Karl Polanyi (1968), George Dalton (1965), Helen Codere (1968), Mary Douglas (1967), Jacques Melitz (1970), Paul Einzig (1966), Melville Herskovits (1952: 245ff.), and M. Panoff (1970) have all had something important to say about it, and their arguments and counterarguments will sharpen our understanding of economics in general.

SUBSTANTIVIST AND TRADITIONAL VIEWS OF MONEY

It again serves our treatment of the subject to begin with the substantivist view of money, to which the formal view will be compared.

Dalton's paper on primitive money (1965) best argues the substantivist point of view. Dalton sees money in industrial Western economies as suited to their special character as integrated market systems (1967: 225.). This money is all-purpose, having the essential qualities of both a medium of exchange (or means of payment) and a standard of value.

Before proceeding with Dalton's views we must pause to consider these two qualities, around which much of the debate revolves. Money as a *medium of exchange* is the easier characteristic to understand. A medium of exchange serves to effect the exchange of most of a variety of goods (never all of them), as goats do among the Sonjo (Gray: 1965), where they are given in exchange for women, land, honey, tools, and a wide variety of other things. So prominent in this role of goats that few things are bartered directly for each other without the mediation of goats. In other words, goats tend to exclusively assume, in the nature of a medium of exchange, the function of mediating exchanges.

Money as a *standard of value,* or *unit of account,* is a more difficult concept. Einzig (1966: 356) asserts that money as a unit of account is quite dissociated from the other role of money. Money as a medium of exchange is physically concrete; money as a unit of account has no concrete existence. So complex is this notion that Melitz (1970) charges that a wide range of economic anthropologists have misunderstood it, including Dalton, Firth, and Belshaw.

Probably the best way to clarify this notion of a standard of value is to consider the following. An economic man, as we know, is trying to mix his consumption possibilities in such a way as to maximize utility. Those things he desires are various, extending beyond the thing whose value he works out on the spot in a barter trade. When he trades good a for good b, he also has in mind relating the value of this good to that of goods $c, d, e,$ . . . , n. He cannot make a rational decision about buying this good unless he can compare it in some way with other goods he desires. This he does through his unit of account. If we say of a peck of potatoes that it is worth 50¢ and of a peck of apples that it is worth $1, we are in each case making an equation of their value in terms of the unit of account called "dollars and cents." The confusion about this concept comes from the fact that we also have goods called dollars and cents which we actually give for apples and potatoes. This situation does not have to exist. One could barter potatoes and apples directly, never using money, and still have a unit of account, as in the Nyamwezi *Kimo-Kitand-Ikumi* system (Abrahams 1967: 40), an abstract method of accounting which equates things such as cattle, goats, and rupees, so that a *Kitand* is equivalent to a bull or five rupees. Melitz feels that the idea of a unit of account is so fundamental to human relations that it must appear in the most primitive states and must have preceded the development of money as a medium of exchange (Melitz 1970: 1031).

To get back to Dalton: he feels that in non-Western economies money is special-purpose, being used to mediate some transactions but not others (Dalton 1967: 255). Even its form is primitive—woodpecker scalps, sea shells, goats, salt, etc.[1]—implying that it is thereby unsuited for commercial transactions of a general type. Primitive money is especially limited by not being usable for redistribution and reciprocal transactions (Dalton 1967: 260), that is, for social exchange. Real money is impersonal but in primitive economies exchanges are personal, and this pseudomoney reflects this in that it is treated personally. Sometimes the money pieces even have names and histories.

The functionalist tendency to try to differentiate primitive from Western societies appears again with respect to money in ways parallel to Dalton. Panoff (1970: 67) remarks of Firth that even though he decided that the definitive characteristic of money was its medium-of-exchange function (1964: 225), he still would not consider his concept of money to include such currencies as that of Tolai, which obviously operates as a medium of exchange. Max Weber (1947: 173–181) likewise sought to

[1] See Einzig's *Primitive Money* for a nearly exhaustive list.

limit the term money to all-purpose money, defining real money as "a chartal means of exchange" (where a chartal is some sort of artifact that enjoys a significant degree of formal value within a group and that can be used in arithmetic calculations). In effect his definition seems to exclude as money almost anything that is not like Western tokens. Bohannan, similarly, denies that Tiv have real money, in that it does not move freely to exchange all things but rather moves in spheres, certain media exchanging only for certain things (Bohannan 1955: 61ff.).

Recently certain substantivists-functionalists have taken more profound positions in defense of Polanyi's thesis. Mary Douglas attempts to distinguish primitive money as "coupons" (1967), on the ground that in a market economy the medium of exchange is free to flow where it will, like the people in the society, whereas in primitive societies, where people are more controlled and interaction more governed and constrained, the medium of exchange is also restrained and restraining. Hence primitive money, or coupons, is relatively more restricted in its flow, and the range of goods it can buy is more restricted. True money emerges as the market develops and as the society becomes less communalistic.

Codere's views (1968) are more complex. Claiming to provide a sounder justification to the substantivist view that there is a difference between money in industrial and primitive societies, she examines money as a symbol, thus focusing on money in much the same way as economists who see it as a unit of account. She concludes (1968: 574) that money should be related to the intellectual dimension of man's existence, in the sense that its quality as a symbol reflects the evolution of the state of knowledge and technology of a people. Money is an intellectual system comparable to mathematics in its range of development from simple arithmetic to complex methods like calculus. To quote her (1968: 575):

> One would not expect the people in a society in which householding was the unit of both production and distribution to have

or to require any but the crudest symbology and calculus of exchangeable goods, while our contemporary mixed social, economic and political system exists through the continuous exchange of every imaginable kind of good and service and requires the technological and intellectual means of both adjusting and keeping its accounts and making economic decisions.

Later Melitz's objections to Codere will be presented, but a parenthetical remark seems in order here. How does such a conclusion square with that of present transformational grammar, which sees each language system (the supreme form of symbolism) as equally developed? That Chomsky finds the reason for this in the physical structure of the mind is beside the point. Is it possible, if Codere's views can be credited, that all men are equally endowed with accounting capabilities and that the difference between men lies not in the difference in intellectual development but rather in the degree to which, and the manner in which, they use their endowment? This would be to argue that in some sense all men need this capability. Symbolizing the relation of values must be a very elementary need in all societies.

Herskovits's position on this question, like his position in general, leans toward the formalist. To him any least common denominator of value, even a consumption good, is acceptable as money so long as it is part of a system of graded equivalents and is used in payment of goods and services. But despite this antifunctionalist, proformalist stance, he rejected the idea of cattle as money because he was committed to the view that they were merely stores of value.

The traditional view of money in anthropology is therefore a compound of functionalist views, which are strongly particularistic in their interpretation of monetary phenomena, and "romantic views," which seem to reject out of hand the idea of the universality of economic processes.

THE FORMAL APPROACH

The formal view of money, following Melitz (1970), stresses first of all the necessity for making a clear distinction between the two primary characteristics of money as a medium of exchange (means of payment, store of value) and as a unit of account (standard of value), a distinction clear to economists (e.g., Einzig 1966: 356) but often, if Melitz is to be believed, unclear to anthropologists. Melitz goes so far as to suggest that the term money be reserved for the medium-of-exchange dimension and that units of account be called simply that, because the explanation for each is different.

To begin with the unit of account, it is not a good but an abstract way of comparing and equating different values. That it is often stated in terms of the medium of exchange is the source of the confusion of the two qualities. But they vary independently. Paper money, depending as it does on the belief of people in its representation of value rather than on any inherent value (though the two things may actually be the same, because it has no inherent value unless you believe in it), is especially prone to this confusion. Yet there are today dollars made of silver and gold which are in fact exchangeable for much more than their face value in paper, illustrating the fact that the notion of a dollar as composed of 100¢ is different from the notion of a dollar as consisting of paper, silver, gold, or whatever. The latter is a good, a valuable good, traded for other goods.

To Melitz, Codere's "symbolic quality" of money is simply this accounting dimension (Melitz 1970: 1025–1026): ". . . at best, her view reduces to the statement that media of exchange possibly can be conceived as symbolizing everything purchasable with them." A unit of account allows calculation between sectors of any economy and therefore, like arithmetic and mathematical systems in general, promotes control. However, one can accept this and also accept Codere's idea (1968: 574) that the conceptual quality of a unit-of-account system (or accounting system) is subject to evolution—for example, in the invention of the double-entry bookkeeping system.

Once the distinction between units of account and media of exchange is clear, the first casualty is the idea of special-purpose and all-purpose money, on which the substantivists' monetary theory is built. Units of account, by their nature, are all-purpose in the sense of being abstract systems, but media of exchange are never all-purpose. One can conceive of an all-purpose money only by confusing units of account and media of exchange.

Money as a medium of exchange is simply a commodity which has become the medium through which things other than itself are exchanged. The reason for this is not mysterious, nor is it necessarily the result of some general agreement by its users. As Panoff notes (1970: 67), Keynes defined money as a commodity with the special characteristics of having high liquidity relative to carrying costs (the latter being wastage or the expense of keeping the good). For example, livestock often operate like media of exchange. Their high liquidity (or easy convertibility) is based on their intrinsic values, particularly the ability to reproduce themselves, so they are always in great demand, and they are also cheap to support. In East Africa, all that one needs to provide for them is a corral for them to sleep in at night to protect them from thieves and wild animals, and some, often meager, pasture. However, we should also be aware (Einzig 1966: 44) that not all liquid goods are money. They may be very perishable or indivisible.

Realizing this, we should no longer be surprised that money takes the form of woodpecker scalps, anymore than we would be if it took the form of gold. The only necessity is that it be something valued by the people who use it. The reason for the valuation is of no concern to the economic analysis. That quality which Keynes attributed to money could then lead to the rise of a variety of kinds of media of exchange. There could be single-commodity money (perhaps silver or gold), multiple-commodity money (silver and gold), and money consisting of inanimate objects like gold or animate objects like cattle, sheep, goats, horses, buffalo, llamas, chickens, and the like. In a particular society it could also happen that no commodity is suitable as a medium of exchange, so that there might be a unit of accounting without any medium of exchange, as in Unyamwezi. Barter would rule in such a situation. I would immediately qualify this last statement by suggesting that the difference between barter and money exchange is not as great as at first appears if we distinguish media of exchange from units of account and see the former as specialized commodities. If there is some definite way to distinguish a medium of exchange from other commodities, the medium of exchange certainly possesses the Keynesian qualities in varying degrees from economy to economy, depending on the elements of liquidity and carrying cost.

Einzig, in *Primitive Money* (1966), has extensively examined the qualities of "primitive" money (he doesn't believe that there is in fact any such thing; money is money). Einzig's book is really written for economists, with the aim of educating them away from some crude notions about non-Western money, but most of it is also instructive for anthropologists since it contains an elementary theory of money. For example, he buries the notion (Einzig 1966: 345) that barter is a more primitive form of exchange, which disappears as volume of trade arises, by insisting that whether barter or media of exchange are used is due to varying circumstances. Money may even arise, he feels, before it has any value in promoting the efficiency of trade. He also asserts that imported objects tend to be currency (Einzig 1966: 350), a claim that has something to say to anthropological ideas about closed societies.

Although these empirical generalizations about the form of money are interesting, Einzig's discussion of the dynamic meaning of variations in money is far more instructive. He notes a division of opinion in economics between those who view money as a commodity and those (nominalists) who feel that money has no intrinsic value. Although one might think that whether money has intrinsic value or not would be important in the prediction of how money acts, Einzig feels that the difference between these two points of view is largely one of emphasis (Einzig 1966: 393), because in the end both see the value of money as related to supply.

We can ignore this controversy, then, and concentrate on certain generally held ideas about the supply of money. The most basic of these is the hypothesis that *the quantity of money is likely to affect its value,* an hypothesis which unites money with other commodities and brings it into the general realm of microeconomic theory. Einzig is much concerned about distinguishing the "intrinsic" value of a given money from its value as money (for example, a cow has intrinsic value as a giver of milk and bearer of calves, but it also has value in East Africa as a medium of exchange). There is some question in my mind about the validity of this distinction. The value of the money is at best a cardinally unmeasurable quality, so the issue can't be settled. And even if it could be settled, I wonder if it would make any difference. If one says that the liquidity of a commodity is affected by the quantity, this would apply equally to any intrinsic or extrinsic value. The only difference might be in the varying degree of elasticity of demand for one quality as opposed to the other. This same question comes up again when we examine Gresham's law (Einzig 1966: 413). In Gresham's law, a debased currency or medium of exchange drives out one that is less debased. But how is debasement determined except in terms of value? What one might more accurately say is that when there are two media of exchange operating simultaneously, the one whose value in exchange is higher than the other when purchasing the same good (which would be determined by the exchange rate of one of the media for the other) would be withdrawn and the "cheaper" of the two currencies would be used, if the liquidity of the two is equal. At the heart of this debate is probably simply a situation in which two or more goods are competing for the position of medium of exchange, the one being chosen being that which gets the most in exchange for the least cost. To speak of debased currencies is a kind of absolute thinking which does not fit in a deductive model.

An increase in the supply of money may generally be expected to cause a decline in its value, which is to say an increase in the price of the things for which it can be traded. This is common knowledge to the man in the (Western) street, but its implications are startling if we begin to see things other than Western money as media of exchange. One of the most interesting examples of this effect outside the West is in East Africa, where the colonial government began a destocking campaign in the 1950's. Reasoning that cattle, sheep, and goats were merely stores of wealth or ceremonial objects, the government decided that an across-the-board reduction in the number of livestock at a rate of 10% would preserve the grass and stop erosion, while leaving the Africans in relatively the same position at the end of the operation. When the program was finally implemented in full force among the Turu (Schneider 1970: 161ff.) it caused widespread agitation, so much so that it was immediately abandoned. The Turu complaint about the program was that it made the rich richer and the poor poorer, which is exactly the case, since by reducing the number of livestock one increased their value, and trade of grain by poor farmers to rich pastoralists was impeded. No doubt there was also a reverse multiplier effect which operates in economic growth, what one might call a substractor, which made the difference in the positions of the farmers and pastoralists an exponential difference rather than a linear one. Einzig's book contains a number of famous examples of the operation of the quantity theory of money in non-Western settings (Einzig 1966: 396): the depreciation of dog's teeth in the Admiralty Islands, of cowries in New Guinea, and of brass rods in the Congo. On the other hand, he notes how the value of cotton cloth money increased in Wadai with a decline in the volume.

If the value of a medium of exchange varies with the quantity of the good, it will also vary with demand for it, so that as a population increases, if the medium of exchange remains constant in supply its value will rise. Value also varies with *velocity*. This represents an increase in the scale of exchanges as the scale of interaction increases; the same quantity of money becomes in effect a larger quantity because it moves around more rapidly.

One special effect relating to the way money acts stems from the fact that it is in great demand. Because the demand is highly inelastic, an increase in supply may not cause any immediate or sharp rise in prices. But, of course, every economy is different, and the quality of its medium of exchange must be individually assessed.

In most non-Western economies, the media of exchange are not controlled by government, so that the market model applies more closely. Because of the high demand for it, production is stimulated. But the cost of production will check production. Empirical research will determine for any particular society what the cost factor is in the production of money, and the answer should be very instructive about the general nature of the economy.

The nature of money is nicely illustrated by a famous article by R. A. Radford on the economic organization of a P.O.W. camp (1945). Radford intended to show that the essential features of economic organization were necessary to any relatively stable aggregate of people, and his discussion also illustrates how money appears and functions. When prisoners were interned in Italy and Germany, they at first exchanged goods haphazardly, the non-smoker giving his cigarettes for chocolate and the non-chocolate eater giving his chocolate for cigarettes. But very quickly barter in terms of the relative values of the goods appeared, and soon after cigarettes emerged as a medium of exchange and standard of value for the exchange of goods and services. Even though all the men in a camp obtained about the same rations, a vital economy for the exchange of goods in terms of demand arose, with the impermanent camps showing a more unstable market than the permanent camps, where the economy was allowed to stabilize. In unstable situations *arbitrage,* the playing off of one sector of the economy against another, arose. This is exactly what a system of accounting, along with price information derived from a medium of exchange, serves to stop. For the persons who got five cigarettes for a can of beef at one end of the camp to discover that they could have gotten ten at the other end builds pressure to generalize information and thus avoid being "cheated."

Once cigarettes emerged as money they acted in every way like money. For example, since any cigarette was for exchange purposes equal to any other, those brands of less desirable quality tended to dominate exchange and the more desirable stayed out of circulation (Gresham's Law). Cigarettes served to exchange most goods in the stabilized camps and acted as a unit of account even when bartering continued for some goods. Arbitrage decreased between sectors of the camp as cigarettes unified the market. Finally, and notably, the fact that cigarettes were also a consumption good caused no problems for their use as money. Radford (1945: 407) felt that they could be viewed as capital when used for investment and profit when smoked.

ROSSEL ISLAND MONEY

The issues at stake with respect to the nature of money are nicely revealed in Armstrong's pioneer investigation of Rossel Island money and the recent debate about his view of the Rossel situation among Dalton, Baric, and Salisbury (Dalton 1965:

269–274; Baric 1964; Salisbury 1966, 1969). Armstrong, an economist, reported the results of several months' study of Rossel Island in the *Economic Journal* in 1924 and in chapter 5 of his *Rossel Island, An Ethnological Study* in 1928. He was convinced that it was money he described (1924: 253) because it served as a medium of exchange and standard of value and because it had no other use (a consideration that we now see was irrelevant). To Armstrong the outstanding feature of the money was that the supply of each type of token was unchanging and the values of the tokens in relation to each other were not simply proportional but were also modified by a time or interest element (Armstrong 1924: 246). Armstrong identified two types of money, "*Dap*" and "*Ko*," both types of shells (the former men's money and the latter women's), each having a specific number of grades, or levels. To him, the value of any level of coin, *x,* in this system was a function of the length of time coin *y* would have to be loaned in order to repay *x.*

A further complication in the system was the fact that certain kinds of payments, for example bridewealth, could be made only with certain tokens. The short supply of the higher denominations was made up for by an extensive credit system, which allowed many more to be circulated than actually existed.

Before proceeding to the discussants of Armstrong's data, we should recognize that (1) he left out much that seems important now and (2) we have no other information on the system. Therefore, the question of whether Rossel Island money is "really" money is probably indeterminable by any definition. The discussion of Rossel Island money is therefore more important for clarification of positions than for answering this question.

Dalton (1965) dismisses Armstrong's conclusions by noting what he considers to be two faults in Armstrong's analysis: (1) he assumes that all shells act as media of exchange and (2) he ranks the shells in value, which the Rosselese do not. Dalton elaborates his argument by insisting that the shells are not media of "commercial exchange" (i.e., they don't unify the market), that there is no impersonal money market (referring to his view that any entrance of personal considerations negates totally any possibility of an economic consideration), and that the various types of shells are used only for certain types of exchanges (and therefore their use is not rational in an economic sense). In short, if all the shells were abolished provision of subsistence on Rossel Island would be unimpaired (Dalton 1965: 274).

Baric (1964) tends to side with Dalton in the sense of rejecting Armstrong's view of Rossel money as true money. She thinks that the attempt to relate levels of tokens through temporal interest is unjustified, and otherwise feels that the tokens did not have the essential characteristics of a real, commercial money. However, she introduces a notion foreign to Dalton but not foreign to this book, the idea that the tokens are a kind of money whose peculiar characteristics are explained by the fact that they are more important to the economy of social exchange than to that of material exchange. The currency, she thinks, operated to double and redouble social links (Baric 1964: 39). The lower levels of coins were liquid and were used to buy goods to make feasts, whose purpose was to raise status. Essentially, in the social-exchange sphere, the system operated as follows: in order to establish a social relationship, such as marriage, a certain token was necessary, and in order to get that token, it had to be borrowed from someone, with whom, therefore, another social link was established. Thus the Island's population became tightly tied together by debtor-creditor relationships. Since social exchange was the center of the system, she feels this explains how the currency could remain constant in amount while people could still become rich in social rank.

Baric's analysis is an improvement on Dalton's in that it tries to understand the obviously "commercial" elements in Rossel money and thereby focuses on the sphere of social exchange, which is so central to peoples such as the Rosselese. It fails by leaving certain important economic questions unanswered. For example, if money operating in the social sphere has a different quality than money in the material sphere, such that its value is indefinite and the tokens not intervally ranked, how can such a currency operate? And how is it possible to operate an economy such that in the social sphere the amount of currency is fixed whereas in the material sphere it must be variable? In fact, of course, since there is an extensive system of loaning, the fact that the supply of money is fixed is not as critical as at first appears. As in our economy, the amount of money can be multiplied even though the supply of the money commodity, such as gold, is fixed or relatively fixed.

Salisbury's reassessment of Armstrong carries the argument beyond Baric to show that, as Baric says, this is centrally an economy of political power, but he does not hedge about the tokens, arguing that they are truly an exact money, as Armstrong said they were (Salisbury 1966: 113). In Salisbury's terms, the manipulation of money seems to be a game played by the Rosselese, the object of which is to maximize the volume of services received from others in exchange for shells. The money regulates the demand for goods and services. This money, insists Salisbury, accepting Armstrong's own words, is a money graded in exact intervals (Salisbury 1969: 89). The money is not very liquid, so that exchanges require extensive negotiations, but it is sufficiently liquid for the job it has to do, namely the exchange of goods and services and the reckoning of compound interest in Rossel Island in terms of this particular social system. Salisbury feels that Rossel Island is not atypical of Melanesia in general (Salisbury 1966: 113), in that egalitarianism is dominant and the intervillage flow of valuables is paralleled by an intervillage system of political rivalries, which are regulated by the valuables. That is to say, goods are given, or money is given, for political rights ("services").

If we review this debate about Rossel Island money in light of the discussion of the nature of money which preceded it, we realize immediately that the important distinction between money as a medium of exchange and as a unit of account was not utilized. What difference would it make to our view of Rossel Island if the distinction were taken into account? In the first place, the problem of liquidity of money would take on a new dimension. Money as a unit of account requires no liquidity whatever, since it is merely used to compare values in different sectors of the market. Certainly the tokens are used in this way to calculate strategies of marriage and political alliance, although this is not brought out in the analysis. Money as a medium of exchange, however, must have some minimum degree of liquidity or there is no point in calling it money. In other words, a lesson to be learned from the debate over money is that like everything else in a formal economic analysis, money is a relative, "moving" thing. That which is money is that which serves most often and by preference to mediate exchange. If it is not liquid it can't sensibly be called money. In Rossel Island, whatever the degree of liquidity of the tokens, they must be the most liquid of valuables if they are to be called money. And if they are not liquid, this still does not prove that Rossel Island has no "commercial" economy if they serve as units of account in barter transactions. But we need not resort to such an extreme position. The tokens obviously are exchanged, and they are liquid, at least in the lower denominations. If the monetary system is otherwise peculiar compared to ours, we may put this to the fact that it is adapted to a special system of material production and values and a peculiar system of social services.

The confusion associated with money has served right up to the present to disguise the function of cattle in East Africa, a subject to which I would like momentarily to turn in order to summarize the cross-cultural view of money.

The East African indigenous monetary system is based on livestock (Schneider 1964a). That livestock are also used for milk, meat, manure, hides, and ritual should not cause us to preemptorily deny them the status of a medium of exchange. Typically, in these East African societies, just about everything can be and is exchanged through the medium of livestock. They are highly liquid, and, as earlier explained, they have low carrying costs. Complicating the system is the fact that not only cattle act as the medium of exchange but also goats and sheep, camels and horses where they exist, and even chickens, not to mention hoes, cowrie shells, and, in recent times, German and English coins of low denominations. That is to say, high liquidity and low carrying cost characterize a few finished goods of metal and shell as well as all kinds of livestock. The medium-of-exchange function of livestock is so strong that right up to modern times livestock are exclusively demanded for brides in areas where the indigenous economy still operates to any degree.

Apparently because the costs of carrying different kinds of livestock tend to be equatable, standardized conversion rates arise between different types of livestock, notably cattle and goats. Over East Africa this rate of conversion varies from five to ten goats for a heifer. In turn, as among the Turu, heifers and steers can be indirectly equated in terms of a conversion rate of five goats for a heifer, so that a steer is worth three-fifths of a heifer because it is worth three goats. In modern times this stable system has begun to be affected by government livestock markets that place higher value on large steers than on cows, whose reproductive ability make them more valuable in the indigenous economies. Arbitrage sometimes occurs between the indigenous and external national economies, whereby traders profit from the fact that steers can be bought cheap internally and sold dear externally. Ultimately this will probably cause a readjustment of the medium-of-exchange function of livestock to bring these now isolated markets into conjunction.

Among the Turu, at least, livestock have also the role of unit of account (Schneider 1970: 66ff.). When speaking of the arranging of marriage a person will calculate the value of a bride in terms of *ndamas* (heifers), although when the actual exchange is made there may be no heifers at all in the bride-price, which may consist of goats and sheep, steers, or other goods. Goats (*mburi*) similarly serve as a unit of account; when calculations are being made, the term takes on a certain definite value in relation to heifers and refers to both goats and sheep and to both sexes of both types of animals, whereas in other affairs there is a different term for all four types of these animals. An illustration of goats as a unit of account can be seen in some calculations made by a group of Turu brothers about division of inheritance. Given the problem of a father who died leaving two heifers to three sons, they solved the distribution of the inheritance by first dividing the two heifers into ten goats, after which they assigned four goats each to the eldest and youngest sons and two goats to the middle son (middle sons among the Turu are discriminated against in favor of the coalition of eldest and youngest). In practice, however, it is unlikely that the heifers would be converted into goats, since the breeding potential of heifers is normally greater than that of goats. That is to say, the exact convertibility of heifers and goats in accounting is not exactly matched in real life, but is close enough to allow the accounting system to operate. In modern times the accounting system adds exact ratios of small English coins to the system, so that one goat is equal to 20 shillings (a heifer being worth 100 shillings). As one might expect, these values are close to those which could be obtained for these animals in the livestock markets in 1960.

Although, as we have seen, the fact that livestock have roles other than that of medium of exchange does not prevent their acting as a medium of exchange, there is a certain empirical interest in the question of how the various roles affect each other. The answer must be that their nonmonetary uses must become ecologically adjusted to their monetary function, and vice versa. The volume of money in these economies must have fluctuated broadly, because there existed a common drive on the part of individuals to increase the number of livestock they had, which caused a steady increase in livestock population until it either pushed the limits of the land or reached a level unable to maintain itself before the periodic droughts. At these times a sharp decline in livestock numbers occurred through starvation and disease, bringing the population back to a lower level, from which it again rose. These variations in volume, one may predict (Schneider 1964), caused fluctuations in prices of goods and services. Among the Turu, far-sighted farmers stored grain against drought, at which time they traded it for cheap livestock from other Turu for whom, before the drought, opportunity costs of keeping up large-scale production of grain proportional to livestock were too high (so that when the drought hit they were long on livestock and short on grain). Droughts, therefore, also had the effect of redistributing polarized assets and keeping the economy stabilized. Similarly, since the basic structure of these societies, as between patrilineal or matrilineal, was dependent on the exchange of livestock, there must have been periodic shifts between the two descent patterns, although the general historical tendency of East African societies to become statistically more patrilineal (Schneider 1970: 145) argues that over time the people have learned to support greater and greater livestock populations.

SUMMARY

Much remains to be learned about money. For example, there are still unanswered questions among economists about the effects on an economy of variations in the amount of money in circulation (Robinson 1971: 77ff.). But for our purposes certain tentative generalizations seem possible as guides to anthropological investigations. The first is that it is necessary that a clear distinction be made between money as a medium of exchange and as a unit of account. In fact, because of the confusion now inherent in the term "money," it might be a good idea to go Melitz one better and abandon the term "money" in favor of the other two phrases. Anthropologists have always been much more conscious of the medium of exchange than of the unit of account, but unit accounting seems to be very important in all societies so that there seems to be a need to direct attention more carefully in that direction. If Melitz is right, some system of accounting is probably universal in human thought. Its investigation would contribute to the investigation of purposeful, rational strategies in human cognition.

Media of exchange seem to vary widely and cry out for empirical investigation in order to clear up questions about how they arise, the extent to which they are or are not in competition with barter (insofar as systems of exchange media and barter can be distinguished), and how they relate to the general socioeconomic structure. It does seem that as a medium of exchange emerges from the general system of commodities exchange it is transformed by the function of medium that it assumes. Salt that becomes money is no longer just the commodity salt. For one thing its demand is enhanced simply by its primacy as a medium of exchange, so that it may continue to have value even when the salt has lost its savor.

Of particular importance is how media of exchange relate to social exchange, a question with which Douglas tried to cope in her essay on primitive money as coupons (Douglas 1967). A medium of exchange has one characteristic that seems at least sometimes to make it quite unsuitable for use in social exchange, namely the mobility which makes possible discharging a debt without further social interaction. One is reminded of Srinivas's (1955) description of the social system of a Mysore Village in which money is not much circulated because payment in land, with accompanying permanence of ties between giver and receiver based on the immobility of the land, is preferred. Put another way, in any society payment for a good with a medium of exchange satisfies the exchange equation in a way that does not involve any continuing relationship between the parties. There may, of course, be all kinds of grades on the continuum between satisfying a value received with cash to partial payment and partial service to complete obligation. But where complete obligation is the form of repayment, there is no medium of exchange involved. Since deference or interpersonal dependencies of varying kinds seem much more prevalent in non-Western, nonindustrial societies, we should not be surprised at monetary systems like those in the Rossel Islands or Tolai, where strange mixtures of obligation and media of exchange emerge and where the actions of media of exchange are not as predictable as in economies like our own, where there is a great striving toward personal autonomy in a cash market. No society, however, can escape social exchange, so that one is encouraged to ponder what might happen to our monetary theory (and Keynesian economics) if it stopped thinking of the questions of inflation and unemployment entirely in terms of media of exchange and tried to integrate into the theory questions of social exchange.

CHAPTER

6 *Applying the Theory*

In the course of discussing the philosophical bases of theory and the nature of microeconomic theory the relation between theory and reality has inevitably been touched on. The task of this chapter is to sharpen the view of this relationship and to show how and in what areas the connection can be made.

MICROECONOMIC THEORY AND REALITY

It seems useful to begin with an interesting exchange between David Kaplan (1968) and Scott Cook (1969) on the question of the applicability of microeconomic theory to reality. Kaplan's position, unlike that of Dalton's, which it resembles in some respects, is that microeconomic theory (or economic theory generally) is not only not applicable cross-culturally, but has not even proved very predictive in Western economy, for which it was designed. An examination of Kaplan's charge will help us to decide where economic theory can be made operational.

One claim Kaplan does not make is that deductive theory is an artifact of Western culture and therefore culture-bound. Ideas, when cast in logical form, can be considered for their truth value irrespective of their socio-cultural context. If two people can agree on the rules of addition, then they will agree on the logical deduction that $2 + 2 = 4$.

The trouble with economic theory, Kaplan argues—at least the deductive micro variety—is that it is so highly "idealized" that there is trouble deciding what reality it could apply to, as if the terms in the model $2 + 2 = 4$ could not be related to anything in the real world that could be called two: two cows, two houses, etc. *Macro*economic theory, he claims, has moved away from this idealized state to assume a much more empirical position (probably because of the fact that its growth has been so closely tied to the solution of practical economic problems). Hence macroeconomics is much more predictive and increasingly divergent in form from micro theory, i.e., more *inductive,* where micro is deductive.

This idealization, Kaplan points out, is not of the variety that one expects in deductive theory, in the form of wild assumptions. The idealizations in economics comprise the things that are being studied, the firms, households, goods, etc., whereas the idealizations of physical deductive theory lie in the area of the limiting conditions, not the objects of study. Illogically, perhaps, he includes the supposed rationality on the part of the actors as one of the things studied that should not be assumed.

Formal theory, Kaplan continues, cannot be tested until it is given substantive content. As long as the elements of the theory cannot be related to any objects in the real world, the theory is nothing but symbol manipulation. In economics there are not even any *rules* for relating the theory to the world. Friedman's (1953) attempt to eliminate the problem by claiming that the assumptions do not have to have any relation to the real world is inadmissible and contrary to what science has always held.

Finally, Kaplan tops off his argument by standing with Dalton and the substantivists in asserting that whenever economic theory has been given empirical content it has proved to be limited to market-organized societies. That is, economic theory is culture-bound, having no logical validity.

In sum, if Kaplan's position is correct anthropology is faced with very severe difficulties in attempting to apply economic theory cross-culturally. The subjects cannot be assumed to be rational, i.e. desirous of maximizing utility; they must empirically be shown to desire to maximize utility (whatever that is). Firms must be identified, markets discovered (perhaps even marketplaces), and the other elements in the theory of the competitive market must be given content. Furthermore, rules for making the identifications must be arrived at. Not anything can be called a firm but only that which the rules of conversion from theory to reality dictate. In the end, Kaplan holds out no hope, for like Dalton he predicts that the behavior analyzed by economic theory is uniquely produced by Western institutions and won't even exist in non-Western contexts. We are rational and profit/utility-oriented because we have institutions that lead us to act that way and that are a distinctive part of Western civilization or, perhaps, of a certain evolutionary stage. Our firms and households are formed under the controls of these institutions. There are no economic men outside the West.

Cook's rebuttal to Kaplan offers a way out of this impasse. It is, essentially, that there are no rules for the application of theory to the real world. Theory and reality are related ad hoc (Cook 1969: 389) by the researcher, who must make a priori assumptions about the relevance of differing methods of approaching the problem. Put simply, one tries a method to see if it works. (Perhaps this is why serendipity is so often involved in discovery.) Cook remarks that for an anthropologist to raise questions about the epistemological status of methods in another field, in this case economics, is equivalent to an economist first inquiring about the validity of anthropological methods before he employs their results in economics. Such questions are illegitimate, as Cook sees it. I would say, rather, that such inquiries are unnecessary. The validity of a field's methods is determined by trying them. There is no insurance in the scientific enterprise against failure.

Since we have concluded that, contrary to Kaplan, there is no reason to believe that economic methods cannot be applied cross-culturally, it follows that either they *may* be applicable or they are certainly applicable. Of these two choices we are driven to the first, since we have no proof that they are applicable, but only a firm feeling that they will prove to be so.

CROSS-CULTURAL MATERIALIST METHODS

Perhaps the most elementary application of economic theory to cross-cultural reality would be through utilizing Lionel Robbins's definition of economics (Robbins 1962) as the study of the allocation of scarce means among alternative ends. It is a study of the possible as it relates to the desirable. Even this simple approach would be useful in anthropological studies, and it is certainly an application, at an elementary level, of economic methods; under the label of *allocation,* it has been successfully employed by Barth (Barth 1967: 667). It merely determines what resources a person or a people have and relates them to their goals in an ad hoc way, much as any prudent householder does when he budgets for his preferences. Even though no formal predictability is involved at this level, this approach can be very revealing.

For example, in Margaret Lantis's account of the introduction of reindeer herding to the Eskimos of Alaska (Lantis 1952) she tries to account for the failure of the attempt and underscores, in the traditional anthropological fashion of focusing on cultural tradition, the discontinuity between Eskimo attitudes about prestige which is tied to individual generosity (Lantis 1952: 145) and the attempts in the herding scheme to make the individual simply a shareholder in a herd with nothing personal to distribute. Lantis's explanation has another dimension, the fact that the market for reindeer was uncertain. In fact, it is difficult in this account to be sure that there ever was a reasonable market, leaving one wondering whether it was the Eskimos' complex of hunting values (Lantis 1952: 146) that caused the scheme to fail or the inability on the part of these Alaskan economic men to relate the means (reindeer herding) to the end (making a "profit"). That Lantis suspects that this is part of the explanation is evidenced by her observations that the failure of the scheme was related to such things as the increase of air freight from the States, which limited the ability of Eskimos to profitably ship meat out (Lantis 1952: 147), the lack of a taste for reindeer on the part of Americans who were the best market (Lantis 1952: 137), and the increasingly high slaughtering standards imposed by the government, leading to lower profits because of higher production costs (Lantis 1952: 137). The only assumption required on the part of the ethnographer for this analysis was that Eskimos *might* be profit oriented, which led to an examination of the means-ends relationship and the conclusion that the failure of the reindeer herding scheme not only might but probably was due to the fact that Eskimos were being asked to allocate time and resources to an enterprise which made no sense except as a profit-making activity in a situation where profit was not really possible.

The economic theory that I have been urging on the reader of this book is but an elaboration of the above method of analysis. The defense for elaboration is the refinement of insight that it will bring. In the Eskimo analysis there was no question that the theory used was made operational. There is no reason to believe that with care more elaborate forms cannot also be made operational.

E. E. LeClair has made an attempt to translate the terminology and categories of microeconomics into a more general, less culture-bound form, than that used in Western economics (Le-

Clair 1962). This is a major attempt to apply economic theory outside the West, and it also has implications for the use of that theory in our own society, since it suggests the use of the theory for a wider range of behavior (for example, in the area of gift giving) than is usual. It will pay us, therefore, to explore LeClair's "translation" of microeconomics.

LeClair begins by accepting as basic the Robbins definition of economics as the allocation of scarce resources among alternative ends. This constitutes *economizing* behavior, and economic anthropology is the cross-cultural study of economizing. The translation consists essentially of finding new terms for the conventional microeconomic categories and broadening the reference of the terms in order to make them cross-culturally acceptable, notably with respect to the inclusion of "prestige" factors. Hence, the household becomes a more inclusive unit, the *consumption unit* (which, he notes, tends in human societies to be kinship based). The firm becomes in LeClair's system a *production unit,* that is, a unit that creates and provides goods but

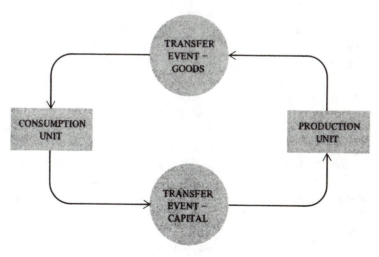

Fig. 6-1. LeClair's Microeconomic Model.

does not directly consume them. The production unit creates *goods*, defined as anything, tangible or intangible, that satisfies human wants. Production units create consumption goods and consume *capital goods*, any goods not directly consumed but used to produce goods. To complete our economic system we have *transfer events*, which corresponds to buying and selling in the micromodel but includes, in addition, giving, bestowing, borrowing, lending, barter, exchange, theft, and appropriation. This last is perhaps the most liberating idea of all since it allows us to deal theoretically with a whole range of exchanges, in both our own and other societies, that are normally ignored. For example, there is good reason to believe that the cattle raiding of many East African pastoral people is best seen as a kind of transfer event rather than as an anomaly, since the Masaai depended on such appropriations to maintain equilibrium in their economy. While LeClair's scheme is deliberately simple, the diagram oversimplifies even further, in that he would allow for transfer events between production units and between consumption units.

LeClair feels that this scheme can be used in two ways, at two levels. The first is purely descriptive, identifying in any non-Western society those social groups which correspond to the consumption and production units (he gives examples in his article, to which might be added from the chapter on social exchange, the groups which exchange gifts for obligations) and describing transfer events. At the more sophisticated level he would use the scheme to describe the dynamics of the system by seeking to identify its fundamental characteristics.

One element of LeClair's scheme seems to be rather purely anthropological, namely the specification of the parameters or conditions within which the economy operates. Economists customarily take for granted many things that should not be taken for granted cross-culturally and that have to be specified in order to better understand why the distribution and production systems take the form they do. These conditions are: (1) the opportunities and limitations of the habitat, (2) the technological possibilities of the people (one should not assume that *any* technology is available, as is often done in growth theories), (3) consumer preferences, which vary widely in human societies, and (4) the rules governing transfer events.

Of course, not all economists are unaware of the special conditions that sometimes obtain cross-culturally. Bert Hoselitz speaks to point no. 2 above in an essay on capital formation in Indian agricultural society (Hoselitz 1964: 372) in which he challenges, in terms reminiscent of Barth's explanation for shifts in social patterns among the Fur after the introduction of livestock (Barth 1967a), the idea that Indian peasants behave as they do because they are "traditional" in their orientation. He argues that we can understand the Indian farmer's behavior by assuming that he is engaged in rational productivity in which the high risk attached to experimentation causes him to be exceedingly cautious about innovation, and lack of knowledge of technological alternatives makes impossible the reduction of the opportunity cost of experimentation.

Returning to LeClair, while he goes far toward relating the micro model to cross-cultural circumstances he stops short of stating explicitly something that follows from constructing the problem his way, namely that the actors in the system are presumed to desire to maximize their preferences, production units are "profit" oriented, and exchanges occur at an equilibrium price. In fact, LeClair may have thought that his model could be valuable even if used only at a descriptive level. But I feel that he saw this cross-cultural model as laying the groundwork for expansion to full-scale equilibrium and dynamic analysis.

In any case, his generalized model is the beginning of a successful cross-cultural operationalizing of microeconomic theory, as can again be illustrated from the Turu. An obvious consumption unit or household is the Turu *nyumba,* or house, within the *xaya,* or homestead. The production unit is again the house, in that the wife, with the help of her husband, purchases livestock to produce manure for crop production, arranges for leasing other wives to increase production of crops and bear children, invests in grain to make beer to sell for profit, and the like. Transfer events include sales of beer, purchase of cattle for grain and vice versa, brideprice payments for leasing of wives, compensation for injury, loans of livestock to kinsmen and special friends in return for subordinate behavior and the like.

Having established this, it remains for the completion of the economic analysis to place magnitudes on the quantities involved in transfer events and to obtain prices, which in Turu economy is easy since (for the most part) they are quoted in livestock. With such information the same types of deductions are possible as are derived from analysis of our own economy.

Scarlet Epstein (1967) carries the process of operationalizing one step further by discussing the kinds of data that anthropologists should collect in the field. In a useful cautionary note, she reminds ethnographers not to be overly ambitious in planning on the amount of data to be collected (Epstein 1967: 159). Epstein indicates that in her experience a field worker and one or two assistants were able to collect detailed statistics for no more than fifty or sixty households in one year of study. In my own experience, merely mapping the farms of a single village comprising about ninety individual units took all my time for every morning for more than a month. As one turns to quantification the breadth of one's view must narrow as depth is substituted for it.

The first step in data collection is to determine the structure and composition of the household (Epstein 1967: 161)—the consumption unit of the theory, which may be different from common residence. For example, in Turu society each individual wife's house within the larger homestead of the male is in important respects an independent consumption unit, contrary to appearances. Similarly, the production units should be differentiated from consumption units. In the case of the Turu the individual houses are also the firms or production units. The consumption unit and production unit, however, need not always be the same. In our own economy they are differentiated, so much so that, as previously noted, LeClair thinks that this fact makes Keynesian theory uniquely applicable to our economy in that investors and consumers must be different people for the theory to work.

I would add at this point that one should keep in mind that economic theory is based upon exchange between differentiated units. If consumption and production units cannot be identified, attention should be given to simply recording exchanging units, leaving the question of whether they are consumption or production units aside.

The next step is to identify the major sources of wealth: crops, animals, and natural resources, such as stone or ores (and, incidentally, status positions). In other words, all desired goods, tangible and intangible, should be denoted. Once this is clear, the fundamental problem becomes to determine the quantity of each form of wealth and its distribution, and the flow of the wealth and prices associated with its exchange. Since time is limited and gathering full statistics on a small number of houses may take too much time, a fundamental decision must be made as to whether the sample of households is large enough for full treatment of one's special problem or whether sampling of the universe to be studied is to be resorted to. This, of course, poses problems of randomness, and one's ethnographic skill must be employed in determining what factors operate to influence the distribution of relevant data in order to conduct a random sample. It may serve in America to stand on a street corner and ask a passerby questions, treating the answers as constituting a random sample, but in a non-Western society it may be that only free men walk the streets while slaves travel elsewhere. In India one must be sure to take caste variations into account. In Africa lineage membership is a basic fact. And in Latin America class ranking based on ethnic affiliations is crucial. Furthermore, in some places women can be treated as having no decision-making part in economic activities whereas in others they are equal to men.

Epstein and I both found that weighting members of the consumption unit according to the amount they consume was necessary. In the Turu case I was trying to establish a minimum level of individual food consumption in order to determine how much of the harvest was available for sale. Epstein used Lusk's coefficient (Epstein 1967: 160), which is as follows:

Men above 14 years:	1.00 (i.e., full consumers)
Females above 14:	.83
Males and Females 10 to 14:	.83
Males and Females 6 to 10:	.70
Males and Females 1 to 6:	.50
Males and Females below 1:	.00

The kinds of data recommended by Epstein for collection are:

1. Production Statistics: degree of self-sufficiency of household; degree to which outside labor is employed; payments for production labor of both a monetary and a nonmonetary kind. What tools are used and how they are obtained. Size and quality of farms and animals. Overhead (i.e., fixed costs).

In the area of production, Epstein was concerned over the fact that in India, where her work was conducted, the amount of personal involvement with persons employed to help in the production process varied inversely with the amount of cash paid, suggesting that part of the payment for this labor was in the form of personal involvement or obligation. This reminds us that the economy for goods cannot be kept rigidly separate from the exchange of personal involvements such as prestige and deference, and some attempt must be made when recording data to indicate this element. Among the Turu it showed up, among other things, in the amount of compensation paid for assault and homicide, which varied inversely with the degree of relationship, suggesting the degree of valuation of obligations. Thus, the closer in lineage relationship a plaintiff was to his assailant the less he charged for compensation, because this might endanger the relationship.

2. Consumption statistics: Household budgets are of special importance. The term budget was encountered in our discussion of microeconomics, where it meant the combinations of consumption possibilities open to a household, given its resources. The term as used here is similar in that it refers to the determination of the flow of income and expenditure in the society under study, i.e., what people actually do with their resources as compared to what they theoretically might be expected to do (the two may or may not coincide). Budget data can be collected on a daily or yearly basis or in terms of some time unit in between, depending on the situation. It can be limited to cash transactions or take into account other types of income and expenditure, including expenditure of time. Epstein feels that budget data is collected with more difficulty in "preliterate" societies, because they rarely employ standardized measures. I would disagree here. It seems logically necessary that people have some kind of standard measures, and in my experience they do have them. In any case, the matter should not be prejudged. It is the ethnographer's job to find out if measures exist and what they are.

In determining consumption data, Epstein warns us, we must be clear when we compare units whether we are comparing consumption units as decision-making units or simply as individuals. Obviously the individual who is not a decision-maker is not as important to analysis as one who is.

Finally, Epstein notes that the nature of productive assets must be carefully worked out for each non-Western society, since this may vary considerably from Western patterns.

We can summarize what Epstein attempts to say as follows: if we start with the static model of an economy, in any given economy we want to collect data that will make possible analysis of that economy in terms of the static model. This means first of all establishing what the household or consumption unit is in the society and what the firm or production unit is. Once that is determined, one must determine what the form of the factors is and what the forms of goods (both tangible and intangible) are. Are the factors, as in our economy, land, labor, and capital (i.e., tools), plus, perhaps, entrepreneurship, as Haveman and Knopf (1966: 36) define this? And if so, what is the nature of the "land," "labor," and "capital"? For example, in Turu society one may conclude, as I did, by defining marriage as a kind of labor market, a fact which is not obvious at the start. Tools of war may be seen as productive capital. Goods, in turn, may be the most apparent things people desire, but prestige, deference, and other social values must also be identified and may be of greater value.

Having established the consumption units and their factors, and the production units and their goods, the next step is obvious: to determine the flow of factors from CU to PU and the flow of goods from PU to CU, or to construct an input-output analysis matrix.

Finally, one must gather data on the exchanges of the goods, specifically the prices paid or the values utilized to make the exchange where there are no prices or where there is no money. In connection with this, of course, the system of units of account, if any, must be detailed.

With this data, we have all the essentials for any level of economic analysis. However, as Epstein implies, it is easy, once the static model is in your mind, to know what kinds of data are needed for economic analysis; it is quite another thing to determine on the spot what empirical facts fit the different categories and to then actually collect the data. This is where the ethnographer's skill comes into play as he delineates the peculiar features of an economy within the framework of theory.

Matthew Edel, in a paper on economic analysis in an anthropological setting, takes us the next step beyond LeClair and Epstein. He sets the stage for his solution to the problem of operationalizing economic theory by quoting Samuelson (Edel 1969: 422, from Samuelson 1947: 7):

. . . in every problem of economic theory certain variables (quantities, prices, etc.) are designated as unknowns, in whose determinations we are interested. Their values emerge as a solution of a specified set of relationships imposed upon the unknowns by assumptions or hypotheses. These functional relationships hold as of a given environment and milieu.

This can be illustrated from our examination of microeconomic theory in a previous chapter. In the theory of the firm, it is plain that if we know the market demand price for a good and the costs of production, and if all other things are equal (that is, if the *ceteris paribus* condition is fulfilled), then we can predict what level of supply of the good the firm will settle on.

Edel points out that economic problems can be set up in two ways, which are mathematically similar though "psychologically separable." That is to say, the problems are derived from the same model but different unknowns are being solved for (Edel 1969: 422):

Either the problem can be one of the allocation of limited resources to competing ends . . . or the problem can be the determination of whether certain targets, which are fixed, can be attained given the means at hand.

That is to say, in the first case we are concerned about making rational choices about distributing available resources so as to maximize profit or utility; in the second we are concerned about whether an end we desire can rationally be achieved, given the resources we have or can get.

Paralleling LeClair and Epstein, Edel explains that the solution to these problems requires knowledge of three things: (1) the wants and preferences of the actors—the things they wish to maximize; (2) the range of production and exchange possibilities open to the actors; and (3) an inventory of available resources and who owns them. Anthropologists have something to contribute towards refining these variables and thus enhancing the predictability of economic analysis while achieving operationality. Economists usually reduce the preferences of the firm and household to profit and income, but as Edel notes, and as we have seen (especially when examining social exchange), preferences may in fact be far more complicated than this. The anthropologist is in a position to specify the range of tangibles and intangibles, like ritual, prestige, and power, that people desire. In turn, indifferent curves, where they can be established to represent these preferences, can help anthropologists determine the strength of competing values. This, of course, is easier said than done because such curves require the fullest possible demand schedules, that is, lists of the quantity of any good demanded at a certain price. Anthropologists are also in a position, by utilizing their specialized knowledge of comparative technology and the laws of culture change, to refine the technological variable. As already noted, economists normally take it as given, which turns out to mean that they assume that all technological means are equally available to all producers everywhere and that the lack of use of a technique is due to opportunity cost. The anthropologist can more realistically indicate not only what techniques are available to a people but also what is involved as a production cost, such as rituals, that might not be seen as such by the ethnocentric Westerner. But the anthropologist also has something to learn from the economists in this matter, for in acculturation situations where new techniques are taught to non-Western people, the failure to use them may sometimes be best explained, as among the Eskimos, as due to the cost of using them rather than to conservative values.

Finally, according to Edel, the anthropologist has a good deal to contribute in terms of operationalizing the resource variable. Economists, strangely, have not explored problems of ownership and variability in resources, which would include cross-cultural differences in how people view resources, such as food taboos on certain types of plants and animals. The variable nature of labor has also not been given the attention necessary in order that theorizing about the use of labor in the production process accord more closely with fact.

The "failure" of economists to be more specific about the dimensions of these variables is, of course, not a failure in the real sense. Dealing as they have been with Western (i.e., their own) culture, they have not had to take into account variability and could afford to treat these variables as constant. But anthropologists are aware that cross-culturally this does not obtain.

How then would Edel actually apply this refined method to a cross-cultural example? We need not explore both of his approaches—means known, ends unknown and amount of means unknown, ends known—because they are different sides of the same coin. One of Edel's better illustrations is of the second kind (Edel 1969: 428). Suppose, he says, that a person requires 200 pounds of grain a year to keep him well fed and the "culture" requires him to spend 165 days a year in rituals. In this circumstance the economists could try to solve for the amount of land needed per capita in order that 200 pounds of grain be produced in less than 200 working days, given the available agricultural techniques. One notes that in this problem, Edel has included the preferences (in this case the desire for sufficient food), the competing demands on the actor (food production and ritual), and the resources available. In other words, this is a problem of relating ends and means in a given set of circumstances. The only thing about the problem that might seem unreal to anthropologists is the need for the actor to give 165 days a year to ritual. A more realistic problem, in the experience I have had, would be something like this: the actor is required to give a certain number of days to annual rituals at the same time that certain critical agricultural activities, such as planting, cultivating, or harvesting, are to be performed.

Actually the anthropologist will ordinarily use an approach which is a variant of these two. He will accept a given situation as representing equilibrium between means and ends, and use that to explain why the social-cultural system takes the form it does and why other forms are precluded. An example is the Eskimo case, where I suggested that the failure to herd reindeer and the preservation of a hunting system stemmed from the inappropriateness of reindeer herding as a means to a profitable end.

SOCIAL EXCHANGE

Technically speaking, all the methods described so far in this chapter can be utilized to study the whole range of economizing behavior, both material and social. For example, the household or basic decision-making unit must be identified. In the struggle for status in the community, one may find individuals acting in this capacity—most usually men to whom women are subordinate, though one may also, as among the Turu, find women playing a separate status game. More commonly one may find larger decision-making units, some as large as a lineage, as Barnett did among the Palauans (Barnett 1960: 39) or as if often true in Africa (Mair 1962: 125).

LeClair (1962: 1199) is most specific about including prestige values in the application of economic theory cross-culturally, but he does not develop this idea sufficiently for our purposes.

Discovering what the social exchange dimension of the system is essentially means determining what the systems of ranking and alliances are. One should recall Bennett's Jaspar and look for (1) systems of dependency relations that contain no element of subordination-superordination but do contain long-term obligations and (2) systems of subordination-superordination, such as Indian castes, Kwakiutl lineage rankings, and American "classes."

It is precisely at this point, historically, that the study of social exchange has been short-circuited, because of the apparent solidarity of systems of rank and kinship, i.e., status. But one must assume, despite all appearances to the contrary, that these rings and hierarchies are ephemeral rather than fixed, temporary and not eternal. Anthropology has since its beginnings had a stake in attributing to patterned social structures a long-term permanence, because permanence of patterns seemed necessary in order to build a social science. Furthermore, in this pursuit it has always had the help of its subjects, who through myth, legend, and various sanctioning devices have insisted on the eternality of their social structures. For example, in Africa the founder of the lineage is often reputed to be the son of the first man. Men of other lineages may whisper that in fact that lineage is a new and even illegitimate enterprise, but those men in turn insist on the invariant character of their own lineages. Hierarchical systems and alliances are in fact temporal and shifting, rising and falling with varying degrees of swiftness and building upon exchanges of women, goods, and clientship as well as upon military might, a kind of economic enterprise in itself.

Because of this, the study of social exchange shifts its attention from the traditional anthropological preoccupation with permanence to signs of flux. Cancian seems to have had a problem with this. In Zinacantan the people presented the cargo system as permanent (Cancian 1965: 28–32); Cancian apparently could not decide whether the number of positions fluctuates or not. In some places he says that the number is fixed (Cancian 1965: 140), but he admits in other places that at least the number of lower positions (those in greatest demand) has increased (Cancian 1965: 187). In Indian studies, the question of the ranking of castes has been of interest for a long time. Scholars seem to be searching for an absolute ranking system, whereas in truth one suspects that, as in any dynamic system, the vying for position leaves the hierarchy somewhat confused at all times. Needham (1962) strives, through insistence on a rule of prescribed matrilateral (from the mother's side) cross-cousin marriage, to find a rigidly institutionalized marriage alliance system in Puram society, whereas, in fact, the system viewed at any time seems to be merely a temporary manifestation of a long-term game wherein connections shift with advantage, although the rules of the game keep marriage alliances from turning back on themselves.

The model to follow in studying a social structure is Leach's (1960) study of the Dry Zone Sinhalese or Barth's (1967a) study of the Fur, where the overt structure is an epiphenomenon of the allocation processes between and within the decision-making units. This, of course, is the heart of the analysis and the place where the investigator's skill comes most fully into play, in imagining the dynamics of the exchange process and collecting data and arranging experiments to check out his suspicions. This does not mean that the surface structure cannot be of long duration, but rather that the allocations and exchanges of value which underpin the structure, and not the length of time that a particular surface arrangement persists, is of primary interest. Few things seem more permanent and resistant to change than Indian castes, yet both Orans (1968) and Harper (1959) have challenged this permanence on essentially economic grounds.

A far more difficult but also far more interesting problem is how to deal with social exchange in quantitative terms. Blau's treatment of this problem suffers somewhat from a lack of quantification of the variables, making it difficult to construct experimental tests. If there is a price on a Zinacantan cargo it must take a form that the game player can use to calculate advantage; to talk without specifying quantities of prestige is to play at economics. I would like to suggest that the problem of quantifying is more apparent than real. If one can bring oneself, like Bennett in his Jaspar study, to reserve judgment on the altruism in such exchanges and coldbloodedly look for the calculations of advantage, one may also, like Bennett, find a subject's notations on his calendar respecting when machinery was loaned and for how

many days, and can get his informants to verbalize about debts
he owes others and debts owed him. The American middle-class
wife can be very specific about the value of meals and services
she has rendered others and what they owe her. The value of
wedding gifts is usually very specifically calculated. As Gray has
argued (Gray 1960: 53ff.) we make a mistake in rejecting the
interpretation of African bridewealth as an economic exchange
on the grounds that if this were so it would not be nice.

Some calculations may not be so obvious and may demand
ingenuity. The rule here is to be bold about deducing or intuiting
value scales. No criticism can be leveled against a researcher, for
imagining what scale of values might be operating in an exchange system. He can be faulted only for not being able to predict, with the scale he derives, actions that might confirm his
guess. For example, Homans, in his study of social exchange
(Homans 1958: 602), had, with Festinger and Schachter, to
intuit a scale of high and low attractiveness and high and low
agreement in order to determine how participants in group action
made decisions about whether to alter opinions or hold steady. In
a study by Candace Jones (1967) of sorority rushing at a mid-
west liberal arts college, the problem was to determine how
rushees calculated where to apply their efforts in seeking acceptance by a sorority. The total value of a particular sorority in relation to other sororities, she intuited, was calculated on the basis
of certain individual values, including possession of campus
leaders and "cool" or attractive members, competitive record in
recruiting members in the past, types of activities engaged in, and
three more minor criteria. To these discrete qualities she then assigned values based on an interval scale such that a campus
leader could be worth a total of up to ten points. In contrast, a
"cool" woman could be valued at a maximum of nine points
(which is to say, the best "cool" member was not worth quite as
much as the best campus leader). The maximum points a sorority
could obtain for having a record of high scholarship amounted to
two points per scholar. She then graded each member of each

sorority on all these values and determined a total score for each sorority, showing its value in terms of what she had guessed were generally accepted values and generally assigned magnitudes. A questionnaire submitted to 100 rushees asking them to rank sororities in terms of their first choices then produced a scale that was exactly in line with the values of the sororities as determined by Jones with her imagined scale of values. This demonstrated the likelihood that the method of valuation she used corresponded significantly with rushees' valuation of sororities in reality. Jones was able to do this because she was part of the community she studied and had been enculturated to the value system she was attempting to understand. For an outsider to obtain such results would be more difficult, although not impossible by any means.

Jones conceived of her study as a kind of game analysis. In economic terms we would revise the results as follows: If we treated the values of certain qualities such as leadership and "coolness" in individuals as subject to demand and not fixed, then the value of any particular sorority would be subject to variation between persons. Not all persons would value coolness as highly as all others. But even if we held this value constant, not all would desire "coolness" with the same intensity. The result would be that when a first choice of sorority was declared, the individual economic woman would make her choice in terms of her particular economic situation. This would result in some people selecting as first choice a sorority chosen second or lower by another. Jones's results, which showed the sororities as ranked according to a "voting" pattern of 50, 25, 15, 4, 3, 3, could not explain why anyone should pick one sorority (the last ranked and second-to-last ranked) along with only two other people. In short, economically speaking, Jones's scale showed that most girls valued sororities in similar ways, but also that 50% varied in their demand for the qualities all of them desired. Some (50%) did not feel they could "afford" the most desirable sororities.

Sometimes value on preference scales exist which are not recognized as such but which, with imagination, can be utilized. In many African societies as well as in American law, there are prescriptions about the amount of compensation that must be paid for losses of various parts of the body (Schneider 1970: 104ff.). In American college sports, letters are awarded for excellence in sports; the size of a given letter may be a function of the value of the sport in comparison with other sports. A novel example of an index to value in social exchange is a study of grading done by the author at a small midwestern liberal arts college during the 1960's. A significant inverse correlation was discovered to exist between the percentage of A's given to students enrolled in all the courses offered by a Department and the number of students enrolled. The cynical conclusion that immediately suggests itself is that Departments such as Classics which are in small demand pay a higher price for students. For various reasons such a conclusion does not hold up. What does appear to happen is that the amount of social exchange in terms of close personal relations between faculty and students that develops in Departments with small enrollments is greater, and the rise in percentage of A's reflects this. The instructor, from his point of view, is not buying a student but rewarding him for excellent performance, without, perhaps, realizing that the excellence of the student's performance is a return for greater input per student on the part of the instructor himself coupled with greater opportunity for the student to express deference. Thus, grades index the quality of the exchange between instructor and student.

When Cancian wrote about Zinacantan cargos, he was able without resorting to inference to work out some relationship between the rank and prestige of a certain cargo and the cost to the occupier of the position. One problem with his analysis is one that should be guarded against. This was the tendency to think of the cost, like the position, as fixed (Cancian 1965: 80). Logically this seems impossible. If the costs are indeed fixed but the economy (as Cancian says) is expanding and the demand for cargoes expanding, then in time the cost would be so low in relation to level of income that anyone could afford to take any cargo. One suspects that the cost of cargoes varies with demand. Similarly, in any study involving status one should work with the assumption, unless otherwise proved, that costs vary with supply and demand. In the literature on Africa the assumption is generally apparent that the brideprice in any given society is fixed. One should assume, on good evidence (Schneider 1964), that it fluctuates with time and region as well as with individual cases.

The fundamental rule to follow in studying social exchange is Radcliffe-Brown's so-called principle of justice (Radcliffe-Brown 1957: 131), that for every good received some good must be returned and for every evil some evil. The problem is to determine the magnitude of the nonmaterial good and evil in the eyes of the individual economic man, and to relate the good or evil received to supply and demand. That is to say, as do Blau, Curry and Wade, and others whom we have discussed above, we must try to fit social exchange to indifference curves just as we do material exchange. A girl of low leadership talents and low attractiveness will repay a low-ranked sorority for its attention to her by giving her allegiance to it. Her low budget of valued talents and qualities and the sorority's similar low store of attractiveness will lead each to value the other within the ineluctable limits of budgetary constraint, thereby generating an overt pattern of social structure.

CHAPTER

7 *The Relevance of Economic Anthropology*

The purpose of this book is multifaceted and complex, as the reader who has plowed through it will perhaps exhaustedly agree. It has tried to establish the outlines of a formal economic anthropology. It has also, more implicitly, urged the value of deductive methods in the study of human behavior. It has tried to extend formal economic methods far into the realm of so-called social behavior. And it has tried to point the way toward operationalizing economic theory in an anthropological context.

THE RELATIONSHIP OF THEORY AND VALUES

There was a time not too long ago when an anthropologist could have rested content with his labors after accomplishing these purposes, when in fact he would have been drummed out of the fraternity had he suggested that he, as an anthropologist, had an obligation to examine the *relevance* of his subject to human welfare. Applied anthropology was anathema. Were not anthropologists scientists, whose investigations were anormative? And were not norms related to one's cultural conditioning, so that one could not make normative recommendations that were not self-serving and even harmful to one's research subjects? So anthropologists contented themselves with describing and analyzing their subjects while also taking a de facto moral position to which they felt committed on account of their personal involvement with their subjects and their subjects' instrumental value to them, that of defending the privacy of their subjects from the normative onslaughts of missionaries, colonial officials, settlers, or whomever.

Alas, those happy days of impartiality are gone. In the last decade the governments of new countries have demanded that anthropologists involve themselves with the solution of practical problems of development (or, alternately, have made anthropologists persona non grata), and Jacques Maquet (1964), attacking from another direction, has taught us that we anthropologists have been kidding ourselves about our impartiality. He has exposed us to the horrible possibility that our method is biased, not anormative, and that we have been using the natives for our own ends and, inevitably, contrary to their own interests. Custer, it turns out, died for the sins of anthropologists as well as other Americans. So the question of relevance—the relation of one's theory to current social problems—must be faced. More specifically, we must answer the question of how our personal desires and values relate to our theory. If our theory is culture-bound, how can it be of any use to peoples of other cultures who desire to achieve ends foreign to us? And if it is not culture-bound, how should it be used?

We may begin by examining first the question of the intertwining of theory and personal values. Is it inevitably true that the social scientist cannot transcend his social and cultural setting and that he is therefore little more than a cultural imperialist abroad and an establishment tool at home? Is theory in some sense independent of its sociocultural setting, or is it merely a pretentious mirror of the predilections of its purveyors? The latter can be only partly the case because logical systems, whether in the mind or in the form of machines, can produce unforeseen and often undesired results. A fully developed, entirely rational theory, a radio circuit, or a machine gun will give us an output, in the form of a mathematical truth, a radio signal, or a bullet, which is dependent solely on the technical structure of the system. Indeed, if one's biases could not be controlled, no system could ever be developed and no technical output would ever be possible. I am reminded of the comment made by one student of revolution (an event notable for its irrationality) that revolutions are good at making ideologies and assaulting establishments, but poor at producing bread. Revolution is a time when moral outrage is meant to take precedence over order, but sooner or later rationality must again prevail or the people will starve.

Nonetheless, bias may occur in two ways. Norms are always intrusive on rationality to some degree, and those who accuse scientists in general and anthropologists in particular of being biased are to some extent and perhaps entirely correct. And, by its very nature, the output of a rational system is capable of being used for any normative end. Theories, therefore, are notoriously subject to distortion by their producers, who sometimes seem to seek to benefit from the prestige (social exchange) associated with an apparently rational theory or device that, however, is unworkable or irrational and therefore poses no threat to its producer.

Robert Merton tells us that science is not just a method but also an institution, a society, constructed in such a way as to control its practitioners and ensure by its ethical system that truth (for which read, output of a rational system) will at least in some measure be produced no matter how uncomfortable to the originators. He detects (Merton 1949: 309ff.) four basic ethical principles in science: universalism, communalism, disinterestedness, and organized skepticism. These principles are intended to ensure that: (1) truth claims are subjected, whatever their source, to impersonal criteria of judgment consonant with observation and previously confirmed knowledge (the ethic of universalism); (2) the substantive findings of scientists will be made available to the scientific community without consideration of personal profit (the ethic of communalism); (3) the search for truth will be devoid of fraud (the ethic of disinterestedness); and (4) judgment will be suspended until the facts are in hand and the evaluation of results is subjected to logical scrutiny (the ethic of organized skepticism). In practice, science, like any society, does not always function entirely in accord with its ethic. Think of instances of scientists claiming truth for their findings contrary to all evidence, hiding information so that it can be used for personal gain, plagiarizing the work of others, or insisting on the unacceptability of new ideas despite their apparent superior logic to accepted ideas.

But if Merton is right that science is a society, its institutional protection of the goals of deductive science, namely the discovery of logical systems, argues indirectly for the existence of such systems and of the possibility that men can transcend the bounds of their societies and cultures to produce scientific output despite the threat of this output to established order.

If, then, discrete theoretical systems can exist, do they exist in economic anthropology? The answer to this question is best given by reviewing the history of the emergence of a logical theory of the competitive market in economics. We are already aware from chapter 2 that the modern theory of the market has grown out of an interaction between theory and fact, in which each gradually has grown toward the other. Another way of putting this would be to say that through the operation of the "institution of science" and other forces, the biases of economists have gradually been forced back as the logic of the theory has been allowed to assert itself. In the 19th century men of the establishment, having found a theory of great logical and technical promise, allowed their biases to intrude into the refinement of the theory by using the theory at an immature level of development as a justification of the established order. Since the theory demanded that labor be free to move where the best wages were paid, this argued for laws against labor unions. Since cartels and monopolies violated the model's assumption of a large number of small firms, the Sherman Antitrust Act was passed. And since the logic of the model proclaimed that a free market would clear itself of all goods, this was conveniently interpreted to mean that it would also produce enough goods and opportunity for everybody, that efficiency and justice were synonymous, hence that those who were poor must be so because they were lazy, since by participation in the market, employment is assured.

In chapter 3 we took note of the Keynesian revision, quoting Dalton to the effect that Keynes's contribution was to show why the competitive market model would not automatically generate full employment, namely, because the market incorrectly assumed that all savings are invested. Keynes's discovery led to the idea that the way to keep the market operating effectively is to pump money back into it, thus increasing consumption and investment ("priming the pump"). Haveman and Knopf, on whom we leaned so heavily in chapter 3, state the situation this way (Haveman and Knopf 1966: 30): A free market, insofar as it corresponds to the theory, is efficient for distributing goods, that is, for equating supply and demand. But effiicency is not equivalent to justice, for the price system will accommodate to whatever distribution of income that exists. For example (Haveman and Knopf 1966: 263), it will reward the factors of production in proportion to their contribution to production whether the factors are in many hands (and thus many are rewarded) or in few hands (and hence few rewarded). In order to alter this situation distribution of income must be guided by value judgments implemented by intervention in the economy on the part of whatever agencies are designated (Haveman and Knopf 1966: 264).

One can appreciate in this discussion the issue involved in Marx's labor theory of value. According to the labor theory of value, the value of a good is or should be proportional to the amount of labor expended to produce it. Samuelson's dismissal of this (chap. 3) on the grounds that in the market the value of a good or factor is a function of the total supply-demand situation should be accompanied by the realization that Marx was intruding normative considerations into the logic of the model by saying that low wages for workers are unfair and should be raised on moral grounds.

In summary, then, the theory of the competitive market must be seen as a logical system that says that in a certain set of circumstances wherein all kinds of conditions are held constant, certain things are predictable. To confuse this logical system with the concrete world in its unregulated and uncontrolled aspect is the subtlest form of confusion of theory and norms. But that confusion continues to be made, even by people such as Haveman and Knopf, who claim to recognize that the model and reality are not the same. This is shown by their claim that the "market-directed society" is a new thing in history. No society is market directed. All societies are open to investigation with this theory. It will fit some societies better than others; it will fit *no* society entirely. One can say similarly that the theory of falling bodies fits no empirical situation entirely but is suited to explain some aspects of most situations. If my argument that we tend to distort theory to fit our predilections is true, one must ask why so many competent economists insist on the idea that the market theory is applicable only to Western societies. I will not attempt an answer but will merely suggest that it seems to relate to the idea that a market system is progressive and so could not be expected to be found among primitive people.

The intricacy of the issue raised here can be further illustrated from a recent article by Robert Solow (1971) on the economist's approach to pollution control. Solow advocates limited use of the market principle in pollution control. That is to say, he is quite aware that the free operation of the market will not solve all social problems, but he feels that it is more efficient than direct control for achieving certain results, in this case control over some forms of pollution. Essentially he feels that if taxes on the amount of pollution that a polluter puts into the water or air are instituted, the polluter will then take the actions necessary to control pollution because he has the incentive of reduced cost (Solow 1971: 500), and the control will be achieved more efficiently than by regulations.

Solow's suggestion is not a confusion of norms and theory because he is not saying that we should do what he describes but only that if one wishes to get the cheapest, most efficient solution to this specific problem, the theory of the market can be usefully employed. One could use the market theory to obtain the opposite results, as has in fact been the case. By leveling no cost on the polluter, we encourage him to dump pollutants as a method of cutting costs elsewhere. Pollution is thereby encouraged because it costs nothing.

Additionally, and paralleling Haveman and Knopf, Solow points out that taxing polluters according to their ability to pay (as opposed to taxing them according to their rate of pollution) is self-defeating. Since the distribution of income (which is what the first tax hits) is not determined by the market, it would be much better to alter income distribution some other way, such as by a system of taxing of the rich and giving to the poor, and let the matter of cost of polluting be handled by the market mechanism in such a way as to take no account of variable income distribution (Solow 1971: 500).

But Solow's article is not merely an exercise in applied economics. Behind it all he harbors the idea, so common to applied economics, that a free market will somehow also produce justice (Solow 1971: 498):

> We would like to insure that each resource is allocated to that use in which its net social value is highest. But if the full costs of some use of a resource do not fall upon the private owner or public decision-maker, but upon someone else, then the resource is unlikely to find its way into its socially best uses.

That is to say, if you charge the polluter for polluting, the net effect of his altered decision-making procedure with respect to allocation of resources will produce the socially most desirable use. But this is saying little more than that efficiency and justice coincide, and we already know that such is not the case. Justice is brought into line with efficiency by an exogenously derived value judgment that ensures that that which is rewarded as most efficient is what is chosen by value judgment. Business is regulated in such a way that its market propensities produce results that are socially acceptable.

So, in the end, we must decide whose idea of justice will prevail, the conservationist's or the polluter's, and regulations or taxes must then be instituted that will alter the operation of the market.

Perhaps the most subtle expression of the relationship of values and theory in economics involves the concept of rationality. A convenient illustration will also provide us with a bridge into the non-Western world, toward which this whole discussion is aimed. Recently Alan Heston, writing about India's sacred cattle (Heston 1971), took issue with Marvin Harris, who had previously discussed the same subject (Harris 1966), over the question of whether the Indians were being rational or not. Harris had claimed that the use of cattle was rational (see Schneider 1971); Heston said it was not. In fact this is an epistemological question. How do you decide if some behavior is rational? Both Harris and Heston are treating rationality as a measurable trait. In fact, rationality is a label for behavior reflecting economic man's assumed propensity to maximize. If we construct the theory so as to conform to the needs of the market model, then we say of an actor that he acted rationally if he took the course of action which maximized his utility. But if we change any conditions of the model, the "rational" course of action, by this definition, is likely to be altered. Hence, that which is rational is defined in terms of the model and has no empirical standing. The question about Indian economic uses of cattle is not whether the people are rational but whether one can predict, using a market model, what they will do in any given situation. This involves operationalizing the model in India—plugging the sacred cattle into it as a parameter and seeing what happens when one predicts.

But generations of anthropologists have gone around the world taking positions on the rationality or irrationality of certain acts performed by their subjects, while blithely unaware of the total confusion between deductive theory and reality that such value judgments represent.

The problem of keeping theory separate from norms and in proper perspective is therefore not an easy one, although one must deduce from the fact that economic theory and the physical sciences have had success and are predictive to some degree that it is possible. Solow's solution to pollution, once one is clear that an exogenous normative judgment must be made, will probably work, and the polluters will reduce pollution as a way of reducing cost, as one would predict. When we move into the cross-cultural sphere we should expect that the problems of keeping our theory and values distinct and the area of applicability of economic theory clearly in focus will be no less difficult, nor any less soluable.

CROSS-CULTURAL APPLIED ECONOMIC ANTHROPOLOGY

The first thing that is apparent when using economic theory cross-culturally is that the long-cherished notion that primitive men are not economic men must be abandoned. Yet most applied anthropology, developmental work, and economic development theory seem to rest on the assumption that economic men exist only in industrialized societies. Because we have emphasized the communalistic (Weber), traditional or tradition-centered (Riesman, Hsu), reciprocative-redistributive (Polanyi), and primitive (anthropology in general) dimensions of our subjects we have allowed ourselves to suppose that they live in a world purified of economic problems. Relations among them, we assume, are personal rather than economic, so no one ever competes with anyone else for scarce goods. Wants are traditionally specified, because a process of natural selection has balanced ecological opportunities and human preferenes so that there is no sense of scarcity or want. Each person desires only that which is in sufficient supply to satisfy unvarying demand. The economy is of the subsistence type, meaning that every household always produces in sufficient quantity to satisfy the needs of its members, and trade is therefore unnecessary except as a social activity. There is no innovation in production or consumption because these are dictated by tradition, leaving nothing for the entrepreneur to do. In any case, there is no capital or savings, so economic growth is impossible. There is a minimum of specialization, with a consequent lack of stimulus to economic activity. There is no status mobility and hence no need for profit-making activity in order to raise one's place in the world. Since population is static there is no expanding market and, again, no stimulus to production.

Perhaps the best that can be said for such ideas is that they served a kind of developmental or evolutionary theory in sociology and anthropology, which, like the analytical method of economics, simplified a complex situation in order to extract certain grains of truth. But such caricatures can no more be taken to represent the empirical situation in any absolute sense than can economic theory. Which is another way of saying that the same situation can be viewed economically to show that all men have certain impersonal relations with others that are competitive and instrumental: think of the Turu man refusing to give a cow to his blood brother, who needs it in order to marry, on the grounds that he has already given one and feels that he has fulfilled his obligations. Similarly, all men have some wants that exceed satisfaction and even, so to speak, transcend cultural training. Think of a Kikuyu middle son who, because of the workings of an inheritance system of primo-ultimogeniture, is left without sufficient land to make a viable farm in his homeland and who must act to satisfy this felt need in some way. Or, to speak to the second kind of want mentioned above, the same man may take advantage of the low opportunity cost of going to work in Nairobi because he does not have a viable farm at home and would like to own a bicycle or radio. Where does the Kikuyu acquire the desire for a radio if there are no radios in traditional Kikuyu society?

Carrying further this refutation of the traditional caricature of so-called primitive societies, no society is so carefully balanced in relation to its habitat that all wants are satisfied, nor is any household able to ensure satisfaction of the wants of its members. Imagine the parameters whose variation can affect the production of food. Rainfall, if insufficient, causes drought, which was periodic in the savannah of East Africa. An extreme tidal condition can wipe out extraordinary numbers of people, as in Bengal in 1970. Heyer has pointed out, in her examination of Kamba peasants (1966: 3) the large number of variables that an African farmer must cope with in planting, comprising in this case 243 possible combinations with respect to crop mixtures, planting time, and weeding. And as I pointed out with respect to the Turu, even in a good year the chances that all households will produce sufficient food to feed their families are well below 100% (Schneider 1970: 81), due to a whole range of variables including the laziness of the farmer, the variability of the rainfall even within a single village, the maddening unpredictability of crop pests with respect to whom they will single out for their attention, and even the randomness of an elephant with respect to the course he chooses to follow through a village and the victim he subsequently bankrupts by his voracious appetite for domestic grain.

To continue, why should we assume that economic analysis is inapplicable to economies that are not growing and innovating? Growth and innovation of the kind we usually seem to have in mind are surely aberrant in world history. And growth and innovation are also relative. That is to say, the exponential expansion of Western economies since the industrial revolution is not the only kind of growth possible. Consider the pattern of growth that might occur in an East African pastoral society, where periodic droughts kill off large numbers of cattle, thereby wiping out a large part of the wealth of the society, and that wealth is gradually replaced by the people's entrepreneurial practices, followed by another drought and a new cycle of growth. This pattern is not that much different from our own business cycles. Innovation, too, is relative to the society in which it occurs. The American businessman who invents a better mousetrap may feel that this innovative act (given the resulting volume of business it engenders) is of a different order from that of an African farmer who plants a field of maize in a society that never knew any grains other than bulrush millet, finger millet, and sorghum, but the relative effect of the latter in an economy of the scale found in East Africa may be greater than that of the mousetrap in America. Innovations of this type have, historically, been responsible for the spread over much of Africa of maize, tobacco, bananas, cocoa, palm trees, millet, sorghum, two types of cattle, sheep, goats, camels, horses, chickens, iron goods, woven cloth, and a host of other kinds of wealth. And within a single society, though invisible to the outsider, are men constantly striving to invent new business strategies, like the Turu cattle dealer who engages in arbitrage between a Turu internal cattle economy, which is cow-centered, and a European livestock economy, which is beef-centered (Schneider 1970: 85).

As for specialization, this is perhaps the most misunderstood area of all. There seems to be a tendency to assume that unless there is overt, literal differentiation of production and consumption units in terms of what is produced and how it is produced, there can be no basis for an economy. Each unit being like every other in appearance, none has anything to offer another, and so an economy cannot develop. But differentiation can be based upon a more important fact, viz., variability with respect to success of the productive enterprise. Hence, although all the homesteads in an African, stateless, segmentary lineage society look just like all the others, a very active economy can and does occur due to the fact that each household varies in the success of its productive enterprises and in its emphasis as between, for example, grain crops and livestock. Consequently, as consumers attempt to balance their preferences and producers to increase their profits, grain flows from the successful producers to the unsuccessful, and livestock flows from those among whom the demand for grain is high to those for whom the demand for livestock is higher.

Finally, the idea of status immobility, which is treated extensively in chapter 4, badly needs reexamination in the light of the theory of social exchange. One is reminded of the extensive literature that has developed around the cargo cults of Melanesia, and Cochrane's thesis (1970) that at the heart of the revitalization movements that have characterized this area since the early part of the 19th century has been status deprivation, not material or "cargo" deprivation as the name given to the cults suggests. The area is marked by an unusual degree of opportunity for status mobility, even more so than in countries like the United States, which pride themselves on the opportunity they afford for making something of oneself. To become a "Big Man," the term generally used by ethnographers to describe the top status, is the aim of most men. Equally important is to avoid becoming a "Rubbish Man," a man of no consequence. In economic terms, the situation that developed after contact with Western colonialists was one in which the Melanesians tried to establish a social exchange relationship with the magistrates and other powerful Europeans in order to incorporate them into the sociocultural system of "Big Men" achievement. But the intruders were immune to these efforts, with the result that all Melanesians came to see themselves as Rubbish Men in relation to the powerful Europeans and could see no way to alter the situation.

Not all non-Western societies are as open to status mobility as these Melanesian systems, but even in India, with its traditionally conceived closed systems, status mobility is gradually becoming recognized. In any case, the rigidity of traditional castes can be seen as a balance of forces rather than as a result of hidebound ideas (Orans 1968: 889).

If a formal economic approach to cross-cultural situations is, therefore, possible in both the material and social realms, how should it proceed? The alternatives proposed by Solow (1971) in his economic solution to pollution would apply equally here. One cannot assert without question that all goals ought to be sought either through the mechanism of command (control) or by the operation of a free market. In some cases price fixing and control of supply and demand is the answer. But this has usually been taken to be the *only* answer in "developing" countries. A market solution is equally appropriate for some circumstances because, as we have seen, the people dealt with are not unused to this framework or unable to work within it.

A good illustration of this point comes from my investigations of destocking in Tanganyika in 1959–1960 (Schneider 1970: 161ff.), to which I previously alluded. The colonial government was faced with a general problem, the erosion of soil, which was threatening to destroy increasing amounts of the better farm land. They ascribed this erosion, rightly or wrongly, to overgrazing by African livestock raisers. The solution to the problem, as they saw it, was to reduce the number of livestock. This solution proceeded on the theory that Africans are not economic men. One could argue this last point and maintain that they did not really think of Africans as unresponsive to the profit motive, but merely chose command as the simplest solution at that time. In any case, the resultant course of action was poor economics, based on an inadequate understanding of African indigenous economies.

The solution was to require each homestead to reduce the number of livestock by 10%, on the grounds that all would thereby be equally affected and left in the same relative position at the end. In doing so, five goats or sheep could be substituted for one cow (cow meaning any bovine, as in English parlance). Furthermore, apparently because they thought of Africans as generally possessing large numbers of livestock, they excluded from the required reduction household herds of less than ten bovine units.

I witnessed the operation of this culling scheme among the Wanyaturu of Singida District through documents which were made available to me in the Government Offices and by examining the aftereffects among the Africans. The scheme was supposed to begin early in the 1950's but was delayed in implementation because of droughts and other problems. When it was finally put into effect about 1954, the effects were negligible because, it was discovered, so many farmers had less than ten bovine units and were thereby exempt from the destocking orders. In 1956 the number of adult men (the household decision-makers and, therefore, the "owners") was about 45,000 in relation to a cattle population of about 210,000, giving an average of four to five head per man and household. If sheep and goats were added, this would raise the average, but not up to ten. In addition, ownership of livestock is highly variable: in one village alone it ran from no livestock owned to more than seventy-five cattle.

The failure of the scheme led to the decision to increase the destocking rate to 15%, which was implemented in 1956 and caused such an uproar that the whole scheme was soon abandoned. The Turu verbalized the difficulty with this new order (which this time did encompass almost everyone) as that its effect was to make the rich richer and the poor poorer. This seemed like rhetoric to the British, who were convinced that people like the Turu kept livestock, and particularly cattle, more as pets than as economic assets. That is to say, since the Turu did not treat livestock economically according to patterns that were familiar to the British, they were not being economic. In particular, the cattle appeared not to be eaten or even milked according to a rational plan, being employed principally for ancestral sacrifices. The cattle were not well fed and the people showed no interest in breeding them up to a more "economical" size and quality.

But if one views livestock as a commodity the effects of destocking can be seen in a different light, one which corresponds to the Turu assessment. Livestock are a singular commodity in the Turu economy, in fact a kind of money, conforming to the definition of money developed in chapter 5. By reducing the number of livestock across-the-board by about 15% a very important change in the total supply-demand situation occurred. Allowing for the fact that even in our own economy we are not altogether clear on the effect to be expected from a reduction of the money supply by 15%, some effect will surely follow, and the most likely is a slowing down of exchange as a result of what amounts to a general rise in cattle prices consonant with the lowering of the money supply. That is, the Turu farmer who raised grain did so in order to exchange it for cattle. The reduction in livestock lowered the value of his grain proportionally and slowed such exchanges, thus making "the poor poorer and the rich richer."

Allowing for the fact that other kinds of command might have been employed which would not have had much unrewarding effects, how could a market solution have been employed? The answer is difficult to give because it is hard to imagine what could have been done to lessen the Turu's demand for livestock. Taxation would be one solution, one that had in fact worked for some years on a low level. As a result of taxing each adult man a certain number of shillings per year, it became economical for the farmer to sell off a certain number of livestock to raise tax money. Resistance to tax increases had been growing, however. Another solution, more problematical but theoretically possible, would have been to *increase* the number of livestock, i.e., resort to inflation of the currency, which in the end would have destroyed it. Among other things, this solution is unworkable because of ecological constraints on livestock population, constraints already being tested by the population if the colonial government was to be believed. A solution which might have been possible, but which was probably ruled out as inhumane, would have been to cease subsidizing the purchase of livestock medicines for trypanosomiasis and allow the tse-tse fly to kill off larger numbers of cattle (such treatment may, in fact, have been the cause of the problem in the first place).

One might argue at this point that a market solution to problems like this is really no easier than command, and that therefore there is no reason to employ the market solution. The rebuttal to that argument is simply that if neither method is easy, then both methods need to be considered. In this case the market method had the merit of at least making possible a better assessment of the situation before acting. Command methods tend to work from unrealistic views of the subjects by those who employ them, views almost guaranteeing failure.

Further illustration of the value of an economic assessment of seemingly primitive situations will bring the point home more clearly. I earlier referred to Lantis's study from Spicer's *Problems in Technological Change* (1952) on the failure of introduction of reindeer herding into Alaska, which failure, I noted, seemed to be due in part to negative Eskimo attitudes toward the kind of activity that reindeer herding demands and in part to the lack of a viable market situation: Eskimos did not take to reindeer herding because it was not profitable. Spicer's book provides other, equally interesting, examples of economic miscalculations. Perhaps the most exotic is the case of the Yir Yoront aborigines of Cape York Peninsula in Australia, who were also previously alluded to. According to Sharp (1952), who wrote this account, missionaries established a station on the coast outside the tribal area and began to import steel axes to pay off and reward Yir Yoront who traveled to the mission to work or trade. The indigenous economy was so constructed that the prime capital was stone axes, made from flint imported through a trade network from central Australia in return for spears made from the barbed spines of sting rays. The flints were shaped by the Yir Yoront men, who therefore had control of the supply of axes. The greatest part of food production was carried on by women, who required for much of this the use of axes. The social economy of the Yir Yoront, therefore, may be said to have achieved its form, in which older men dominated younger men and men dominated women and children, on account of the singular importance of axes for production combined with their control by older men by virtue of the above division of labor. When steel axes were introduced, the fact that they improved the input-output relationship compared to stone axes, because stone axes did not cut as efficiently and cost more to produce, was not as important as the fact that the increased supply of axes and their dissemination to practically everyone destroyed the economic basis of the social structure. According to Sharp, the Yir Yoront were unable to recover from this social earthquake, so that today they are effectively demolished as a society.

Another interesting case in Spicer's book concerns the Spanish Americans of New Mexico. The author, Apodaca (1952), argues that the failure of the introduction of hybrid corn into this closed community was due to the fact that the people did not like the taste and consistency of hybrid corn for making tortillas. Be that as it may, the economic situation described in the account raises some unanswered questions. Several things seem apparent. In the first place, before hybrid corn was introduced the supply of corn to the community was, on the whole, adequate; there seemed to be no suffering. When planted, as it was for about four years, hybrid corn increased yields about fourfold over the old corn. But there was no market for the corn outside the community (Apodaca 1952: 36), and while the people were used to using surplus for feeding cattle it seems apparent that the magnitude of the increase oustripped the ability of the livestock to consume it. What justification could there be for increasing yields under these circumstances? Whatever the taste and texture of the corn, the economic consequence of increasing the supply of the most important food crop by fourfold over the normal demand for it seems to have been, as one would expect, a decline in its production. Griliches (1957) found that the spread of hybrid corn among American farmers generally was facilitated by profitability and slowed by lack of profitability, which seems to support my conclusion.

A final case from Spicer is of special interest because it demonstrates so well the economy of social exchange. This is John Useem's analysis of a "strike" on Angau, Palau in the Micronesias after the Second World War (Useem 1952). This Palauan situation conforms nicely to Salisbury and Brown's characterization of status games played in the Pacific, referred to in chapter 4. Men and their clans, or lineages, compete for position and titles, which requires control of goods, including glass money (Barnett 1960: 37ff.). Within the villages, clans are ranked and there is continual tension as the various clans strive, as corporate groups headed by a chief decision maker, to improve position.

The delicate balance of forces in this situation was upset by the appearance after the war of the American military government, which decided to mine phosphate fertilizer for export to Japan in order to assist Japanese postwar recovery. First, the "chief," i.e., a person recognized by the colonial administration as head man but who in the indigenous system was merely the head of one of the high-ranking clans, was asked to provide men for this work. He, of course, selected men of his own clan, whose wages would be pooled to raise the clan's status—for example, by getting control of the children of the men of the clan through payment of brideprice (Barnett 1960: 47). Then, upon discovery of an American soldier who had settled on the island, recruitment was redirected through him—not only for ordinary workers but also for "skilled workers," who were paid more—on the grounds that he would be better able to understand the needs of the military government and to translate them into action. The soldier, of course, recruited members of his own clan, which was lower than that of the "chief," thus threatening the status of the "chief's" clan.

From this point on the course of events is simply stated. The "chief," frightened by this preemptory threat to his clan's position, was prompted to actually promote a "strike" against the military government. The unmanageability of the heightening tension led to the shutting down of the mine and the cessation of "development" on Angau.

Without further investigation of this situation it would be impossible to say how social exchange could have been manipulated in order to get phospate mined while at the same time preserving peace. It seems obvious that the rewards for mining should have been made available on a competitive basis, as was traditional, rather than, in effect, giving windfall benefits to one group. There would still have been tension, but it would have been contained so long as all clans saw the new opportunities as equally accessible.

But as we focus on "the solution," we should not forget that to the Angauese, whether the mining of phosphate was successful or not and whether there was "development" or not were really irrelevant to the central issue of maintaining a viable system of social exchange. From that point of view, the end result of all this for them was probably fortuitous. So to speak, the Palauan solution to the problem of interference with their social games was to eliminate the American military government and its development program (which, unwittingly, they did!).

The exotic nature of some non-Western economies and the peculiar consequences of random interference in these economies are well illustrated by the situation with respect to marriage in Africa (see especially the recounting in Mead [1955: 96–126] of the economic consequences of British abolition of so-called sister-exchange marriage among the Tiv). If one assumes that African marriage is an institution like that of the West, then whatever economic interpretation it might be subject to will ordinarily be discounted or even deprecated (Gray 1960; Fortes 1969: 249). African marriage, however, has startling economic implications. The general pattern of African marriage is that a man of a corporate lineage goes to another lineage to seek a wife. He is forced to do so even if he does not want to do so by the rule of exogamy, which, in effect, makes marriage to any women of his lineage incestuous. When he has found a woman he bargains for her with her controllers (her father or her brother and her mother). Seldom is the payment sufficient to transfer to the husband complete and utter control of his wife, as the Romans did, although it happens in some cases. In most cases he obtains varying degrees of rights over her; at the least he has control of her sexual activities. He may also obtain the right to incorporate her children by him into his lineage as opposed to their being incorporated into the lineage of her brother. Next he may obtain rights to her labor and produce in the sense that although she has practical control over the produce of her house, she can maintain de facto control only as long as she stays married to him. This right and the right to control children tend to go together, and this combination of productive assets in the woman, the bearing of children and production of crops, is often equated by pastoral Africans with the economic function of cows (female bovines). A woman may be spoken of as a cow because of this.

The point I am making is that to the African producer, women are a critical factor of production, acting partly as capital (producing children) and partly as labor (producing crops). There is no other labor market that amounts to anything in most cases. One cannot hire other men's labor in significant amounts to work in one's fields. Therefore, in order to expand production in the face of an expanding market, and in order to make a living in a more general sense, the producer must be free to expand the number of wives (factors). Imagine the devastation caused in such an economy by a prohibition on polygyny. Imagine similarly the problems involved in reduction of population, with girl children having the economic importance just indicated. The importance of the male population for augmenting the lineage should not be underestimated either, for the value of the lineage is both social, in the sense developed in the chapter on social exchange, and economic, in the sense that members of the same lineage cooperate for short-term labor-intensive activities.

The solution to the population problem is similar to the one encountered with respect to livestock reduction. How can one make it cheaper and more profitable to have fewer children? What market solution is equivalent in this case to the economic control of pollution? Since other forms of population control work poorly, perhaps this market approach is worth pursuing.

WHAT OUGHT ANTHROPOLOGISTS TO DO?

At the beginning of this chapter I posed the problem of the involvement of anthropologists in developing solutions to human problems by arguing that normative goals and analytical methods are conceputually separate. I insisted that even though scientists are normatively involved just like all other persons, their analytical method, if pursued with vigor, can give results that transcend norms. In the light of this and in the light of the examples of cross-cultural applicability of economic analysis, where do we stand with respect to the question of what the anthropologist ought to do?

The answer must begin wtih the acknowledgment that no analyses are value-free, in the sense of having no normative implications. Whether the investigator realizes it or not, his analysis has implications for himself and others that may be positive or negative. Since the analytical method may transcend the desires of its users, there is no guarantee that the scientist will be pleased and positively rewarded by the results of his investigations. Atomic scientists during the war seem generally to have been horrified by the success of their analysis and manipulation of atoms. Equivalent horrors may be expected from social scientific analysis. Even results that may strike one as neutral, having a curiosity interest but no strong normative implications, may have hidden negative or positive implications. For example, it is an interesting scientific curiosity that African marriage is equivalent to the labor market. It is perhaps not so immediately apparent that if one were desirous of developing a national African economy and decided that freeing people from their indigenous economies would force them into new enterprises, banning polygyny might in many cases have this effect by destroying the basis of the indigenous economic system. Or suppose that Sharp is right about the Yir Yoront and that in Australia sheep herders want cheap labor, what is to prevent the herders or the government from dumping steel axes, or their equivalents, on the Australian aborigines, thereby destroying their economy the way the Germans hoped to destroy the British economy during the war by dumping on England cleverly forged pound notes in the millions?

If knowledge has the indicated power to influence events and is not integrally tied to "good" or "bad" results, then it can be employed to any end. And if the implications are indeterminate, should activities designed to uncover new knowledge be suppressed? Such a solution has been tried but has been only moderately successful. The general trend in human history seems clear from anthropological investigations: new ideas emerge and are utilized in an inexorable fashion, momentary attempts to stop them them being overridden by changing fashions about what is good and bad and the propensity of men to try to maximize control of energy, as well as by the impossibility of preventing creative thought.

In the end, one suspects, the solution is that which has always been employed when new ideas are discovered: The new element is socialized, i.e., exploited for the working of the system, the "good" of the system. New knowledge, then, can have only temporary threatening effects. In the end it is controlled by turning it to acceptable uses, which means most generally uses which support rather than threaten the social group. The group of concern may, of course, be defined as a world community as well as a local community.

Economic analysis will be employed cross-culturally because

it is available and powerful. It will be used against people but it will also be controlled. This sounds Pollyannish, to be sure, but there is no point in posing the alternative of its threat to humanity even if it were probable, which it is not. The Turu economy, for example, is no longer viable in an expanding world economy and society. The Turu, like so many other peoples in Africa and elsewhere, will be demolished one way or another and replaced by a national Tanzanian system. I somehow feel that the necessarily painful readjustment will be less painful for them and maybe even made enjoyable, as it was for the Chagga and Ashanti, if we recognize that the Turu are economic men who can be made to desire what is inevitable if it is made profitable. If we continue to regard them and treat them as traditional men, we shall surely, as in the past, cause pain. If truth transcends particular social systems, so does the desire for satisfaction and even what satisfies. The Turu, Africans, and people in general don't dislike change. They simply want change to make economic sense. Working from this position, we may make the road for them easier—an interpretation of relevance that, I suspect, we can all agree on.

GLOSSARY

Abstract Economics: The analysis of behavior by means of economic models and theories rather than substantively (i.e., institutionally). Synonymous with theoretical, formal, and deductive economics.

Accelerator: This concept from Keynesian economics should be considered side by side with the *multiplier.* The accelerator refers to the fact that the level of investment rises with rise in income, the multiplier to the fact that the marginal propensity to consume also rises with income. If the income level is manipulated in various ways, an economic system can theoretically be made to explode (*inflation*), implode (*deflation*), or dampen. This concept, then, belongs with *dynamic theory* rather than with *statics* because it is a *positive-feedback* phenomenon.

Accounting: A bookkeeping method which by using a *unit of account* compares the state of various areas of an economic enterprise and infers thereby the state of the total enterprise.

Actors: The decision-makers in an economic system, whether they are individuals or not.

Aggregate: A term used to indicate a pooling of something, notably such things as income or utility (aggregate income) in contrast to income or utility considered for a single commodity market (*partial equilibrium analysis*). Used principally with dynamic or macroeconomic analysis.

Algebra: See *Calculus.*

All-Purpose Money: According to substantivists (see *Substantive Economics*), money that serves to exchange all goods in any economy rather than only some goods, as is true with *special-purpose money.* Because of this, substantivists maintain, all-purpose money is suited to market economies and special-purpose money to non-

NOTE: Italicized terms are defined elsewhere in the glossary.

market, noncommercial economies. Formalists maintain that money, defined as a *medium of exchange,* is never all-purpose.

Alliance: In social exchange theory, a relationship between two parties that differs from a *paternalistic* relationship in that neither party is subordinate. Rather an equalitarian relationship exists, by virtue of the fact that each one owes *obligations* to the other.

Alliance Theory: A kind of social theory within social anthropology that focuses on alliances formed between groups (usually *lineages*) and persons through marriage. To be contrasted with *descent theory.* Of special importance to alliance theory are *marriage rules,* notably the rules of *patrilateral* and *matrilateral cross-cousin marriage, Kariera marriage,* and the *Kachin system.*

Allocation: A term favored by F. Barth to refer to economizing acts as they lead to the creation of *social structure.*

Altruism: To substantivists, the giving of gifts without calculation of return. To formalists in the area of social exchange (Mauss, Blau), the giving of gifts under the guise of noncalculation where return, particularly of *obligations,* is expected.

Analytical Method: According to Rapoport, the method of all science. In this method pairs of variables are related as *functions* and these functions are then related to each other through differential (and, I would add, simultaneous) *equations.*

Arbitrage: The act of taking advantage of the lack of coordination between the markets of two different economies or sectors of one economy in order to profit thereby. For example, the exchange of glass beads for gold between an economy that values beads little and gold much and one that values beads much and gold little. Presumably, if the two economies were conjoined the great demand for beads in one sector paired against the great demand for gold in the other would lead to an equilibrium of supply and demand with respect to gold and beads, thereby eliminating arbitrage.

Assumption: (see *Axiom*).

Average Cost: In the theory of the *firm,* the cost of a unit produced by a firm at any point in production, arrived at by dividing the total cost (*fixed* plus *variable costs*) by the number of units produced. Average cost is important along with *marginal cost* in calculating the level of output for a theoretically rational firm.

Avunculocal Residence: The residence pattern of living with one's mother's brother, found in some *lineage*-based societies, particularly those with *matrilineal descent,* i.e., descent traced through the mother. In this system, a woman at marriage goes to live with her husband at his father's residence, but her son, when he marries, returns to live with his mother's brother. The system makes sense if we realize that mother's brother is simply reclaiming the children of his sister, over whom, by virtue of matrilineal descent, their father has no rights.

Axiom: A theoretical statement whose usefulness can be established only by testing some of its logical consequences. In formal economics, it is axiomatic that men desire to maximize utility. One does not attempt directly to establish the truth of that statement (even if the axiom is testable). In *statics* it is also axiomatic that the system is closed (see *closed system*). *Assumptions,* by contrast, are testable propositions whose magnitudes are assumed while attention is devoted to the variables of central interest, and *hypotheses* are testable statements (predictions) logically derived from a system of axioms and assumptions.

Barter: The exchange of one good for another without the intervention of *money.* But since money is itself a good, and since money varies in the degree to which it acts as a medium of exchange, the difference between barter and money exchange is relative rather than absolute.

Bilateral Descent and Inheritance: The system of reckoning descent and receiving inheritance through both mother and father, in contrast to *patrilineal* and *matrilineal descent,* in which a person reckons through the father only and mother only respectively.

Bilateral Monopoly: One of various monopolistic situations deviating from the classical competitive market model. In monopoly itself there is one seller and many buyers; in monopsony, many sellers and one buyer; and in bilateral monopoly, one buyer and one seller.

Bloodwealth: The compensation paid for causing bodily harm or death to someone.

Brideprice: Wealth conveyed to the family of or owner of rights in a woman in reciprocation for obtaining control over her. Ordinarily this should be considered to be a mutual exchange or *lease* of *capital* rather than a quitclaim sale, because upon the death of the woman the brideprice is usually returned.

Budget Line: In indifference analysis, a linear *curve* expressing all the various combinations of resources or means available to a consumer. Establishing a budget line is necessary in order to determine the rational conumption point on an indifference curve.

Calculus: That branch of mathematics which concerns itself with rates of change in variables, in contrast to, for example, algebra, which is concerned merely with the relation of static variables. Central to calculus is the concept of the *derivative,* a number expressing the slope of a curve and therefore, in a generalized sense, a rate of change. An example of an important use of calculus in economics is the determination of the *accelerator* and *multiplier.*

Capital: Goods that are not consumed themselves but are used to produce other goods (for example, money). In microeconomic theory, the machines used in production, which are one of the *factors of production.*

Capitalist: One who seeks to profit by producing goods which are in demand through control of the necessary factors. The capitalist applies capital to production. He is the *firm* decision maker in the market model.

Capitalist Society: A society which allows capitalists to operate. To be contrasted with a society in which individual decision makers are not allowed to control the *factors of production.*

Cardinal Utility Theory: That type of consumer demand theory which assumes that utility is intervally measurable (see *Interval Scale*). To be contrasted with the more modern *indifference analysis,* which assumes utility to be only ordinally measurable. That is, in the former you know exactly how much more utility one good has than another, whereas in the latter case you know when one good has more utility than another but you do not know by how much.

Cause: In the analytical method, that relationship between two variables such that as one alters the other alters in a predictable way. The ascription of causality depends on holding all other variables constant. If this were not so, one could not ascribe any effect to any particular variable.

Ceteris Paribus: Literally, "all other things being equal." This term refers to the holding constant of certain variables in a model in order that the logical relations between other variables may be ascertained. For example, supply is a function of price, all other things being equal (i.e., held constant).

Choice: The action of an actor who finds himself faced with more than one path to a desired end. A concept important to economics because, given the assumption of utility maximization, one can predict which of the available paths the actor will choose.

Classical Economics: Microeconomics, or *static* economics. The economic theory of the founders: Adam Smith, Ricardo, and others.

Classificatory Brothers: Cousins (i.e., persons of the same generation with respect to a common ancestor) in societies which equate cousins and brothers.

Closed System: A system of variables, in which change or movement in any variable is found to be dependent on change in other variables within the same system. For example, in a heating system, the furnace's output causes the thermostat to react, which in turn, eventually, causes the furnace to act, etc. To an important degree, theoretical systems must be closed in order to make logical conclusions possible. Hence theory looks at real systems as closed (by holding all *exogenous variables* constant) when in reality the only truly full closure imaginable is that of the entire universe. (See *statics.*)

Command: Term denoting consumption, exchange, and supply decisions which come from political directives rather than market forces.

Commercial Exchange or Economy: An economy in which all inputs to production are paid for with money and only money is received for outputs; equivalent to the competitive market.

Communalism: In Max Weber's typology, the polar opposite of associationalism. In a communalistic society people belong to a single group, which is multipurposed, and cooperation is dependent on affectivity. In an associational society like the United States, people belong to many groups, each with a single purpose, and cooperation is built on self-interest.

Comparative Method: Essentially an inductive technique, this is the extracting of generalizations about behavior by means of comparison of a wide range of different types of societies. The generalization that the family is universal comes from the comparative method.

Comparative Statics: A form of static analysis in which a static system is observed as it responds and adjusts internally to a change in a *parameter.* For example, the effects on a market for agricultural products of a change in supply due not to a decline in demand but to drought. Drought is an exogenous variable since the amount of rain received by the crops in the model would in ordinary static analysis be held constant.

Compensation: A kind of payment associated with violation of a person's property rights. Legal judgments require compensation for, e.g., injury to the body (see *Bloodwealth*).

Competitive Market Theory: The *classical* segment of economic theory; static analysis under perfect competitive conditions.

Complex Systems: In alliance theory, marriage systems, like those in Western industrial societies, in which the only marriage rule is negative (i.e., incest taboo) and the mixing of segments of a society is accomplished "statistically," that is, randomly through chance meetings of potential spouses. To be contrasted with *Elementary Systems*.

Constant (see *Variable*): In a system of interrelated variables, a variable which is not allowed to vary its effect on the *dependent* and *independent variables* while they are being observed. A constant does not literally have to remain unchanged but must maintain a relationship to the other variables such that it does not interfere with the singularity of their interaction. For example, in the theory of the firm, the unit cost of labor is not allowed to vary at the same time as the cost for the *amount* of labor employed is allowed to vary. If the cost of labor in real life does vary, the amount of variation is taken into account and its effect discounted, which is another way of holding this element constant.

Constant Outlay Line: In theorizing about the most economical combination of factors to use for production, a line maping all possible combinations of factors which the firm can afford. The line is then related to an *isoquant curve,* which describes all combinations of resources which are equally productive. The point at which the outlay line and isoquant curve are tangent is the rational combination of factors to use for production.

Constraint: See *Rules*.

Consumer: In the classical model, the household (or the *consumption unit* in anthropology). This is the decision-making unit for consumption.

Consumption Unit: The same as the *household* in the *classical model*.

Contract Curve: In *bilateral monopoly* analysis, that series of points at which the indifference curves of the two parties are tangent, which, when connected, form a curve which represents all rational solutions to a bilateral contract. Also called the *Pareto Optimum*.

Corporate Group: A group whose members act in one respect or another as a single decision-making unit.

Corporate Lineage: A corporate group whose membership is defined in terms of unilineal descent (matri- or patrilineal) from a common, apical ancestor.

Cost: In the theory of the firm, a concept referring to those inputs of *factors,* both variable and fixed, for which revenue must be used in payment and which are necessary to produce goods. The difference between such payments and total revenue determines profit ($P = R - C$).

Coupon: In Mary Douglas's view, primitive money is a kind of coupon rather than a medium of exchange, rationing goods to consumers. This stems from her essentially substantive view of primitive society as redistributive and reciprocal rather than market oriented. Money in this setting is a device for effecting distribution in accordance with social good. On the other hand, to Friedman, all money is a kind of rationing device in that it rations goods to those who have the money to pay for them.

Credit: Ordinarily thought of as trust. In social exchange it is essential because the giving of obligations occurs over time.) See *T Factor.*)

Cross-Cultural Analysis: See *Comparative Method.*

Culture: Ideas and behavior passed from generation to generation. That is, cultural behavior exists most often by virtue of transmission through learning rather than by invention every time it is required. In economics, the machines used in production are culture. New forms for machines are not invented simply because they are useful, cheaper, or needed and their availability is usually fortuitous.

Curve: In the *analytical method,* a line connecting coordinates on a graph. Curves are graphic expressions of *equations* and need not be actually curved; e.g., *linear equations* appear as straight lines.

Decision-Making Theory: Any theory of behavior (notably game theory and formal economics) utilizing the fact that actors must continually choose among alternative courses of action. By including an assumption about the orientation of actors toward ends, the course of action that will be chosen can theoretically be predicted.

Deductive Economics: Synonymous with *Abstract Economics.*

Deductivism: In contrast to inductivism, a theoretical or analytical approach (see *Analytical Method*). This type of theory isolates from the real world a set of facts to study, imagines the way these relate, expresses these relations as *functions*, and then tests this theory by generating *hypotheses* and testing them. The inductive method is primarily classifying, inducing generalizations from a wide range of facts (see *Comparative Method*).

Deference: A value given in the form of an obligation (using Goldner's term) for otherwise unreciprocated material or instrumental values.

Deflation: A period during which the purchasing power of the monetary unit is rising relative to costs, as when the volume of money is declining and money is thereby increasing in value on account of its increasing scarcity. Contrast this to *inflation*, where costs are rising or inflating faster than buying power. Since the level of output on which a firm settles depends on the relation between revenue and cost, one can see that whether the economy is inflating or deflating will have important effects on production.

Demand: The desire for a good or goods, expressed as a certain price per unit that the actor is willing to pay relative to the quantity desired. When graphed, a *demand schedule* gives us a downward-sloping curve showing declining marginal value. That is, the more units he is offered, the less he is willing to pay per unit.

Demand Function: $Q_d = f(P)$, meaning "The quantity demanded is a function of the price"; that is, the quantity of a good demanded by households varies with variation in price.

Demand Schedule: A list of goods desired by consumers showing how much they are willing to pay for varying amounts of them.

Descent Theory: Associated with structural-functional anthropology, this type of theory focuses on unilineal descent groups or corporate lineages with a view toward explaining their continuity.

Dependent Variable: In a functional equation, the left-hand variable [e.g., Q_d in the equation $Q_d = f(P)$], whose values depend on the values arbitrarily assumed by the "independent variable" (P in the example above). The concept is relative; thus one could reverse the function to read: $P = f(Q_d)$.

Derivative: See *Calculus*.

Development: A concept referring to the movement of an economy from a presumably traditionalist to a market type. The concept is essentially ethnocentric and the process is basically merely a process of acculturation (i.e., culture borrowing). Development, in a nonethnocentric sense, is *dynamics.*

Differentiation: The process of specialization or of differential distribution of essential resources in a society, which causes interaction between segments because each segment, in order to maximize utility, requires goods from other segments.

Diminishing Rate of Marginal Substitution: In indifference analysis, the decline in utility of a good as the amount consumed increases in preference to other goods.

Division of Labor: Specialization of skills, a basic element in *differentiation* and one which, according to Levi-Strauss, is created out of whole cloth in order to make society possible. The most common division of labor, present in all human societies, is the sexual division of labor.

Dowry: Ordinarily contrasted with *brideprice,* dowry is wealth conveyed from the family or owner of a bride to the groom or family of the groom. Dowry seems to occur commonly where the "status" or power of the bride and her family is raised by the marriage.

Dynamics: In contrast to *statics* and *comparative statics,* the viewing of the equilibrium state of a system on a time scale, in which the equilibrium does not result from the interplay of variables at a given time but is rather a consequence of a previous state of the system. Change is endogenous and not due to alteration of parameters. The *multiplier* effect is an example of dynamics: The present state of a system depends on the income of the actors in the previous state.

Dysfunction: A term peculiar to structural-functional analysis, and denoting an effect on a total social system by one of its parts that tends to diminish the system rather than reinforce it.

Ecology: The study of the relation between the habitat of a society and the social structure. In anthropology the term is associated with a school of thought that sees the social structure as balanced with the habitat in such a way as to serve the needs of the people and the society.

Economic Analysis: That form of the *analytical method* employed in *Abstract Economics.*

Economic Man: Man seen in the single dimension of those of his actions designed to relate his means to his desires. In order to develop predictive theories of economic behavior, economists assume that man in this dimension desires to maximize *utility.*

Economic Sociology: According to Smelser, the application of the general frame of reference, variables, and explanatory models of sociology to that complex of activities concerned with the production, distribution, exchange, and consumption of scarce goods and services.

Economizing: In the process of relating one's means to one's ends, selecting that combination of means and ends which maximizes utility. In indifference analysis, economizing means selecting for consumption that combination of goods represented on one's indifference curve by the point at which the curve is tangent to the budget line.

Economy: There is no single established meaning of the term. For example, to some it means that portion of all social behavior devoted to production, exchange, and consumption; to others it means all behavior, seen in the dimension of relating means to ends. To some it refers to economizing "material" means; to some both material and "social" means or obligations.

Economy of Scale: The increase in profit or utility that comes with increase in the size of the productive enterprise and consequent decline in costs. Mass production is an example of economy of scale, as is pooled labor for cultivation in an African village.

Edgeworth Box: Refers to the form of graphing used to represent *bilateral monopoly.*

Efficiency: Distinct from justice or the just distribution of resources, efficiency refers simply to the accomplishment of the movement of the total supply of goods in the market to whatever demanders there are.

Elasticity: That relation between the units in which price is expressed and the units in which goods occur such that as the price changes, the demand for the good changes at a percentage rate greater or less than the percentage of price change. For example, a small price increase in cigarettes leads to no decline in demand.

Elementary Systems: In Levi-Strauss's marriage theory, those systems in which positive marriage rules direct people's marriages so as to effect mixing between social segments and thus give the society greater survival value. Elementary systems occur in smaller tribal societies. *Complex systems,* relying more on chance to effect mixing, are found in Western industrial societies.

Embedded Economy: Derived from Karl Polanyi's writings, this term refers to a system of production and distribution that serves the needs of the society, in contrast to a disembedded economy, as in industrial or capitalist societies, which serves only the needs of the entrepreneurs.

Empiricism: Frequently used as a synonym for inductivism, it refers more generally to observation of facts and experimentation in contrast to theory building.

Endogenous Variables: Variables that exist within one's model. Contrasted to *exogenous variables,* which are outside the model (i.e., are *parameters* to the model).

Ends: In economics a nonteleologic concept referring to the actor's expressed or implied preferences, to the attainment of which his means are related.

Entrepreneurship: Considered by some to be a factor of production along with land, labor, and capital, this is managerial ability in a firm or production unit.

Epiphenomenon: See *Surface Structure.*

Epistemology: The area of philosophy concerned with the question of how we know something and the limits of knowing. Certain epistemological claims must underly any theory: for example, the claim that we know if we can predict.

Equation: In mathematics, an expression of equality between two magnitudes, symbolized by the equal-sign ($=$).

Equilibrium: A concept which in structural-functional analysis means essentially a steady state, but which in economics means a balance of stresses. For example, the price which in a competitive market will clear the market is called an equilibrium price, because all demand is satisfied by it and all supplies are cleared by it to the demanders. In mathematical terms, it is a state in which a simultaneous equation is solved. An important difference between structural-functional equilibrium and formal equilibrium is that formal equilibrium could theoretically be a different point each time.

Exchange: Buying and selling. See also *Transfer Event.*

Exogamy: A rule proscribing marriage *within* some group. In tribal societies exogamy usually takes the form of lineage exogamy.

Exogenous Variables: See *Endogenous Variables.*

Exponential Change: Change which occurs at an increasing rate, so that its path, if plotted, would be a bowed curve rather than a straight line. Inflation would be exponential change if the rate of price increase over certain equal time periods increased, for example, in the following way: period 1 — 2%, period 2 — 5%, period

3 — 7%, period 4 — 10%. In other words, an exponential change pattern is that of an explosion.

Exponential Equation: A nonlinear *equation;* that is, one containing a variable raised to some power, such as x^2 or x^3. When graphed, an exponential equation produces some form of bowed curve, whereas a linear equation (one without powers, or exponents) produces a straight line or unbowed curve.

Extrinsic Rewards: In Blau's social exchange theory, equivalent to wealth (goods), both material and social, in contrast to *intrinsic rewards* such as love, which to him are noneconomic because noncalculable.

Factors of Production: Those goods which are used to produce other goods. Usually designated as land (or resources), labor, and capital (machines), factors may also include entrepreneurship or anything else used in production.

Filiation: As distinct from kinship, which is the legal dimension of relatedness, this refers to the biopsychological dimension. That is, a person can be filiated to another without being his kin, as in a unilineal descent system where legal relatedness is to only one side of the family but a child feels related to the parent from the nonlegal side.

Final Demand: Demand for consumption goods by those who will actually consume them (as opposed to those who use them for production or profit).

Firm: In classical economics, that sector of the total economy which produces goods for consumption by the household. In economic anthropology the firm is designated the *production unit.*

Fixed Costs: In the theory of the firm, those costs (overhead) which must be incurred before production can even begin. In contrast to *variable costs,* which are costs adjusted to the level of output (like the amount of labor employed), fixed costs are the capital goods needed to produce for which a fixed price must be paid regardless of the level of output. For example, to grow wheat one must first buy land.

Flow: The movement of goods and payments in a competitive market, forming a closed circuit.

Formal Economics: Synonymous with *Abstract Economics.*

Free Market: An economy in which distribution of goods is accomplished by the free play of supply, demand, and price rather than by *command,* or dictated supply, demand, and price.

Friendship: The equalitarian attitude of mutual respect resulting from a social exchange arrangement in which the parties are mutually obligated. See *Obligations.*

Function: A relationship between two variables such that to each value of one (the *independent variable*) there corresponds a unique value of the other (the *dependent variable*).

Functionalism: That view of society, associated with structural-functional theory in social anthropology and its cousin in sociology, in which all its parts are seen as having the effect of maintaining the whole system.

Game Theory: That type of decision-making theory which views the actor as seeking an end consisting of a payoff, which gives him a maximum return consistent with minimum risk (minimax payoff).

General Equilibrium Analysis: a form of *static* analysis in which the various sectors of a market system, the household's demand for goods and supply of factors, and the firm's demand for factors and supply of goods—all of which are separately treated under partial equilibrium analysis—are now combined into a single model of general equilibrium in order to predict prices, given the particular conditions in these partial markets.

Gift: A good given not in exchange for money or another good but for obligations (i.e., social goods).

Gift Giving: See *Gift.*

Good: Anything of value, either material (e.g., labor) or social (some obligation), which is traded in the *market.*

Gresham's Law: The theory that a "debased" currency will drive out a good currency (e.g., paper will drive out gold).

Household: See *Firm.*

Hypothesis: (see *Axiom*).

Ideology: Evaluative ideas, ideas about rights, in contrast to theory, which is nonevaluative.

Imperfect Substitutability: When determining what to produce, the condition in which shifting factors from one kind of production to another results in a decline in efficiency because factors are to some extent fitted to the kind of production they are doing and cannot be substituted for another kind without cost.

Incentives: See *Ends.*

Incest Taboo: A rule, said by many to be universal in human societies although expressed in different ways, that one must not have sexual contact with or bear children by certain classes of relatives. To be distinguished from a rule of exogamy, which may not condemn sexual contact but will not allow marriage within a certain class of relatives.

Income: In static theory, payments received from firms for factors. In other words, income is payments received by households, in contrast to revenue, which is payments received by firms.

Independent Variable: See *Dependent Variable.*

Indifference Analysis: Analysis of consumer demand based upon determination of combinations of goods to which the consumer is indifferent, i.e., which have the same utility for him. Indifference analysis allows analysis of demand without assuming that utility is absolutely measurable. (See *Cardinal Utility Theory.*)

Indigenous economy: In anthropological settings, the more or less self-contained economy operating in a native society before it is affected by Western trade. Thus, one may say that among the Turu livestock, finished iron goods, and cowrie shells served as money in the indigenous economy before being partially replaced by German and British coins.

Inductivism: See *Deductivism.*

Industrial Economy: An impressionistic term for free-market or Western economies.

Inelasticity: See *Elasticity.* That relation between the units in which price is expressed and the units in which goods occur such that a change in price brings a percentage change in the number of units of the goods offered which is smaller than the price change. For example, if one raises the price of an inelastic commodity like cigarettes, demand changes hardly at all.

Infinite Elasticity: See *Elasticity.* That extreme condition in which a single percentage point change in price brings a complete change in demand from no demand to demand for all that can be produced.

Inflation: A situation in which the demand for goods is increasing at a rate faster than the rate of increase in supply. See *Accelerator.*

Innovation: The invention of a new idea (e.g., machine or type of crop). In anthropology there is controversy over whether some innovations are invented in parallels between isolated societies or whether all innovations are random and essentially unrepeatable. Anthropologists generally agree that parallels are uncommon. This means that in economic anthropology, one can normally assume that if a people are not acquainted with a certain cultural idea, whether a machine or a strategy for maximizing utility, they cannot be expected to invent it but will have it only if it is diffused to them from another society. However, they may invent machines and strategies of their own.

Input: In static terms, an economy is conceived of as closed, which means that all volumes and changes in one sector are equalled or balanced off in others. If we conceive of the economy as having only firms and households, then factors are inputs to firms from households, the firms producing outputs that are inputs to demanding households.

Input-Output Analysis: Referring specifically to the type of analysis developed by Leontief, this is the study of how inputs of factors in one area of production as well as to output of an economy are related to output in *other* sectors in that sector. The point is that because of the relatively invariant connection between inputs and outputs and because every sector of the economy is connected to every other one, any input change in one sector directly or indirectly affects output in all sectors.

Input-Output Variable: In the theory of the firm, supply is a function of the price of the good under scrutiny, the price of other goods in the market, and the *I-O,* or input-output variable. This refers to the productivity of a machine relative to the amount of input. For example, the same amount of labor input into an axe and a chain saw will have much greater output in the case of the chain saw.

Institution: A key concept in sociology and social anthropology, it is nevertheless poorly defined and the subject of much controversy. Generally speaking, an institution is some relatively discrete area of social life (e.g., politics) having a set of rules and goals particular to it. Institutions are not synonymous with groups.

Institutional Economics: In the history of theoretical controversies within economics, that point of view which is equivalent to the *substantive economists* in anthropology.

Instrumental Relations: Those relations between people in which one or both parties use the other to gain some end. The relationship is impersonal, or if personal *pseudogemeinschaftliche,* pretending to be concerned about the welfare of another person in order to get him to cooperate with one's purposes.

Instrumental Value: Meant to substitute for "material" values when contrasting the material and social economies, this refers to the classification of values into two types, those which are *instrumental*, including some nonmaterial values such as labor or service, love, and information, and those which are social or are *obligations,* i.e., expressions of subordination to someone.

Interest: In static analysis of factors, payment for capital as compared to wages as payment for labor and rent as payment for land or natural resources.

Interval Scale: The scaling or ranking of something in intervals that are exactly equal, as compared to ordinal scaling, where the size of the intervals is variable, or nominal scaling, where the position of the units in relation to each other and the intervals are not known.

Intrinsic Rewards: See *Extrinsic Rewards.*

Investor: One who risks capital in a production enterprise.

Irrationality: In theoretical terms, irrationality refers to behavior (decisions) which does not conform to the assumption that the actor desires to maximize utility. In the real world it means taking a course that will not achieve a stated goal.

Isoquant Curve: A curve expressing the outputs to be expected from different combinations of factors, e.g., machinery and labor. Typically the curve is bowed because new combinations lower the efficiency of the factors of production due to *imperfect substitutability.*

Jural Rules: Sanctioned rules, laws, or *norms* which act as constraints on the decision-making process. For example, for a person seeking to make a marriage, the *incest taboo* is a jural rule.

Justice: Justice in the sense used here refers to distributing income according to peoples' ideas about how it ought to be distributed as opposed to distributing it according to the dictates of the free market. The two do not necessarily coincide, so the market is not necessarily just.

Kachin System: The system of marriage practiced among the Kachin of Burma, among whom there are reputed to be three levels of class. People sometimes marry in circles within classes as dictated by the rule of *matrilateral cross-cousin marriage,* and sometimes marry between classes, with the men marrying up and the women down.

Kariera Marriage Rule: Found among the Kariera tribe of Australia (and elsewhere), this is the rule that a man must not marry a member of his own *moiety* (these societies have only two moieties) and must not marry a woman of his own section (sections crosscut the moities; there are also only two sections). The result of following this rule is that man nearly always marries a woman who is simultaneously his mother's brother's daughter and father's sister's daughter and who is from the moiety and section from which his grandfather got his wife.

Keynesian Theory: Generally the system of theory derived from John Maynard Keynes (1936), which questions the validity of classical closed-market models, particularly with respect to the question of employment. Keynes argued that the equilibrating, static model would not automatically bring full employment. He showed that the model for full employment had to be dynamic.

Labor Theory of Value: Originating with the founders of classical theory and abandoned by them but retained by Marx, the theory that the value of a good is a result of the amount of labor put into its production. The theory ignores the fact of the degree of scarcity of labor, which in the market model would cause the price of labor's product to vary.

Law of Diminishing Marginal Utility: Specific to *cardinal utility theory,* this is the "law" that the utility to a person of increased consumption of a particular good declines at the margin, so that the second unit has less utility to him than the first, the third less than either the second or first, and so on.

Lease: A contract conveying rights in a piece of property for a specified term.

Levirate: The practice characteristic of patrilineal descent groups in which the men operate to some degree as a corporate group for passing rights in a wife on to her husband's heir (usually his brother) at the time of his death.

Lineage: A group of men and their sisters whose membership in the group is defined in terms of unilineal descent from a named, apical ancestor. The effect of tracing descent unilineally, once the founding ancestor is designated, is to automatically create a discrete group.

Linear Equation: See *Exponential Equation.*

Linear Programming: Also called mathematical programming, an algebraic technique utilized in *decision-making* which allowed determination of the various mixes of processes of production and kinds of crops which will give optimal desired output. For example, Heyer used linear programming to determine the optimal mix of crops for a Kamba farmer in order for him to maximize production in terms of expected or desired return.

Liquidity: The degree of ease with which a certain good can be converted into another. Most commonly thought of as the ease with which a good can be converted to money.

Logic: The system of rules governing formal, deductive reasoning.

Logical Positivism: According to Krupp, that form of positivist philosophy which requires that all theoretical terms be made operational, and which would therefore exclude such "mystical" notions as maximization.

Logical System: A theoretical or deductive system.

Lorenz Curve: A curve which expresses the distribution of income in a population.

Lusk's Coefficient: A coefficient in a scale of numbers expressing the amount of food consumed during a given time period by children and women in proportion to a fully grown man, for whom the coefficient is 1.0.

Macroeconomics: That branch of formal theory dealing with macro-variables, i.e., variables which are *aggregates* rather than specific variables: for example, aggregate labor costs as compared with labor costs for production of a specific product. This approach is associated with *Keynesian theory* and *dynamics.*

Marginal Cost: In contrast to average cost, which is the cost of any one unit, determined by dividing the total cost by the number of units produced, marginal cost is the cost of producing one more unit at any given point.

Marginal Propensity to Consume: In Keynesian theory, the hypothesis that as income rises, the propensity to consume also rises. See *Accelerator.*

Marginal Revenue Curve: In the theory of the firm, the curve which expresses the change in revenue to be obtained by producing one more unit. Equivalent to the *marginal cost* curve in the firm's consumption of factors.

Magnitude: Expression of size. When we speak of the need to obtain magnitudes of variables in field work, we are speaking of obtaining amounts, such as the amount of crops grown, the number of livestock raised, etc.

Marginal Utility: The utility to be obtained by consuming the next unit of a good. See *Law of Diminishing Marginal Utility.*

Market: The total supply-demand situation and the opportunities for exchange, by whatever means and in whatever place, of goods for payments. Also, a marketplace.

Market Community: That community or society within which there exists a complete *free market* system of firms and households united into a system of supply and demand.

Market Directed Society: Synonymous with *Free Market.*

Market Economy: Synonymous with *Free Market.*

Market Mechanism: The automatic distribution of supplies of goods to demanders through the operation of the pricing system, which reflects, theoretically, the supply-demand situation. Another way of speaking of this is as the "invisible hand" which sees that just enough goods are produced to supply all demand despite the fact that there is no overt direction to the supply process.

Market Solution: Synonymous with *Free Market.*

Marriage Rule: A rule which directs the marital flow of women in a particular society. Marriage rules can be negative or positive, and the latter can be of two types: direct (two groups exchanging women) or indirect (three or more groups sending their women around in circles). See *Matrilateral Cross-Cousin Marriage Rule, Patrilateral Cross-Cousin Marriage Rule.*

Material Economy: The economy seen only in its material or *instrumental* dimension and taking no note of social values.

Material Wealth: Wealth which is *instrumental* or material as opposed to social wealth or *obligations.*

Materialism: In formal economics, exclusive analysis of the material or instrumental economy while ignoring the social.

Materialist Formal Economics: See *Materialism.*

Mathematical Function: See *Function.*

Mathematical Model: A set of equations which are integrated into a logical system but which have no necessary empirical referents.

Mathematical Theory: A *theory* without any necessary empirical referents.

Matrilateral Cross-Cousin Marriage Rule: The rule in some societies that a man must marry his mother's brother's daughter (although usually the terms "mother's brother" and "mother's brother's daughter" mean not necessarily the actual brother and his daughter but classes of relatives equivalent to these people).

Matrilineal: See *Bilateral Descent.*

Matrilocal Residence: The taking up of residence by a married couple at the home of the bride's mother.

Maximization: The selection from a group of two or more alternative paths that path which will insure the actor the most utility.

Means: Resources that may be used to obtain some valued goal. Economics as the study of how people relate means to ends takes as its problem those situations (which comprise most situations) in which the means are insufficient to obtain all desired ends, so that economizing of means must be practiced.

Mechanical Explanation: An explanation of an actor's course of action that invokes rules or ideology as the motivating force rather than an orientation to desired ends.

Mechanical System: A system which operates by means of people dogmatically following rules and ideologies rather than by specialization and *mutual contingency,* the latter called an organic system. See *Role playing.*

Medium of Exchange: To be differentiated from a *unit of value,* this is a means of payment or store of value—a commodity that has come to act as a medium for the exchange of other commodities because it has high *liquidity* relative to carrying cost.

Micro Model: Shorthand expression for the microeconomic, static model of an economy which is concerned with individual enterprise.

Microeconomics: That branch of formal economic theory devoted to static analysis of partial and general equilibrium.

Minimax Assumption: See *Game Theory.*

Mix: Refers generally to the combining of resources or goods in proportions that maximize profit or utility. In economics, determining the right mix of resources and goods is a basic problem in maximizing.

Mobility: When referring to the factors of production, an attribute for the market mechanism to work. Labor must be mobile and go where wages are best. Land must be mobile in the sense of being marketable and not restricted from sale.

Model: A system of logically related variables. When the variables have no empirical referents, it is a mathematical model: when the variables have empirical referents it is an empirical model or natural theory. The market model refers to some measurable activities in the real world and so is of the latter class.

Moiety: One of the divisions of a society that has only two all inclusive divisions, between which women are exchanged in marriage. In such a society we may speak of moiety *exogamy*. (See *Kariera Marriage Rule.*

Money: A concept so variable in meaning that it is almost useless. To some it is both a *unit of account* and *medium of exchange*. To Melitz it is merely a medium of exchange, not to be confused with a unit of account. Keynes defined medium of exchange as a commodity having high liquidity relative to carrying cost. Substantivists generally feel that true money does not exist outside Western industrial economics because primitive money does not serve to exchange all things. See *All-Purpose Money, Standard of Value, Unit of Account, Coupons, Primitive Money, Medium of Exchange.*

Monopoly: See *Bilateral Monopoly.*

Multiplier: See *Accelerator.*

Mutual Contingency: A social situation in which two or more parties interact not because interaction is morally required or specified by rules (e.g., the rule that one must marry a member of the other moiety in a tribe) but because the interaction is mutually beneficial. Hence, the actions of one party are contingent on what the other party does, and vice versa. Cf. *Mechanical System.*

Needs: To be distinguished from ends, "needs" is more usually used teleologically. That is, in economics one specifies that the actors are assumed to desire to achieve an optimum relation between means and ends. Theoretically, what a consumer needs is outside the concern of economics, for which needs are given. See *Teleology.*

Negative Feedback: A process in a closed system whereby the action of one element causes a reaction in another element leading to a reestablishment of the status quo ante in some form. The interaction of furnace and thermostat is an example. Positive feedback, by contrast, is an accelerating, exponential process such as an atomic explosion, in which the action of an element causes reactions that accelerate rather than dampen the process. See *Accelerator.*

Norm of Reciprocity: The phrase is Gouldner's and denotes *reciprocity* as a rule rather than as a mutually contingent relationship. Gouldner calls the norm a "starter" because he believes that society begins with people giving *gifts* because they are required to do so, and then evolves into a market exchange system in which people exchange things because they find this profitable. See *Mutual Contingency.*

Norms: This term has two very different meanings. It may mean a rule or law, or it may refer to a statistically prominent repetitive pattern.

Nucleation: Turning back on itself, in contrast to branching out. For example, in alliance theory, marriage with father's sister's daughter is said to cause nucleation because it reinforces ties with another clan with whom ties were previously established while avoiding the development of more far-reaching alliances, whereas in mother's-brother's-daughter marriage, far-reaching, nonnucleating ties are established.

Obligations: A term derived from Gouldner and employed generally in this book to cover values which are noninstrumental or nonmaterial. Social obligations are compliance with the demands of another given in exchange for some benefit. *Power* is the condition over the receiver obtained by the giver of the benefits.

Operationalization: The fitting of a model or mathematical theory to a real situation—e.g., fitting the equation $x = y^2$ to the path of an actual rocket, thereby making possible deductions within the theory about the action of the rocket.

Opportunity Cost: In analysis of production possibilities, where attention is paid to what to produce, opportunity cost takes cognizance of the fact that as resources are shifted to producing something else the efficiency of the resources, which continue to be used to produce the original product, declines and costs rise.

Optimization: Synonym for *maximization.*

Ordinal Scale: See *Interval Scale.*

Organic System: See *Mechanical System.*

Output: See *Input.*

Overhead: See *Fixed Costs.*

Ownership: Control to one degree or another of rights (not things). That is to say, property is rights to the use of values, material and social. Ownership in any value is seldom complete. One may own partial rights in it or one's rights, even if complete, may be limited in time. For example, inheritance laws, which in effect confiscate some of the rights of a deceased person, are an expression of the limits of the deceased rights to the term of his life. *Status,* by this definition, comes under the heading of property.

Parameters: Variables on the border of the system of variables under study i.e., exogenous variables. For example, the number of firms in the market is a parameter of the usual static market model. Parameters are normally held constant in static analysis, in contrast to variables within the model (endogenous variables), which may or may not be held constant according as an hypothesis demands.

Pareto Optimum: In the analysis of *bilateral monopoly,* the condition that maximizes the joint advantage of both parties, represented by the tangent point of the indifference curves of the two parties.

Partial Equilibrium Analysis: See *General Equilibrium.*

Paternalism: In Bennett's terminology, that form of interaction between two actors in which one, the subordinate, pays with obligations for instrumental values received from the superordinate.

Patrilateral Cross-Cousin Marriage Rule: The rule, in some societies, that a man must take as his wife the daughter of his father's sister.

Patrilocal Residence: The taking up of residence by a married couple at the home of the groom's father.

Patrilineal: See *Bilateral Descent.*

Payoff: See *Game Theory.*

Payment: In static analysis, any wealth (money or whatever) exchanged by the firm for factors and by the household for goods.

Polygamy: Practice of having multiple wives (polygymy) or multiple husbands (polyandry).

Positive Economics: That form of economics which draws upon positivistic methods, i.e., is deductive and theoretical (See *Abstract Economics*).

Positive Feedback: See *Negative Feedback.*

Potlach: Specifically, the name for the process in Kwakiutl or Northwest Coast Indians society by which a man incurs from others extensive *obligations* by giving them gifts in excess of their ability to repay immediately. Mauss generalized the term to the process in any society by which a man gains power by giving gifts to others and thereby obligating them to him.

Power: A relationship between two or more actors in which one (the powerful person) is owed *obligations* or dependence by another.

Preferences: Synonymous with satisfactions, *ends.*

Preference Scale: A ranking of the order of desirability of preferences. It should be noted that a preference scale is both variable and relative. The order of desirability of values fluctuates with consumption as the utility of goods varies at the margin. And each consumer has his own preference scale.

Prestige: A term that in the literature of economic anthropology seems to be synonymous with the ownership of *obligations* in others.

Price: The payment a demander is willing to give for a good and the revenue a producer is willing to accept for a good.

Price Fixing: In static analysis, the holding of price at a constant level, in contrast to the free-market situation, where it is allowed to fluctuate in accordance with supply and demand.

Primitive: In anthropology, a term which refers to a *mechanical system,* one in which tradition rather than *mutual contingency* rules.

Primitive Money: According to substantivists, money which does not serve to mediate all exchanges or sufficient exchanges to serve as a regulating device for supply and demand.

Primo-Ultimogeniture: An inheritance system in which the majority of the property descends to the eldest and youngest sons as a team and in which middle sons are given little or nothing.

Principle of Justice: In Radcliffe-Brown's thought, a principle, universal in human societies, that like should be given for like—good for good and evil for evil.

Production: Any act of transforming materials by means of the application of factors.

Production Possibilities Curve: A curve, concave to zero, which expresses the fact that to shift resources from one kind of production to another involves *opportunity costs.*

Production Unit: In economic anthropology equivalent to the *firm* in statics.

Profit: In *statics,* that revenue which is in excess of fixed and variable costs.

Property: See *Ownership.*

Rationality: See *Irrationality.*

Reality: Whatever is designated as empirical, in contrast to what is designated as theoretical.

Reciprocity: While this term has several meanings, some unclear, it is generally synonymous with *gift giving* in the anthropological literature or *social exchange* in this book. That is, it is the giving of deference or *obligations* in return for value received. See *Redistribution.*

Redistribution: In Polanyi's substantive economic anthropology, that kind of reciprocity in which wealth is gathered to a political center and then redistributed to the people in return for obedience to the ruler-distributer. As a type of gift giving it is to be contrasted with Polanyi's "reciprocity", which is reciprocity without inequality of status.

Relevance: Generally speaking, the relation of theory to the solution of practical problems for the general good. Relevance is a relative concept.

Rent: In statics, the form that payment for land or resources takes.

Resources: Factors of production were originally designated in statics as land, labor, and capital. Mineral wealth and the like are now usually aggregated with land as a factor called "resources."

Revenue: Payments received by a firm.

Rights in Personam: In Radcliffe-Brown's theory, rights in a person as a social being, as opposed to *rights in Rem*, or rights in a person as a material thing.

Rights in Rem: See *Rights in Personam*.

Ring: Alliances of more than two persons; i.e., more than two parties tied together in indirect and direct relations of mutual contingency.

Ritual: Symbolic and dramatic action having to do with ensuring social and personal equanimity. Ritual can be thought of as instrumental for these ends and therefore as a desired, valuable good to which resources must be diverted in order to maximize utility.

Role Playing: A concept having implications for the substantive-formal debate, in substantive terms this is mechanical action in the sense of a *Mechanical System*. In formal terms, and in the terms meant by Belshaw, it is behavior which is strategic for reaching goals in the manner of a game player in an *Organic System*. The repetitiveness that inheres in role playing, and on which structural-functional thinkers focus, would be thought of as an epiphenomenon (*surface manifestation*) of the fact that the number of paths to maximum utility is small and therefore they are all frequently used. See *Mechanical System*.

Rules: Constraints on decision-making behavior in any society which are socially imposed rather than being derived from other sources, such as nature (a mountain as a barrier). The *incest taboo* is such a rule.

Satisfactions: Synonymous with preferences, *ends*.

250 ECONOMIC MAN

Savings: In statics, the difference between income and consumption.

Scarce Means: As the resources used to maximize profit or utility, means can be scarce, so that in order to reach a given end they must be used most economically.

Scarcity: A concept over which much ink has been expended. In substantive terms it is absolute, in the sense that it represents the net amount of good which is less than that required to support the social system. Formally, scarcity refers simply to insufficiency of means to reach a certain end, or insufficiency of ends to satisfy all demand. Scarcity is relative to demand, which changes with supply, tastes, and other variables. Ironically, formalists therefore claim scarcity to be universal, while substantivists hold it to be "instituted," since under natural conditions a society adjusts its ends to its means.

Scientific Law: In inductive thought, a statement of a pattern which occurs invariably or relatively invariably (since invariance is probably impossible). In deductive thought, a predictable condition, given the truth of the theory. The term is also used to identify critical principles of a particular theory, such as the *Law of Diminishing Marginal Utility* in cardinal utility theory.

Section System: Specific to the structure of most Australian aboriginal societies, this refers to a way of grouping people that crosscuts moieties. For example, in a four-section system, the simplest form, the society is divided into two moieties crosscut by two sections. There are also eight-, sixteen-, and larger section systems.

Sectors: A loose term designating subparts of a "closed system." Thus in statics we may talk of the production sector, the household sector, the agricultural sector, or the manufacturing sector.

Segmentary Society: A kind of social structure in which the society is divided into homogeneous and balanced segments that aggregate at higher levels into larger balanced segments in a nesting pattern, on the model of a geneology. As the term is usually used, it means societies in which groups are defined by unilineal descent.

Serendipity: The accidental discovery of a scientific principle in the course of an investigation designed to discover something else.

Service: Specifically, human time devoted instrumentally to someone's production ends in return for wages. Service should be differentiated from the giving of *obligations,* as in *reciprocity,* and from the giving of information and love. See *Instrumental Value.*

Simultaneous Equations: Two or more equations satisfied by the same sets of values of the unknowns.

Social Anthropology: That branch of anthropology focusing on human behavior through the concept of society (rather than the concept of culture). Social anthropologists may generally be classified as descent theorists, alliance theorists, and transaction theorists.

Social Differentiation: That type of *differentiation* in which the interaction (*mutual contingency*) of two or more actors includes an element of obligation and not only instrumental values. That which sociologists mean by society is to social exchange theorists the complex system of interaction based on obligations or rights of some persons in the deference of others, i.e., social differentiation.

Social Economy: As compared with material economy, that area of the economy consisting of *social exchanges.*

Social Exchange: The system of exchanges involving *reciprocity,* which includes, generally the exchange of nonmaterial goods.

Social Organization: A term which in formal theory means *role playing,* i.e., strategic actions designed to reach ends, but which is sometimes loosely used as synonymous with *social structure* (which is more inclusive than organization).

Social Structure: In social anthropology, the patterned interaction of people in its totality, which forms a closed system or society.

Social Value: To Solow, and probably to economists in general, a good consequence for society derived from some particular kind of market equilibrium. For example, the reduction in industrial pollution consequent on taxing the amount of pollution, as a result of the manufacturer's desire to reduce costs.

Socialization: Teaching a child or foreigner the ways of a society. With respect to new (and perhaps potentially dangerous) knowledge, the subjugating of its use to the good of society by asserting social controls over its use and users.

Society: The key concept in sociology and social anthropology, it refers generally to the view of human beings as mutually dependent, whether this dependence is *mechanical* or *organic.*

Sororate: The practice, characteristic of some patrilineal descent groups, by which the men operate to some degree as a corporate group in order to replace with a substitute a woman of their group who has died while married to a man of a different group.

Special-Purpose Money: See *All-Purpose Money.*

Standard of Value: Synonymous with *Unit of Account.*

Statics: That form of analysis synonymous with general and partial equilibrium analysis in which, in contrast to *dynamics,* the analysis is timeless and concern is focused on the way the variables within the model relate. In *comparative statics,* the relationship between the variables in the model is observed as it is affected by changes in the parameters of the model. Statics is to dynamics as algebra is to calculus.

Status: The general meaning is a set of rights and obligations which apply to some person (e.g., professor, or pitcher), but the term has the connotation also of rank difference based on *obligations.*

Status Deprivation (See *Status*): In Cochrane's terms, the condition in which one is unable to obtain obligations from others. Melanesian cargo cults are said by Cochrane to have arisen among people who feel status deprivation because they cannot obligate Europeans to them.

Status Immobility: Synonymous with *Status Deprivation.*

Stratification: Any established system of differentiated ranked statuses. (See *Social Differentiation.*) There can be a system of differentiated unranked or equal statuses.

Structure: See *Social Structure.*

Structural-Functional Theory: See *Functionalism.*

Subsistence: A poorly defined term which seems to mean a production situation in which producers are barely turning out enough to eat or do not choose to produce more than they can eat, so that no economy in the sense of markets and exchange, is possible.

Subsistence Economy: See *Subsistence.*

Substantive Economics: That theory which asserts that outside Western, capitalist economies, the production, distribution, and consumption of food are achieved by moral direction and are conducted for the purpose of maintaining society, not for personal profit.

Supply: In statics, that amount of goods which a firm is willing to produce as a function of the price demanders will pay.

Supply Curve: Typically upward sloping, the supply curve represents the theory that producers will produce more and more for the market (rising supply) as the price offered rises.

Supply Function: That function which states that the quantity of goods a firm is willing to supply is a function of the price, or $Q_s = f(P)$. A supply function can be made more complicated by including in it other prominent variables such as *I—O*, or the input-output possibilities of the machines employed, and P_n, or the price of other goods.

Surface Structure: Borrowed from Chomskian linguistics, this term is similar to *epiphenomenon* as used by Barth, in that it refers to the fact that observed social events may be reflections of allocation processes. For example, the *levirate* is a social pattern which is an epiphenomenon or surface structure of the exchange of a bride for livestock (brideprice), in that the amount of wealth exchanged and the number of people involved (two corporate groups) makes the marriage of a woman to her dead husband's brother economic and possible whereas in cases where no brideprice is paid this does not happen and the woman returns home when the husband dies.

Surplus: In common parlance surplus refers to an excess of something in relation to the needs of people. In analytical terms, surplus refers to various things, for example, the excess of assets over liabilities. The formal meaning is entirely different from the common meaning, because the idea of surpluses that are over and above the needs of the system is impossible to entertain, in the logic of the model where any production in excess of demand is discontinued.

Syllogism: Generally speaking, a logical statement in which certain conclusions derive inexorably from the premises. The point is that a syllogism allows one to deduce certain statements and states of affairs that might otherwise not be imagined.

Systems Theory: A kind of deductive, analytical method which is designed to theorize about theories. In other words, it is a higher-level theoretical system than those (such as economic analysis) which are specific to certain phenomena (such as the allocation process).

Tautology: A type of logical statement flawed by the fact that the conclusion is a repetition of something in the premises and the argument is therefore circular and uninformative. For example, if we define men as animals who are bipedal in locomotion and then study this class of animals for distinctive features and conclude that one is that they are bipedal in locomotion, we have merely restated a premise of the investigation.

Teleology: A type of generalization or scientific "law" which ascribes purpose to events. For example, "the function of the family is to maintain stability in society," where the purpose of achieving a future state, social stability, is ascribed to the family. A more formal way of putting it is to say that teleological statements have the form, "X exists because it is necessary for the existence of Y." Many evolutionary assertions are teleologic. For example, the idea that man is the "highest" of the animals contains implicit within it the idea that any forms preceding and leading up to man existed for the purpose of producing man. Teleologic statements are not necessarily illogical, but they are analytically primitive and should be differentiated from functional statements (see *Functionalism*), which avoid any ascription of purpose.

Theoretical Economics: Synonymous with *Abstract Economics.*

T Factor: A phrase utilized in this text to denote the element of trust that is involved in any credit relationship, particularly one in which obligations are returned for goods. The giver of the goods must trust the receiver to return the obligations, so that social relations are necessarily trusting whereas direct material exchanges are not. See *Credit.*

Theory: Logico-deductive analysis, proceeding from general principles or formulas, offered to explain some set of phenomena.

Total Cost: In the theory of the firm, the combination of fixed and variable costs.

Total Prestations: In Marcel Mauss's theory of the *gift,* a situation existing in the most "primitive" societies, where *rings* or *alliances* occur in which all material goods are exchanged in return for obligations, which themselves are paid off either by deference or with material gifts, which incur counterobligations from the former obligator. The point is that in this type of gift giving, in contrast to *potlach,* no status differentiation occurs, because the exchanges of goods, material and social, are balanced.

Total Revenue: The amount of revenue received by a firm, calculated as the total quantity of units produced multiplied by the price at which each is sold. To be contrasted with average revenue and marginal revenue, the average revenue received per unit sold and the revenue received for the last unit manufactured.

Total Revenue Product: The curve expressing *total revenue* at any point in the production process.

Tradition-centered: In Francis Hsu's typology, that type of society, like traditional China, in which people conform to tradition and do not assert individuality. That is to say, the polar opposite of an individual-centered society.

Traditional: A common sociological expression utilized by Riesman, having a meaning equivalent to Hsu's *tradition-centered.*

Transcendence: As used with respect to scientific method, the term means that conclusions may be reached by use of the method that are not apparent in the premises (i.e., not tautologic) and may, therefore, constitute new knowledge. For example, by the use of psychological methods one may discover that one is selfish, even though the thought is repulsive to one. In astronomy, deductive models allowed us historically to conclude that the earth moved around the sun, though the idea was ideologically repulsive.

Transaction: Used by Belshaw and Barth in a way that is synonymous with *Social Exchange.*

Transfer Event: Equal in Le Clair's thought to *exchange* in the traditional economic sense. However, transfer events include kinds of exchanges not ordinarily considered in economics, such as theft, appropriation, and conquest.

Trust: See *T Factor.*

Unit of Account: A unit expressing value in some abstract sense, used to compare values in various sectors of an economy for purposes of bookkeeping and the making of allocation decisions involving the whole of an economy or enterprise. To be distinguished from *money* or *medium of exchange.* The unit of account may have the same appearance as the medium of exchange (e.g., the dollar as a unit of account and a dollar used to buy something), but they are independently variable.

Unit of Value: Synonymous with *Unit of Account.*

Utility: That quality of goodness or desirability inherent in desired goods but which is not the goods themselves.

Value Judgment: A statement which evaluates the goodness or oughtness of something, as contrasted with a purely logical statement. For example—Logical statement: $X = Y$; evaluative statement, X ought to equal Y. Evaluative statements are generally thought to be untestable, whereas logical statements have the potential of being tested. The choice of ends by a consumer is an example of a value judgment. *Formal economics* says nothing about what a consumer ought to want, but only the rational way to get what is wanted. Normative economics, welfare economics, and political economics deal with the ought.

Variable Costs: See *Fixed Costs.*

Velocity of Money: The frequency with which money is used in exchanges. The supply of money in an economy may be taken to be the quantity multiplied by the velocity.

Wants: Synonymous with *preferences, ends.*

Wealth: The total of desirable (i.e., valuable) goods, both social and material, possessed by someone or existing in an economy. In static theory it is the total of resources or valued goods in an economy and is a constant. In real life it is highly variable from time to time and person to person. That which is scarce and desirable and hence wealth to one person is not wealth to another.

BIBLIOGRAPHY

ABRAHAMS, R. G.
  1967 *The Peoples of Greater Unyamwezi, Tanzania*, International African Institute, London.
ALCHIAN, A. A. AND W. R. ALLEN
  1968 *University Economics* (2nd ed.), Wadsworth Publishing, Belmont, Calif.
APODACA, ANACLETO
  1952 "Corn and Custom," in Spicer, 1952.
ARMSTRONG, W. E.
  1924 "Rossel Island Money: A Unique Monetary System," *Economic Journal* 34: 423–429. (Reprinted in Dalton, 1967.)
ARMSTRONG, W. E.
  1928 *Rossel Island, An Ethnological Study*, Cambridge Univ. Press.
BARIC, LORRAINE
  1964 "Some Aspects of Credit, Saving, and Investment in a 'Non-Monetary' Economy (Rossel Island)," in Firth and Yamey, 1964.
BARNETT, H. G.
  1938 "The Nature of the Potlach," *American Anthropologist* 40: 349–359.
BARNETT, H. G.
  1960 *Being a Palauan*, Holt, Rinehart, New York.
BARTH, F.
  1959 "Segmentary Opposition and the Theory of Games: A Study of Pathan Organization," Journal of the Royal Anthropological Institute, *Man* 89: 5–21.
BARTH, F.
  1964 "Capital, Investment, and the Social Structure of a Pastoral Nomad Group in South Persia," in Firth and Yamey, 1964.

257

BARTH, F.
1966 *Models of Social Organization,* Royal Anthropological Institute, London.
BARTH, F.
1967 "Economic Spheres in Darfur," in Firth, 1967.
BARTH, F.
1967a "On the Study of Social Change," *American Anthropologist* 69: 661–669.
BECKER, HOWARD
1956 *Man in Reciprocity,* Praeger, New York.
BELSHAW, CYRIL
1965 *Traditional Exchange and Modern Markets,* Prentice-Hall, Englewood Cliffs, N.J.
BELSHAW, CYRIL
1968 "Theoretical Problems in Economic Anthropology," in Maurice Freedman (ed.), *Social Organization: Essays Presented to Raymond Firth,* Aldine Atherton, Chicago.
BELSHAW, CYRIL
1970 *The Condition of Social Performance,* Routledge & Kegan Paul, London.
BENNETT, JOHN
1968 "Reciprocal Economic Exchanges Among North American Agricultural Operators," *Southwestern Journal of Anthropology* 24: 276–309.
BERLINER, J. S.
1962 "The Feet of the Natives are Large: An Essay on Anthropology by an Economist," *Current Anthropology* 3, No. 1: 47–61.
BERNDT, R. M. and C. H. BERNT
1964 *The World of the First Australians,* Univ. of Chicago Press.
BLAU, PETER
1955 *The Dynamics of Bureaucracy,* Univ. of Chicago Press.
BLAU, PETER
1963 *The Dynamics of Bureaucracy* (2nd ed.), Univ. of Chicago Press.
BLAU, PETER
1964 *Exchange and Power in Social Life,* Wiley, New York.
BOAS, F. H. CODERE
1966 *Kwakiutl Ethnography,* Univ. of Chicago Press.
BOHANNAN, PAUL
1955 "Some Principles of Exchange and Investment Among the Tiv," *American Anthropologist* 57: 60–70.
BOHANNAN, PAUL
1963 *Social Anthropology,* Holt, Rinehart, New York.

BOHANNAN, PAUL AND PHILIP CURTIN
1988   *Africa and Africans* (3rd ed.), Waveland Press, Inc., Prospect Heights, Ill.

BOHANNAN, PAUL AND GEORGE DALTON
1965   *Markets in Africa: Eight Subsistence Economies in Transition* (revised edition) Natural History Library, Anchor Books, Doubleday & Co., Inc., Garden City, N.Y.

BOHANNAN, PAUL AND LAURA BOHANNAN
1968   *Tiv Economy*, Northwestern University Press, Evanston, Ill.

BOULDING, KENNETH E.
1955   *Economic Analysis* (3rd ed.), Harper & Brothers, New York.

BRONFENBRENNER, MARTIN
1966   "A 'Middlebrow' Introduction to Economic Methodology," in Sherman Roy Krupp (ed.), *The Structure of Economic Science*, Prentice-Hall, Englewood Cliffs, N.J.

BROWN, PAULA
1970   "Chimbu Transactions," *Man* 6: 100–117.

BUCHANAN, J. M. AND G. TULLOCK
1969   *The Calculus of Consent*, Univ. of Michigan Press, Ann Arbor.

BUCHLER, I. R. AND HUGO NUTINI
1969   *Game Theory in the Behavioral Sciences*, Univ. of Pittsburgh Press.

BUCKLEY, W.
1968   *Modern Systems Research for the Behavioral Scientist*, Aldine Atherton, Chicago.

BURLING, ROBBINS
1962   "Maximization Theories and the Study of Economic Anthropology," *American Anthropologist* 64: 802–821.

CANCIAN, FRANK
1965   *Economics and Prestige in a Maya Community*, Stanford Univ. Press.

CHOMSKY, NOAM
1968   *Language and Mind*, Harcourt, Brace & World, New York.

CLARKE, DAVID L. (ED.)
1973   *Models in Archaeology*, Methuen, London, and Barnes and Noble, New York, 1973.

COCHRANE, GLYNN
1970   *Big Men and Cargo Cults*, Clarendon Press, Oxford.

CODERE, HELEN
1950   *Fighting With Property: A Study of Kwakiutl Potlach and*

Warfare, 1792–1930, Monographs American Ethnological Soc., J. J. Augustin, New York.

CODERE, HELEN
1968   "Money-Exchange Systems and The Theory of Money," *Man* 3: 557–577.

COOK, SCOTT
1966   "The Obsolete Antimarket Mentality: A Critique of the Substantive Approach to Economic Anthropology," *American Anthropologist* 68: 323–345.

COOK, SCOTT
1969   "The 'Anti-Market' Mentality Reexamined: A Further Critique of the Substantive Approach to Economic Anthropology," *Southwestern Journal of Anthropology* 25: 378–406.

COOK, SCOTT
1970   "Price and Output Variability in a Peasant-Artisan Stoneworking Industry in Oaxaca, Mexico: An Analytical Essay in Economic Anthropology," *American Anthropologist* 72: 776–801.

CURRY, R. L., JR. AND L. L. WADE
1968   *A Theory of Political Exchange,* Prentice-Hall, Englewood Cliffs, N.J.

DALTON, GEORGE
1961   "Economic Theory and Primitive Society," *American Anthropologist* 63: 1–25.

DALTON, GEORGE
1965   "Primitive Money," *American Anthropologist* 67: 44–65 (Reprinted in Dalton, 1967).

DALTON, GEORGE (ed.)
1967   *Tribal and Peasant Economies,* Natural History Press, Garden City, N.Y.

DEMSETZ, HAROLD
1967   "Toward a Theory of Property," *American Economic Review,* 57, no. 2: 347–359.

DINWIDDY, CAROLINE
1967   *Elementary Mathematics for Economists,* Oxford Univ. Press, London.

DORFMAN, ROBERT
1953   "Mathematical, or "Linear," Programming: A Nonmathematical Exposition," *American Economic Review* 43: 797–825.

DOUGLAS, MARY
1967   "Primitive Rationing," in Firth, 1967.

DRUCKER, P. AND R. HEIZER
1967   *To Make My Name Good,* Univ. of California Press, Berkeley and Los Angeles.
EDEL, MATTHEW
1969   "Economic Analysis in an Anthropological Setting: Some Methodological Considerations," *American Anthropologist* 71: 421–433.
EDEL, MATTHEW
1970   "Karl Polanyi's Concept of Non-Market Trade," *Journal of Economic History,* 30: 127–130.
EGGAN, F.
1955   "The Cheyenne and Arapaho Kinship System," in F. Eggan (ed.), *Social Anthropology of North American Tribes,* Univ. of Chicago Press.
EINZIG, PAUL
1966   *Primitive Money* (rev. ed.), Pergamon Press, Elmsford, N.Y.
EPSTEIN, T. S.
1967   "The Data of Economics in Anthropological Analysis," in A. L. Epstein (ed.), *The Craft of Social Anthropology,* Tavistock, London.
EPSTEIN, T. S.
1968   *Capitalism, Primitive and Modern, Some Aspects of Tolai Economic Growth.* Australian National Univ. Press, Canberra.
EVANS-PRITCHARD, E. E.
1952   *Social Anthropology,* Free Press, New York.
EWERS, J. C.
1955   *The Horse in Blackfoot Indian Culture,* Smithsonian Institution, Bureau of American Ethnology Bulletin 159, Washington, D.C.
FIRTH, RAYMOND
1964   "The Place of Malinowski in the History of Economic Anthropology," in Raymond Firth (ed.), *Man and Culture,* Harper & Row, Harper Torchbooks, New York.
FIRTH, RAYMOND (ED.)
1967   *Themes in Economic Anthropology,* Tavistock, London.
FIRTH, RAYMOND AND B. S. YAMEY
1964   *Capital, Savings, and Credit in Peasant Societies,* Aldine Atherton, Chicago.
FOA, URIEL
1971   "Interpersonal and Economic Resources," *Science* 171: 345–352.

FORTES, M.
1969   *Kinship and The Social Order,* Aldine Atherton, Chicago.
FOX, ROBIN
1967   *Kinship and Marriage,* Penguin, New York.
FRANKENBERG, RONALD
1967   "Economic Anthropology: One Anthropologist's View," in Firth, 1967.
FRIEDMAN, MILTON
1953   "The Methodology of Positive Economics," in Milton Friedman, *Essays in Positive Economics,* Univ. of Chicago Press.
GERARD, H. B.
1954   "The Anchorage of Opinions in Face-To-Face Groups," *Human Relations* 7: 313–325.
GODELIER, M.
1971   "Salt Currency and the Circulation of Commodities Among the Baruya of New Guinea," in George Dalton (ed.), *Studies in Economic Anthropology,* American Anthropological Assn., Washington, D.C.
GOODFELLOW, D. M.
1939   *Principles of Economic Sociology,* Routledge & Kegan Paul, London.
GOULDNER, A. W.
1960   "The Norm of Reciprocity: A Preliminary Statement," *American Sociological Review* 25: 161–178.
GRAY, ROBERT
1960   "Sonjo Bride-Price and the Question of African 'Wife Purchase,'" *American Anthropologist* 62: 34–57.
GRAY, ROBERT
1965   "The Sonjo-A Marketless Community," in Bohannan and Dalton, 1968.
GRILICHES, ZVI
1957   "Hybrid Corn: An Exploration in the Economics of Technological Change," *Econometrica* 25:4.
HARPER, E. B.
1959   "Two Systems of Economic Exchange in Village India," *American Anthropology* 61: 760–778.
HARRIS, MARVIN
1966   "The Cultural Ecology of India's Sacred Cattle," *Current Anthropology* 7: 51–60.
HART, C. W. M. AND A. PILLING
1960   *The Tiwi of North Australia,* Holt, Rinehart, New York.

HAVEMAN, R. H. AND K. A. KNOPF
1966 *The Market System,* Wiley, New York.
HERSKOVITS, MELVILLE J.
1940 *The Economic Life of Primitive Peoples,* Knopf, New York.
HERSKOVITS, MELVILLE J.
1952 *Economic Anthropology,* Knopf, New York.
HESTON, ALAN
1971 "An Approach to the Sacred Cows of India," *Current Anthropology* 12: 191–209.
HEYER, JUDITH
1966 "Preliminary Results of a Linear Programming Analysis of Peasant Farms in Machakos District, Kenya," East African Institute of Social Research Conference Papers, Kampala.
HILL, POLLY
1970 *Studies in Rural Capitalism in West Africa,* Cambridge Univ. Press.
HOMANS, GEORGE
1958 "Social Behavior as Exchange," *American Journal of Sociology* 63: 597–606.
HOSELITZ, BERT F.
1964 "Capital Formation, Saving, and Credit in Indian Agricultural Society," in Firth and Yamey, 1964.
JONES, CANDACE
1967 "The Game of Rush" (unpublished manuscript in possession of the author).
JOY, LEONARD
1967 "An Economic Homologue of Barth's Presentation of Economic Spheres in Darfur," in Firth, 1967.
KAPLAN, DAVID
1968 "The Formal-Substantive Controversy in Economic Anthropology: Reflections on Its Wider Implications," *Southwestern Journal of Anthropology* 24: 228–251.
KEYNES, JOHN MAYNARD
1936 *The General Theory of Employment, Interest, and Money,* Harcourt, Brace & Company, New York.
KNIGHT, FRANK H.
1941 "Anthropology and Economics," *Journal of Political Economy* 49: 247–268.
KRUPP, S. R.
1965 "Equilibrium Theory in Economics and in Functional Analysis as Types of Explanation," in Don Martindale (ed.), *Functionalism in The Social Sciences,* American Academy of Political and Social Science, Philadelphia.

KRUPP, S. R.
1966   "Types of Controversy in Economics," in S. R. Krupp (ed.),
       The Structure of Economic Science, Prentice-Hall, Engle-
       wood Cliffs, N.J.
LANTIS, MARGARET
1952   "Eskimo Herdsmen," in Spicer, 1952.
LEACH, E. R.
1960   "The Sinhalese of the Dry Zone of Northern Ceylon," in
       G. P. Murdock (ed.), *Social Structure in Southeast Asia,*
       Tavistock, London.
LEACH, E. R.
1961   *Rethinking Anthropology,* Athlone Press, New York.
LECLAIR, EDWARD E., JR.
1962   "Economic Theory and Economic Anthropology," *American
       Anthropologist* 64: 1179–1203.
LECLAIR, EDWARD E., JR. AND HAROLD K. SCHNEIDER
1968   *Economic Anthropology: Readings in Theory and Analysis,*
       Holt, Rinehart, New York.
LEE, RICHARD
1969   "!Kung Bushman Subsistence: An Input-Output Analysis,"
       in D. Damas (ed.), *Contributions to Anthropology: Eco-
       logical Essays,* Queen's Printer, Ottawa.
LEONTIEF, WASSILY
1963   "The Structure of Development," *Scientific American,* Sep-
       tember, pp. 2–14.
LEVI-STRAUSS, CLAUDE
1956   "The Family," in Harry L. Shapiro, *Man, Culture, and So-
       ciety,* Oxford U. Press.
LEVI-STRAUSS, CLAUDE
1963   "Social Structure," in Claude Levi-Strauss, *Structural An-
       thropology,* Basic Books, Inc., New York.
LEVI-STRAUSS, CLAUDE
1969   *The Elementary Structures of Kinship,* Eyre & Spottiswoode,
       London.
MAIR, LUCY
1962   *Primitive Government,* Penguin, Pelican Books, New York.
MALINOWSKI, BRONISLAW
1961   *Argonauts of the Western Pacific* (revised 1984), Waveland Press,
       Inc., Prospect Heights, Ill.
MANSFIELD, D.
1970   *Microeconomics: Theory and Application,* Norton, New
       York.

MAQUET, JACQUES
1964 "Objectivity in Anthropology," *Current Anthropology* 5: 47–55.

MAUSS, MARCEL
1925 "Essai sur le don, forme archaique de l'échange," *L'Année Sociologique*.
1954 *The Gift*, Free Press, New York.
1967 *The Gift*, W. W. Norton, New York.

MEAD, M.
1955 *Cultural Patterns and Technical Change*, New American Library, Mentor Books, New York.

MELITZ, JACQUES
1970 "The Polanyi School of Anthropology on Money: An Economist's View," *American Anthropologist* 72: 1020–1040.

MERTON, R.
1949 *Social Theory and Social Structure*, Free Press, New York.

MOENCH, R. U.
1971 "Wealth, Expertise and Political Entrepreneurship," *Journal of Asian and African Studies* 6: 37–48.

NASH, MANNING
1961 "The Social Context of Choice in a Small Society," *Man* 219: 186–191 (Reprinted in LeClair and Schneider 1968).

NEEDHAM, RODNEY
1962 *Structure and Sentiment*, Univ. of Chicago Press.

ORANS, MARTIN
1968 "Maximizing in Jajmani Land: A Model of Caste Relations," *American Anthropologist* 70: 875–897.

PANOFF, M.
1970 "Marcel Mauss's *The Gift* Revisited," *Man* 5: 60–70.

PARKINSON, C. NORTHCOTE
1957 *Parkinson's Law*, Houghton Mifflin, New York.

PARSONS, TALCOTT AND NEIL J. SMELSER
1956 *Economy & Society*, Free Press, New York.

PIDDOCKE, S.
1965 "The Potlach System of the Southern Kwakiutl," *Southwestern Journal of Anthropology* 21: 244–264.

POLANYI, KARL
1944 *The Great Transformation*, Holt, Rinehart, New York.

POLANYI, KARL
1947 "Our Obsolete Market Mentality," *Commentary* 3: 109–117.

POLANYI, KARL ET AL.
1957 *Trade and Market in the Early Empires*, Free Press, New York.
POLANYI, KARL
1968 "The Semantics of Money-Uses," in *Primitive, Archaic and Modern Economics*, Doubleday & Co., Inc., Garden City, N.Y.
POSPISIL, LEOPOLD
1963 *The Kapauku Papuans of West New Guinea*, Holt, Rinehart, New York.
RADCLIFFE-BROWN, A. R.
1950 "Introduction," in A. R. Radcliffe-Brown and D. Forde, *African Systems of Kinship and Marriage*, Oxford Univ. Press, London.
RADCLIFFE-BROWN, A. R.
1952 *Structure and Function in Primitive Society*, Free Press, New York.
RADCLIFFE-BROWN, A. R.
1957 *A Natural Science of Society*, Free Press, New York.
RADFORD, R. A.
1945 "The Economic Organization of a P.O.W. Camp," *Economica* xii: 189–201. (Reprinted in LeClair and Schneider 1968).
RAPOPORT, ANATOLE
1968 "Foreward," in Walter Buckley (ed.), *Modern Systems Research for the Behavioral Scientist*, Aldine Atherton, Chicago.
RIKER, W. H.
1962 *The Theory of Political Coalitions*, Yale Univ. Press, New Haven.
ROBBINS, LIONEL
1962 *An Essay on the Nature and Significance of Economic Science*, Macmillan, London.
ROBINSON, JOAN
1963 *Economic Philosophy*, Aldine Atherton, Chicago.
ROBINSON, JOAN
1971 *Economic Heresies: Some Old-Fashioned Questions in Economic Theory*, Basic, New York.
SAHLINS, M.
1965 "On the Sociology of Primitive Exchange," in M. Banton (ed.), *The Relevance of Models For Social Anthropology*, Tavistock, London.

SAHLINS, M.
1968   *Tribesmen*, Prentice-Hall, Englewood Cliffs, N.J.
SALISBURY, RICHARD
1962   *From Stone to Steel*, Melbourne Univ. Press.
SALISBURY, RICHARD
1966   "Politics and Shell-Money Finance in New Britain," in
        M. J. Swartz, V. W. Turner, and A. Tuden (eds.), *Political
        Anthropology*, Aldine Atherton, Chicago.
SALISBURY, R.
1969   "Formal Analysis in Anthropological Economics: The
        Rossel Island Case," in Buchler and Nutini, 1969.
SAMUELSON, PAUL
1947   *Foundations of Economic Analysis*, Harvard Univ. Press,
        Cambridge.
SAMUELSON, PAUL
1967   *Economics: An Introductory Analysis* (7th ed.), McGraw-
        Hill, New York.
SCHNEIDER, HAROLD K.
1964   "A Model of African Indigenous Economy and Society,"
        Comparative Studies in Society & History 7: 37–55.
SCHNEIDER, HAROLD K.
1964a   "Economics in East African Aboriginal Societies," in Mel-
        ville J. Herskovits and M. Harwitz, *Economic Transition
        in Africa*, Northwestern Univ. Press, Evanston, Ill.
SCHNEIDER, HAROLD K.
1970   *The Wahi Wanyaturu: Economics in an African Society*,
        Aldine Atherton, Chicago.
SCHNEIDER, HAROLD K.
1971   "Comment on Heston's 'An Approach to the Sacred Cow
        of India,'" *Current Anthropology* 12: 205–206.
SCHNEIDER, HAROLD K.
n.d.   "Brideprice in Africa" (ms.).
SHARP, L.
1952   "Steel Axes for Stone Age Australians," in Spicer, 1952.
SIMMEL, GEORGE
1950   *The Sociology of Georg Simmel*, Free Press, New York.
SMELSER, NEIL J.
1963   *The Sociology of Economic Life*, Prentice-Hall, Englewood
        Cliffs, N.J.
SOLOW, R. M.
1971   "The Economist's Approach to Pollution and Its Control,"
        Science 73: 498–503.

SPICER, EDWARD H.
1952   *Human Problems in Technological Change,* Russell Sage Foundation, New York.
SRINIVAS, M. N.
1955   "The Social System of a Mysore Village," in McKim Marriott (ed.), *Village India,* American Anthropological Assn. Memoir 83, Washington, D.C.
STIGLER, A. J.
1942   *The Theory of Competitive Price,* Macmillan, New York.
SUTTLES, W.
1960   "Affinal Ties, Subsistence, and Prestige Among the Coast Salish," *American Anthropologist* 62: 296–305.
USEEM, JOHN
1952   "South Sea Island Strike," in Spicer, 1952.
VAYDA, A.P.
1961   "A Re-examination of Northwest Coast Economic Systems," *Transactions New York Academy of Sciences,* Series II, 23: 618–624.
WEBER, MAY
1947   *The Theory of Social and Economic Organization* (Translated by T. Patsons), Free Press, New York.
WILLIAMS, ROBIN
1960   *American Society* (2nd ed.), Knopf, New York.
WORSLEY, P. M.
1956   "The Kinship System of the Tallensi: A Revaluation," *Journal of the Royal Anthropological Institute* 86: 37–76.

Index